CRIMETIME

Ex libris
Michael J Kelly

Mark van Leewarden

CRIMETIME
FROM UNDERCOVER COP TO INTERNATIONAL INVESTIGATOR

MARK VAN LEEWARDEN

Foreword by Alan Duff

Quentin Wilson
PUBLISHING

This book is dedicated to:
My perfect wife Ainsley
My children Charlotte and Ben
And my late friend Roo

First published by
Quentin Wilson Publishing
105 Moncks Spur Road
Redcliffs 8081
Christchurch
New Zealand

email: wilson.quentin@gmail.com
www.quentinwilsonpublishing.com

First published 2021

Text copyright © 2021 Mark van Leewarden
The author asserts his moral right to the work.

ISBN 978-0-9951438-6-9 (Print)

A catalogue record for this book is available from the
National Library of New Zealand.

This book is copyright. Except for the purpose of fair review, no part may be stored or transmitted in any form or by any means, electronic or mechanical, including recording or storage in any information retrieval system, without permission in writing from the publishers. No reproduction may be made, whether by photocopying or by any other means, unless a licence has been obtained from the publisher or its agent.

Where the work of others has been included, every effort has been made to trace copyright holders and to obtain their permission for the use of copyright material. The publisher would be grateful to be notified of any permissions or acknowledgements that should be incorporated in future reprints or editions of this book.

Editor:
Jane McKenzie

Front cover photo:
Police surveillance image

Frontispiece author photo:
Ben van Leeuwarden

Front cover concept:
Ben van Leeuwarden

Final cover and page design and page layout:
Quentin Wilson Publishing, Christchurch, New Zealand

Typeset in 11.5/15.5 pt Adobe Garamond Pro
Printed by Your Books, Wellington

Contents

FOREWORD	by Alan Duff	7
ONE	"Has he got one leg?"	9
TWO	"Emu, you've gotta go back in."	23
THREE	"What'll we do now?"	34
FOUR	"You need to come clean, son, or things could go badly."	46
FIVE	"We're all on a fishing trip in the Sounds."	52
SIX	"It's a secret message, man."	55
SEVEN	"We've got some shit going on with the Angels."	66
EIGHT	"Fuck with the bull and you'll get the horn."	75
NINE	"If you sit by the river long enough, the bodies of your enemies will float by."	87
TEN	"I didn't do it. I don't believe she's dead."	95
ELEVEN	"Run it up the flagpole and see who salutes."	101
TWELVE	"You're not in the Schooner anymore."	113
THIRTEEN	"Shoot to kill."	117
FOURTEEN	"There's a guy out there who looks exactly like Mark Phillips."	125
FIFTEEN	"Badness grows like rice in the fields."	139
SIXTEEN	"You guys will also be killed in the explosion."	149
SEVENTEEN	The legal mile.	154
EIGHTEEN	"This will change investigation and security forever."	162
NINETEEN	"Very bad times have befallen us."	181
TWENTY	"My client wants his money back."	191
TWENTY-ONE	"Something bad has happened with the case."	197
TWENTY-TWO	"Trust comes on foot but leaves on horseback."	204
TWENTY-THREE	"This place is getting a hold on us."	213
TWENTY-FOUR	Drive a black Mercedes. Tell lies.	226
TWENTY-FIVE	"Would it be fatal if I was to tell you I had been in the police?"	237

Foreword

by
Alan Duff

I FIRST READ OF MARK's extraordinary story in the *New Zealand Herald* online while living in France some five years ago. I made contact with a view to maybe write his story because it was so fascinating. We met and I decided to have a crack.

Sadly, my attempt fell well short. I know why: It was his story, he had lived it, especially that one year undercover with some of Auckland's most hardened criminals. He was only twenty. You talk about good acting. This young man acted brilliantly because every long, usually drunken day, his life was in danger.

It would only take someone from police training days to recognise him and recall old times. And he was dead. Or for some drunk paranoid crim to point the finger and call him a "nark". Narks in every criminal society are the worst form of life that must be obliterated. Mark withstood this intolerable pressure for a whole year.

A year that ended in him witnessing an actual murder. He was right there. He knew the guy who did it, and his girlfriend victim. But love had its nose in here too, as unwittingly he crossed paths with his future wife, a constable attending the scene of the murder. Meeting later as members of the same Auckland Police squad, they have now enjoyed thirty-plus happy years of marriage.

The private investigator Mark van Leewarden is also another incredible story, more often than not fraught with danger chasing fraudsters around the world and frequently nailing them.

Read this book and marvel at one very courageous, determined, even relentless, genuine good guy.

◀ ONE ▶

"Has he got one leg?"

"I got word to take you out." The sentence was delivered in a flat, menacing tone.

Wana Nepia was a senior man in the scene and had plenty of mana. He was thoroughly familiar with violence: how to inflict it and its effects. It wasn't surprising he had been given the contract to take out this nark. The nark being me.

Hearing those words activated every street-survival instinct I had developed over the last year as an undercover agent. Questions hurtled through my mind. *What's next? What should I say? What's my escape route? Who else is around? Is he carrying his favoured handgun? How serious is this?*

Wana was six foot two, powerfully built, and more than capable of delivering on his threat.

I'd only come into the Schooner Tavern that day because Roo, my operator, had implored me to. Although it sounded sensible when he asked me, now it seemed ludicrous. The rationale for turning up was that if I didn't, I would clearly be seen as a nark. My running mate Rick had committed a murder with a switchblade only days before and the word on the street was I had given a statement to the police homicide team.

Of course, I had. I was a police undercover agent deployed in this scene to take down hardened criminals, including Rick and, for that matter, the stand-over merchant Wana who was in front of me.

"Mate, we've done a heap of deals and you're still walking around," I said in my most earnest and incredulous voice. "Come on, brother, you know I'm not a nark."

I'd always got on well with Wana; we were pretty close, or so I thought. We had done four deals together previously when I had bought TVs and cocaine from him. The week before we had committed a burglary together. He cased the joint and I stood on his shoulders and catapulted through an insecure window. We got away with electronics and jewellery without a problem.

At my plea, Wana's face softened slightly, or softened as much as possible for a Maori thug's face with boob spots around the eyes and framed by a neck tattoo.

"Yeah, that's right. I've never had a problem with you," he conceded.

"Of course, mate, and why the fuck would I be here if I'd just been down the cop shop?"

"Yeah, but the word's been given and there's eighty grand in it for me."

"You know in your heart it's wrong, man," I said.

"It's true, I've never had any heat from shit we've done."

The ominous sense of inevitability in the air dissipated somewhat. The conversation was swinging my way.

"Plus we go way back," I reminded him. Not exactly true, but a year in the scene is easily extended in the target's mind through shared drug use, partying and doing deals together.

"Yeah, bro, that's true."

Bingo! My breathing started to normalise.

I also detected in Wana that killing me, or anyone in fact, was not really on his agenda, unlike Rick.

I'd seen Wana mete out violence before, dealing to a punk eighteen-year-old Black Power member who bleated about the price I offered him for a stereo system. Wana had been acting as my backstop when I did my usual dealings as the Schooner fence of stolen property. The backstop is a fundamental prerequisite in asserting your status as the pub's fence and maintaining a climate of fear in those you deal with. The prowess of your backstop enhances your own position. Burglars would turn up to see me. I'd check out the property in the boots of their cars, or they would bring it into the bar. TVs, stereos, jewellery, leather jackets, silver, firearms, drugs — it was all fair game. If I didn't know values I would take a sample away and my friendly local Crown valuer would give me a hand.

I paid cash up to no more than forty per cent of the value of the item.

It was sometimes a fine balance paying low enough to preserve the legal presumption it was stolen but enough to make it attractive. My one redeeming feature over my real fence competition was that I was always flush. Courtesy of the Queen, I always had a wad of cash at the ready.

At the offer of forty dollars the punk said it wasn't enough. This comment, and his smart-ass attitude, was disrespectful. Even if you wanted to let it pass, such an action cannot go unchallenged. It is damaging to your street cred, your cover and ultimately your survival.

My words, "Fuck you and fuck your attitude, you're gonna pay," were a sufficient signal to Wana of the desired next step.

When the punk left the Schooner and exited onto Quay Street, Wana followed him out the door. He caught up with him in the adjacent covered car park. When I arrived Wana had finished with the chain and was kicking the punk to the body. There wasn't much fight in him by this time and he was left to nurse his injuries. One of those we later found out was a broken leg.

An efficient and rapid display of violence from Wana and a lesson for other punk burglars coming to sell hot gear. Fencing stolen property is business and your rep is everything. Like every facet of street crime there is no room for weakness.

In this context Wana was having second thoughts about taking up the contract on me. The game wasn't over yet, though, and it certainly wasn't full time. Pensive, he peered into his beer glass as if the amber liquid might provide some portent of what action to take. For Wana, there was no middle ground with this call. I was either a nark or I wasn't. If he decided I was a nark then the drab surroundings of the Schooner might be the last thing I'd see. If I wasn't, I was walking back into the sunshine on Quay Street.

What Wana didn't know was that I had been present up until the murder Rick committed went down and accordingly was a key prosecution witness.

On Labour Day, 22 October 1979, I had picked Rick and his lady Paula up from their flat in Sandringham to head into the city and get on the piss. I had another criminal associate with me, Joe Kapa, a recently patched Black Power member. I drove over in my government-supplied Mitsubishi Lancer, a perfect car for the scene as it was nondescript and didn't attract police attention.

Rick, a strongly built Maori aged thirty-three, thirteen years older than me, was a major crime figure in Auckland. He presented as the personification of evil: long, shoulder-length black hair and smoking-black deep-sunk eyes. He stood about the same height as me, five foot eleven. Rick had lost his left leg below the knee in a motorcycle accident while riding with the Hell's Angels, and wore a prosthetic limb. His arms bore the mandatory full-sleeve tattoos and his hands wore boob-spot tattoos indicating time spent in prison. In his case eighteen years, with the last stint spent in D Block of Paremoremo Maximum Security prison.

D Block held the worst and most violent members of the New Zealand criminal scene. Time spent in D block gave you kudos, a passport to entry among upper-level street criminals.

Not being able to relate time in prison could be a difficulty for undercover agents attempting to penetrate a scene. No agent has been in prison; it is simply too dangerous to place an agent in jail. Saying you have served time when you haven't is like playing Russian roulette.

Rick's criminal history covered dishonesty, violence, robbery and extensive drug offending. When I met him he was primarily dealing cocaine, his drug of choice. When it was available, he would taste or shoot up heroin.

I had met Rick within the first three weeks of my deployment. My initial digs were in Parnell and it was the local pubs that I frequented. Parnell was a bit of a yuppie scene, but drug dealers were in evidence because of the potential clientele.

I was drinking in the Alexandra Tavern on Parnell Road, about halfway up on the right. The plan for my operation had involved specific criminal targets and covering specific areas. The reality was I was tossed into Auckland and told, "Go for it; hook on to whoever you can."

I was playing pool in the back bar of the Alex, which was the seedy part of the establishment. The cool movers and shakers drank in the front bar bordering Parnell Road where they could be seen. Rick challenged me to a game and that's how our relationship started.

Every agent seeks a top-line running mate who can drag him through the scene and make introductions to key players. Frankly, I could not have met a better person and the fact it was so early in the operation was a major bonus.

At the time I didn't realise the significance of the meeting or the status within the criminal world my new running mate held. That night, as was my usual practice, I reported to my operator and gave him a rundown of the day's events. I also made handwritten notes about every day of the deployment and secreted these where I was staying. These were for subsequent use as evidence. My favourite hiding place for the notes was inside the towel rail in my bathroom. The hiding place had better be good, because if those notes were ever found things would deteriorate rapidly.

When I told Roo that I had met a "Rick" and gave him a brief description, he became quite animated and asked, "Has he got one leg?"

I said, "Fuck, I don't know."

"You sure he doesn't have one leg?" Roo said in an excited tone. I thought then that this dude must be important.

"I don't know, he might have had a bit of a limp," I responded.

"Fuck, if that's Ricki Goodin, he's the main man. You need to get right alongside him. He'll take you everywhere."

I met Rick again the next day, his identity was confirmed, and from then on we became tight associates and in due course friends.

Rick's lady, Paula, would have been an attractive woman when she was younger. At twenty-eight, though, she looked much older. The ravages of hard-core drug use had taken its toll. A Maori with long black hair, her body was now too skinny, but a few more kilos would have served her well in her previous job as a stripper in Wellington.

She had a distinctive Japanese-style snake tattoo right down her back. I'd never seen a tattoo like that. No doubt many a Wellington strip club patron would have been mesmerised by that reptile.

In the scene, women can be your most dangerous threat. In my case Paula was at the top of the list. You learn from operating undercover that female intuition is real and dangerous. You may possess every accoutrement of criminality and a watertight cover, but it can all be pierced by an inquisitive female. Paula knew there was something not quite right with me, but she couldn't pinpoint what it was. She told Rick, "You need to watch him. I'm suspicious, but cops don't have tattoos or wear earrings like that."

When Rick told me what she said, I just blew it off and nothing really changed between us. This was 1979 and tattoos were not as ubiquitous as they are now. My gold pendant left earring was also unusual.

One night Paula rolled out her culinary repertoire and cooked a mince feed for Rick and me. This was the one and only meal she cooked. I like mince and can happily consume the most basic fare. Paula's mince was in another realm, though. It was composed of minced something and fat. To call it inedible would be unfair, but it was certainly at the lower end of the scale as far as delicacies went.

When we had finished eating, I thanked Paula for what she'd done. This is what decent middle-class country boys do. Not in the criminal scene. From Paula's reaction I knew my thanks were out of place and I had made a mistake. Rick's expression conveyed the view that that's what she was supposed to do and she should be doing more.

In the street-criminal scene women were not regarded highly. They were never involved in doing business, should look good and be on their backs when required. Their mouths should be kept shut unless spoken to, or a cuff could be coming their way.

Despite this, their influence in the scene was significant. It was not unusual for crims to be cajoled and stirred up by their birds. Particularly so if they didn't like someone or saw them as a threat to their man. A well-placed "He's disrespecting you," "He ripped you off," "He's an undercover," "He's hitting on me," or "That fucker's got to be knocked over," could do wonders in instigating swift action and advancing a bird's objectives. I was beginning to learn then, and it crystallised in later years, that in most convoluted investigations there would be a woman somewhere influencing the turn of events. Cherchez la femme.

Joe, Rick, Paula and I headed into the city. Paula looked a little more shit-faced than normal considering it was pretty early in the day. Joe had been a loyal associate for some time. He was Maori and slightly built but he could look after himself. Joe was nineteen and from a brutally violent background. This had driven him into gangs and crime. He had a particularly strong bent as a burglar, and did nicely stealing electronics. He had yet to be caught, but that was to change through his involvement with me. It was handy to be associated with gang members. It provided another arrow in my quiver of criminality.

Our first stop that day was the Lion Tavern in Fort Street. The Lion was a criminal hangout but not as hard-core as the Schooner. It was occupied by straight people who could get a bit of a taste of the underworld and maybe score some gear. It was one of my stomping grounds and we were all known there. I didn't do much fencing bizzo there — any burglars who fronted I would normally put off until I was next back at the Schooner. Drugs were different. I did deals there on pills, cocaine and small amounts of heroin. The druggies were thicker on the ground in the Lion.

A few months into the scene, when I was getting established, I would carry a sawn-off shotgun under a long leather coat. Carrying that and entering the Lion with two backstops and a couple of good-looking hookers put the frighteners on most people I encountered. There was a table in the middle of the bar by the dance floor. That was our table. I would sweep in with Rick and our crew and if anyone at the table knew us they would move straight away. If they didn't know us, or chose not to move, they were unceremoniously told to fuck off. A headlock was used in the absence of immediate compliance. We would take their piss too.

Exhibiting that sort of power and the feeling it created was a surreal experience, and I could see how it would become addictive. At the time it was intoxicating.

I had to stop carrying the shotgun because, as I became more important and significant in the scene, I came to the attention of the police. Those police interested in me of course had no idea I was a cop working undercover — they were just doing their job. Under no circumstances could you, or would you, admit to a cop or anyone else what you were actually doing. *Deny, deny, deny. Your life may depend on it.*

Two cops in particular took an interest in me. Detective Sergeants John Hughes and Tony Lynch. Hughesy had a reputation as a tough uncompromising detective. A former boxer, he would not back down from anyone, including the most vicious criminals. He knew I was doing plenty of business in stolen property and drugs, and he made it his mission to put heat on me.

The heat ramped up to a degree where it was affecting my business. As Hughesy could not be told who I was, I just had to deal with it. Every time he saw me in the Lion he would tip me out. Usually accompanied by Tony Lynch, he would approach me with my associates, tell me to come with him and take me through the bar out onto Fort Street. There he would search me, including making me take my boots off. He would then generally hassle me about what I was doing. As I held decent wads of cash in my boot to pay for gear, it was inconvenient. I didn't want to get caught with anything, either, especially not a firearm or narcotics. Being arrested would be difficult.

The other side of the coin is that it didn't hurt my cover to be escorted from the pub by senior detectives. It was a different story if you got attention from uniform cops. They were simply regarded as fleas. The only cops that meant anything in the scene were detectives, whom we called Ds or demons.

We left the Lion and got to the Schooner around 11am. I resumed the day's drinking with my usual tipple — a quart bottle of Lion lager.

Alcohol was a constant, day in day out, and heavy drinking the norm. I'd always start with beer and after three or four switch to bourbon and Paeroa. When they were around and I felt like it, I'd drop pills as well. The huge amounts of alcohol, shit food and lack of exercise took their toll. I put on about two stone during the course of the operation.

By the time I switched to bourbon, I normally had a good buzz on and was nestled into my criminal persona. On one occasion in Parnell

Road I was so wasted on alcohol, cannabis and a pill concoction that I fell down a set of wooden stairs leading to someone's house. Upon impact at the bottom and rolling away from the stairs, I came face to face with an Alsatian tied to a clothes line. The dog barked at me. My response, which I thought was totally appropriate at the time, was to bark back.

But no matter how wasted I was, I always knew what I was doing. Somewhere in the back of my mind a self-preservation brake operated born of training, fear and anxiety. I would never be loose enough to make admissions about my true role.

Rick had a rum and Coke, as did Paula. We sat around chewing the fat and Paula dropped a few chewies. I don't know how many she took but she had certainly taken some at home as well before we picked her up. After a couple of rounds of drinks she was slurring her words and became unsteady on her feet.

Chewies was the street name for Tuinal prescription pills. In 1979 there was a heroin vacuum on the streets of Auckland and the rest of the country. This was caused by the demise of the Mr Asia syndicate. Terry Clark, a New Zealander, had been a major player in the international drug scene, moving large quantities of heroin through Singapore into Australia and New Zealand. His homeland was a beneficiary of his worldwide success. Clark, who based himself in Australia, had taken over the syndicate after putting a hit out on the boss, Marty Johnstone. Clark thought Johnstone was about to nark and roll over to the cops in New Zealand. This view was correct. Johnstone had also been ripped off in a deal in Thailand, losing Clark a considerable sum.

The contract on Johnstone was taken up by his best friend, who shot him in the head, cut off his hands and dumped him in a quarry in Lancashire. This murder was one of around a dozen attributable to Clark.

Clark's lawyer was Eb Leary, a flamboyant Auckland-based criminal barrister. He was a dapper man and master of oratory, but involvement with Clark was his undoing. When appearing for clients he strode through the courts like some dominant lion of the law. His eloquent addresses were such that the court stenographers used to look forward to working in the courtrooms where he appeared.

Eb's stellar career collapsed when in the late Eighties he was struck off by the Law Society after he introduced another client to Clark: the clients began drug-dealing together. He was also found guilty of trying to deceive the Inland Revenue Department and a Drug Trafficking Commission. Eb was to pose major problems for me and my operation.

The New Zealand end of the Mr Asia operation was run by Peter Fulcher, a burglar and safe-cracker who had worked his way up into the drug world. He distributed syndicate heroin and cocaine to lower-level street dealers and acted as an enforcer. He was quick to violence, a baseball bat being his tool of trade.

I met Fulcher briefly but never got a chance to properly connect with him and develop a relationship. His reputation as one of the country's highest profile and most dangerous criminals preceded him. Although with an undoubted sense of menace, he presented as a physically slight and relatively short European in his mid-thirties.

The Auckland streets were awash with heroin and cocaine in 1978 and generating millions for the Mr Asia syndicate, but by the time I was deployed in 1979 the situation was different. The syndicate ructions had taken their toll on the drug supply lines. With the lack of heroin on the streets came the rise of alternatives to feed junkies' habits. The junkies turned to pills such as Tuinal, Decanol and Secanol. These drugs came in tablet form. To get the best hit, junkies crushed the tablets and injected them intravenously. These drugs were dangerous, and a fine line existed between a superb high and death from an overdose.

The most favoured and best of these drugs was Tuinal, at that time a Class C controlled drug. Demand was high for chewies and prices were jacked up. Chewie dealers were making good money. There was one major supplier who kept the market satisfied, a chemist from Parnell. He was making considerably more cash in the illicit drug scene than from his pharmacy and supplied the majority of the Auckland drug scene. He became one of my targets.

The junkies were attracted to a clean outlet like the chemist instead of having to forage on the street trying to score from chemist-shop burglars. With the demand for pills had come a spate of chemist-shop burglaries and robberies. The problem was so bad that the police resorted to physical surveillance of high-risk pharmacies and setting up alarms that directly activated in patrol and Criminal Investigation Branch (CIB) crime cars.

Decanol tablets were called pinkies on the streets: if shot up they produced a good hit. Secanol tablets were called dolls. All three were barbiturates and highly addictive. Other drugs on the street at the time were Methadone, Pethidine, Palfium and Mandrax (mandies). Heroin and cocaine were still about, but only in small amounts. Methamphetamine was not used at the time — that scourge was still on its way.

The problem for junkies when forced to switch to new drugs was assessing how much they needed to get the right hit. With heroin, they knew quantities and strengths. Heroin was often cut by dealers down the chain so it would go further and mean better returns. The cutting changed the strength. Despite this, junkies were used to the variances and knew their effect.

It was different shooting up pills. Getting their drug concoction right required experimentation, sometimes with fatal consequences. Early in my deployment I met four hard-core junkies who were all friends and stayed together. Of the three men and one woman, only one was alive when I finished. Two had overdosed and one had jumped off Grafton Bridge thinking he could fly.

After three rounds of drinks at the Schooner Rick said, "This place is fucken boring, let's fuck off to the Station." This was the New Station Hotel in Anzac Avenue. This proved to be a fateful call.

The New Station Hotel covered two levels, a public bar on the downstairs Beach Road floor and the Harbour Lights lounge on the top floor, with an entrance from Anzac Avenue. I parked the Mitsi on Beach Road and we entered the public bar. We scored drinks and assembled around the pool tables. Most of the people I associated with were handy at pool after spending inordinately long hours in bars.

Stools were lined up in a semicircle mirroring the bar. Rick and Paula took seats at the bar. We ordered drinks, top shelf by now, and Joe and I took seats at a table opposite the bar. By this time Paula was really out of it. She had obviously dropped a heap of chewies which were really kicking in.

She tried to sit on the stool but her co-ordination abandoned her and she missed the seat completely, catching herself on the bar rail before falling. Rick was not impressed. "What the fuck do you think you're doing?" Paula's slurred response was unintelligible.

Joe and I began chilling at the table, talking about important matters such as narks. Joe said, "Disrespectful pricks, narks and fucking fleas need to go. They gotta be knocked over."

"Yeah man, you're dead right," I replied.

"And fucken undercovers of course," he added.

"Yeah, right on. No mercy," I said.

"You know that tall fucker with the hat who was in the Schooner? He's an undercover."

This was a regular topic of conversation. Numerous times I would be told by associates that this person or that person was an undercover. At the time I was deployed there was one other agent working in Auckland, Oyster, who had been on the same undercover seminar as me. He was about the only person they didn't name.

Rick left the bar, came over to where Joe and I were sitting and said to me, "I need that fucken blade, man."

He was referring to a switchblade knife that I had taken off him about three weeks previously. Rick customarily carried the knife. Roo had discussed with me that this was probably not good for the operation as Rick was already on bail for serious charges and if he got snapped with the blade, he would end up in jail. We didn't want that — I needed Rick on the street to advance the operation.

When I took the blade off him, Rick said, "I'll give you the nod if some fucker gets out of line and I need it back."

I didn't see any problem with giving the switchblade back to him now — but how wrong I was.

After a couple of hours in the public bar we left and took the lift up to the Harbour Lights lounge. Rick and Paula sat at a table by the jukebox and Joe and I sat at a table across from them. The arguments between Rick and Paula became more heated.

As time passed more people drifted into the bar and a few extra rounds slid down. Paula became progressively more wasted. Remaining properly seated became impossible and she continued to slump to either side of her chair. By now she was ranting and abusive.

Rick became extremely agitated at her behaviour. This had been brewing during the course of the day. I couldn't hear exactly what was being said but then Rick yelled, "You fucken bitch!" Paula had snarled something at him and simultaneously slumped off her chair towards him. He roughly pushed her backwards and slapped her across the face. She fell off her chair and began to cry.

When she got herself back up, she unleashed a litany of swearing directed at Rick. He became incensed and slapped her twice more on each cheek. "You're a fucken disgrace, you fucken bitch."

At Rick's actions Joe became agitated. He stood up from the table but didn't move. "He fucken better watch himself," he said. "She doesn't deserve that."

This was a big call from someone like Joe, even to start to disapprove of what Rick was doing. Joe was only young and hadn't been around that long. Rick was a senior crime figure who commanded respect. If he wanted to cuff his woman, that was his call.

It was a mark of Joe's staunchness that it looked as if he was going to do something about what was happening. Paula made some inaudible but derogatory comment towards Rick. This resulted in her being punched in the face, which properly floored her.

At this Joe rushed at Rick yelling, "You fucken prick!" He got Rick in a headlock, tipped him from his chair and they spiralled away towards the dance floor, wrestling as they went. Rick got in a couple of short jabs to the body but Joe wouldn't release him. They fell to the ground. Rick was under Joe and his head hit the wooden floor hard. With Rick dazed, Joe unleashed brutal and fast punches to his face.

In the mêlée, Rick's artificial leg came off. Although he kept wrestling and punching, this left him at a disadvantage. Joe was not as big but was younger and fitter. His Black Power background meant he was used to street fighting. He was getting the better of Rick in this scrap.

When the fight started the barman began yelling that he was calling the police. Things were quickly becoming very untidy. When the barman repeated the word "Police" I intervened in the fight and pulled Joe off Rick. "We're getting out of here, now!" I told Joe.

By this time Rick was like a rabid dog, complete with the saliva and snarl. Joe and I left him sitting on the dance floor, minus his leg, and hurried to the lift.

As we passed him, the barman was gesticulating frantically and yelling that the police were coming. My immediate objective was to get away before they arrived. Rick was angry, defeated, humiliated and in a frenzy. I needed to get away from him as well.

The lift dropped us to the Beach Road level. The Mitsi was parked just along the road. I drove and we left the city heading out to Panmure. Out there, south of the city, was one of our favourite haunts, a bar and nightclub called Cleopatra's. We headed there.

◀ TWO ▶

"Emu, you've gotta go back in."

I USED THE COVER NAME Mark Munro. My cover story was that I was from the South Island and was a rich kid living on trust funds. Somewhere along the way, I had basically gone rogue and turned to crime. I had a government-supplied driver's licence in my cover name and a false address. My supplied car was registered in my cover name, with my Parnell address. I didn't need a bank account, as I always had plenty of cash.

The key with cover stories is that the basics need to be watertight, but the details should not be too specific. Once I got into the scene and started rolling, my cover was only really challenged once. If anyone ever did start asking probing questions the classic response was, "Who the fuck are you, a policeman?"

This could be delivered forcefully, and generally a retort was never forthcoming. The most dangerous people you could encounter were those who knew you in the past and were aware you had joined the police. Sometimes police you had trained with could stupidly or inadvertently cause exposure issues.

My code name was Emu. Every undercover agent has a code name. It is a protective device. Your operator and those within the Criminal Intelligence Section (CIS) who are aware of the operation only use your code name. By this means no actual names, not even cover names, are referred to, thereby preserving confidentiality. Secrecy is the only thing that protects you.

There were no mobile phones when I was deployed so I had set times during each day when I would call my operator, Roo. I had to call every day. If no call was received, Roo would go on alert, as there could be a problem. When I called I would always say my code name first before anything else. He knew then categorically it was me and that it was cool to speak. If I said, "Hey Uncle Paul, it's Mark," he would know there was someone else with me.

I might use this tactically, so the conversation was purportedly regarding a deal where an associate could listen, or alternatively there might be something wrong. When I didn't say my code name, Roo would listen very carefully to ascertain what was happening.

I knew Roo so well it was easy for us to speak in riddles and be understood. Over the course of an operation you get to know your operator extremely well. You are working in life-and-death situations, so you need complete trust and faith in your operator. He is your only link to the real world. The relationship you have is quite unlike anything else.

Every day Roo and I would speak about what happened during the course of the day. These conversations would last at least an hour, sometimes longer when plenty was happening. We discussed individuals and operational tactics. How to relate to a particular individual and what would be said to him, leading up to a deal, could warrant detailed discussions.

There was also a direct line into the CIS from where the undercover operations were based. I could use this if I needed something urgently, if there was a problem, or I couldn't get hold of Roo. That line was answered "Hello" and normally by Bernie. An old-school detective nearing retirement, Bernie was like an old trusted uncle. Dealing with him was comforting.

Aside from those contacts, I didn't interact with anyone. I lived and breathed the criminal life. Essentially I lived as a criminal and over time I felt like a criminal. Gradually there is a progression whereby your social mores begin to become jumbled. Almost by osmosis your criminal persona seeps into your being.

In conjunction with this comes an unwitting change in personality and behaviour. Although you are not personally aware of it, the outward transmogrification into criminality is witnessed in stark relief by your family and friends. During the year I was deployed I returned to my parents' home in the South Island on three occasions for R&R, or rest and relaxation. Each time I went back I was further subsumed by the criminal persona I had chosen to adopt.

On my last visit home for R&R before terminating, my sister startled me when I was changing an LP. I didn't see her approach and was surprised when I saw her. My instinctive reaction was to strike out at her, which is what I did. It was more by good luck than good management that I didn't connect with her face. When I was at my local home-town pub, I was approached by the local heads who wanted to score heroin. My mutation from small-town country boy to big-city criminal was complete.

There was only one other total-immersion police undercover programme at the time, and that was run by the Canadians. Most other jurisdictions had operations lasting only a matter of weeks, or a cop would simply put on a leather jacket and go and do a buy. These types of deals were normally set up by informants and the offender would be crunched and arrested after the buy went down.

Your real first name is generally always used in a cover name, as it is very difficult to respond to something other than what you have used all your life. Although my cover name was Mark, in the scene I used to get called Marcus. Rick christened me with that handle, but I'm not sure why. It was a name that stuck after my deployment, into the CIB and beyond.

The most serious threat to my cover came in the Schooner. I had been deployed for about two-and-a-half months and was starting to get myself well established as a fence. I was drinking at a leaner one afternoon with Rick, Wana, and another associate, Charlie Shelford. Charlie was a large Maori, mid-thirties, who looked like a boxer. He had a fearsome reputation for violence and therefore made a good backstop. I used him in this capacity on a couple of occasions. I liked him; he was a good guy and had a really good-looking fox of a younger cousin whom he kindly introduced me to. He had access to a few young burglars and later in the operation hooked me up with some good stolen-property deals.

Also in the bar was Wana's nephew, Steve, a nineteen-year-old budding gangster. He had a couple of mates with him and was standing at a bar leaner about twenty metres from us. I had seen Steve once before and he presented as an arrogant, egotistical little prick. I think he was envious of my developing relationship with his uncle, whom he regarded as a hero. All the time within the scene, I was constantly assessing people, their demeanour, and what risks they might pose to me and the operation. I knew instinctively that Steve could be a problem.

Steve proceeded to saunter over to our leaner. On his way past us to the bar, and directed at me, he said, "There's a fucken few too many undercovers in here."

I tried to remain impassive but this was a major challenge. I murmured, "What the fuck's up with that prick?"

My mind was racing, however. How was I going to respond to this direct challenge to my position and reputation? I knew that this was a seminal moment in the operation. I had advanced to a reasonable degree in penetrating the scene, but how I reacted to this situation might well determine the future course of the operation. The most important players in my scene were standing around me.

Complicating the issue was Steve being Wana's nephew. Different potential scenarios barrelled through my mind. I bristled with awareness, trying to capture the mood around me. Once a bit of time had elapsed without any comments about what Steve had said, I left the leaner to go and have a piss. This ruse would give me an opportunity to crystallise my course of action.

At the toilets, as was customary, I entered a cubicle. In the scene you never pissed at a urinal: it was too dangerous. Standing with your back to the door you are vulnerable to attack. Alternatively, if you are going to get someone done, do it in the toilets — maybe they won't be so careful.

Once I had decided what to do, I left the toilets and headed back through the bar. I could see Steve and his associates standing at the leaner on the other side of where we were. When I had left the bar I noted that Steve had his back to our leaner. He was luckily still in this position when I emerged from the toilets.

I walked purposefully past our leaner towards Steve. As I approached his leaner, I picked up a bar stool. The Schooner bar stools had steel frames with an upholstered top. The frames were box steel with sharply defined edges.

Walking rapidly, I swung the stool behind me above my shoulders and then smashed it down onto Steve's head. He dropped like a puppet whose strings had been cut.

Steve lay unconscious at the base of the leaner. Blood seeped from the back of this head. His mates looked at me, but took no retaliatory action. They knew who my crew was and knew something serious had happened that they would rather not become familiar with.

I turned and walked back to where my henchmen were standing. I took my place at the leaner. No one said anything. After a pause Wana said, "Another beer?"

From that day I never had another challenge to my cover. Violence was the central premise. As an agent you had to prove you could look after yourself and therefore survive. Once this was established you could use others to dispense violence on your behalf if necessary. The rules were simple: you looked after your brothers, protected your women, remained staunch, never ripped off anyone who didn't deserve it, and exhibited a zero tolerance for fuckwits.

On the car trip out to Panmure, Joe and I discussed what had happened at the Station. When we got to Cleopatra's he was still wound up about Rick and the fight. "He fucken deserved that, Marcus," he said.

"What's done is done, bro," I replied. Even with a few drinks on board I had a feeling of disquiet. "Let's have a good time and forget about it."

Joe and I hit the piss pretty hard for the rest of the night. We cracked on to a couple of good-looking chicks, but it came to nothing as both of us were rolling drunk. The early hours of the morning were a blur, but I remembered being kicked out by the bouncers. I weaved from the bar to the Mitsi paralytic-drunk and drove Joe back into town. I always drove drunk. That's what you did; it was part of the deal.

The Police Department was clear: you were on your own as regards prosecutions for drink-driving. There would be no intervention in the prosecution of agents who were caught. You would be charged and dealt with after your operation. The rough interpretation of this edict to the undercover agent on the street was, "Drive pissed, but don't get caught."

My version of the edict was put into play one night in Parnell Road. I had been drinking at the Alexandra Tavern and had made my way inebriated from the pub after closing. The Mitsi was parked outside the pub, facing down Parnell Road. This necessitated my having to do a U-turn to head towards my flat in Corunna Avenue, off St Stephens Avenue. Naturally, in my condition, I dropped the clutch and screeched through the U-turn.

Unfortunately for me, prowling up Parnell Road at this very moment was an Auckland City Council traffic car. At that time the council employed its own traffic officers to enforce road rules within the city boundary. He fell in almost directly behind me. My worst fears were realised when I saw his light bar activated and heard the siren.

At the top of Parnell Road is a set of lights. The lights were red, so I stopped and the traffic car drew up behind me. I had my left indicator on displaying that I would turn left into St Stephens Avenue and stop. That's what I did, stopping about forty metres down.

He stopped behind me. I stayed in my car and intently watched my rear-view mirror for movement from his car. It was quite difficult because of the red-light wash from the roof, plus my vision was a bit blurred. I saw the door open and he stepped out on to the road.

Right then I threw my door open and took off running down the road. I cut on an angle from the roadway on to the footpath. To my surprise he was right behind me. I was pretty fast, even half-pissed with boots on. He stayed on my tail and I had to weave to prevent him grabbing my jacket — but at about a hundred metres he slowed down and my escape was complete.

I heard him in the distance yelling into his radio, "Ten-nine, ten-nine. I need dogs!"

I kept running down the road but no longer at a sprint. I scanned the houses I was passing and when I saw one with a good drive leading to the rear, I cut into the property. I ran down the drive to the rear boundary wooden fence and clambered over. There were lights on in the house but I didn't care. When I jumped over the fence, I landed in the vegetable garden of another property. I dropped down between the rows of veggies to catch my breath. As I lay there, I contemplated my options.

My digs were in an old house that was split into three flats. Corunna Avenue ran at right angles from St Stephens Avenue. I figured I could make my way through the back yards of properties all the way up to Corunna Avenue and emerge about where my house was. There wasn't much room for error. The longer I roamed the area, the higher the risk of canine intervention.

I jumped the fence into the next property. I skirted around the swimming pool and climbed over the next fence. At about this time, I heard a dog barking. It wasn't that close, but was close enough. The dogs could cover ground quickly, but I had done a loop and there was a bit of ground for them to cover. I kept running through properties and fell over a couple of times encountering backyard obstacles.

Dropping over the fence into the last property, I could see street lights through the trees. That's got to be Corunna Avenue, I thought. I burst through a hedge and on to a driveway which, sure enough, led on to my street. I broke into a full sprint on the open street and quickly reached my flat. Bursting through the door, I left the lights off, went into my bedroom and stripped down to my jocks.

I waited in the darkness. Knowing that my car was registered to my address, I figured they would turn up at some stage. I was still puffing and my heart rate was pretty high. I was sweating from the exertion and had cuts on my legs.

After about fifteen minutes there was a knock at the door. I let a suitable amount of time pass and then answered it. Standing in my jocks I did my best sleepy eye-rub and tried to suppress my heavy breathing. In the doorway were two ACC traffic cops in uniform. One was an older guy with sergeant's stripes; beside him was a younger cop, the one who had chased me. There was no sign of a dog van.

The older cop said, "Are you Mark Munro?"

"Yes."

"Were you driving your car tonight?"

"No."

The sergeant turned to his fast, but not fast enough, younger colleague. "Is this him?"

"I'm not sure. He had a brown jacket."

The sergeant turned back to me. "Do you have a brown jacket?"

"No," I said. "I lent my car to a mate tonight. I hope nothing's happened to it."

"No, but it will be impounded," the sergeant said in a slightly miffed, disapproving tone.

"Well, if that'll be all, gentlemen," I said, and closed the door.

I dropped Joe at his place in Kingsland and drove to my flat in Sandringham. By the time I got home it was around 4am. I fell into bed and went out like a light.

An hour later, which only felt like minutes to me, all hell broke loose. Simultaneous with my bedroom door being smashed, my window flew open. Instantly there were two figures dressed in black standing over me. Torchlight danced around the room before the light came on. I couldn't grasp what was happening. Shock raced through me like some rogue wave.

Squinting under the light and coughing, I took in my surroundings. Standing before my bed were two Armed Offenders Squad cops wearing black paramilitary uniforms and balaclavas and holding shotguns.

"Anyone else here?" one asked urgently.

"No," I said in a croaky voice that sounded like someone else's. "What the fuck's going on?"

"Your mad fucken mate Ricki Goodin has stabbed his bird. She's dead."

"Dead?" I said incredulously, as if repeating the word might change something. "Fuck, that's bad," I said to the room in general.

"We've been searching the city looking for you. We thought he might have taken you out as well. We need to get you down to Central to make a statement."

I had a shower, changed and was escorted down to the Auckland Central police station. My cover was still in place. The ramifications of what had happened began to circulate in my mind. Foremost of which was the switchblade. I had given the knife back to Ricki and that was undoubtedly the murder weapon. If I hadn't given the knife back Paula would still be alive.

On arrival at Central I was met by the detective inspector in charge of the case. He gave me a briefing, explaining that they had found the murder weapon buried in a garden in Anzac Avenue. It was the switchblade. Rick had been caught at the scene and was in custody. Paula had been stabbed three times, the fatal strike entering her heart. I made a full statement of all the circumstances leading up to the killing.

From an operational perspective, the murder was a crisis. Roo and I had a roundtable to discuss options. Talking this through would involve imbibing more rum than our sit-downs usually demanded. I travelled out to his place out west in Massey. Spread out in his lounge with our bevvies and the ever-present potato chips, we mulled over the options.

We were coming to the end of the operation anyway. This development meant the timetable needed to be brought forward. It was agreed pretty early that termination was the only option, which meant winding up the operation, withdrawing the agent (me), executing search warrants and making arrests. The risks of my remaining deployed were just too high.

Rick, at the scene and following the murder, had been spoken to by detectives. As expected, when interviewed he made no admissions and refused to co-operate on anything. He did not believe Paula was actually dead and had to be taken to the morgue to confirm her death.

With my running mate out of the game it would be difficult to make further traction operationally. We had close to a hundred offenders in the book and as far as we were concerned there were no major players outstanding. I had done deals with all the major targets.

Leading up to termination, considerable background work is required to ensure that the day you finish has maximum impact. One primary issue is: where is everyone living? Will they be at the address on termination day? What's the address location like? Who else is likely to be there? Are there fences? Are there dogs? What's the lighting like? What are the entry/escape routes? What's the likelihood of firearms being present? Will there be hard drugs at the address? If so, is provision required to smash toilet outlets in the event gear is flushed? Detectives assigned to the termination would profile supplied addresses.

Roo's strong view was that I needed to remain in the scene to gather as much information as possible for the lead-up to termination. This would mean doing a raft of fresh deals with offenders to get updated intelligence. His blunt appraisal was: "It's fucken dangerous, mate, but you've got to front up back at the Schooner as if it's bizzo as usual. It'll show the fuckers you're not a nark, too."

I wasn't so sure. If even a hint got out that I had made a statement, let alone that I was an undercover cop, I would be brown bread. It would certainly be safer to get out now. I could shoot down to the South Island and then come back for termination day. If a few targets weren't around on termination day, they could be mopped up later.

"Emu, you've gotta go back in," Roo reiterated.

Every single one of the cells in my body was in agreement that this was not a good idea. There were no dissenters. However, there was also a burning drive to do the best job possible. I had already invested a year in the operation. The success of what I'd done was a personal driver. I didn't want to compromise the job at the finish. My decision to go back was ultimately determined by my respect for Roo. He thought it was the right call and I was going to run with that. This eliminated none of my apprehension.

My thinking turned to when I would go back to the Schooner and how events might unfold. I thought about taking my shotgun or blade but decided against it.

What neither Roo nor I knew was that I was to be compromised in the worst way possible by the very department I was out there risking my life for.

Rick instructed as his defence counsel none other than Eb Leary, Terry Clark's lawyer. This was a major case and Rick was well known in the criminal underworld, so naturally Eb became his lawyer. Eb was anxious to know as much as he could about the Crown's case and the strength of the witnesses' evidence. Neither Roo nor I were sure why, but for some inexplicable reason Eb was provided with a copy of the statement I made, conduct so outrageous that it beggared belief. What was bewildering was that no one mentioned to Roo that my statement had been given to Eb. The statement, although in my cover name, was damning against Rick. It detailed every aspect of the lead-up to the murder and fingered Rick as the perpetrator. The link with the murder weapon was incontestable.

There is little doubt that Eb told Rick about the statement and probably showed it to him. So Roo's assessment and mine of the best way forward failed to incorporate one critical fact: my criminal associates now knew I was a nark.

◀ THREE ▶

"What'll we do now?"

I HAD GONE TO CANTERBURY University in 1977 to study law. I was unsettled and couldn't get my teeth into study. I was living in a hall of residence and had been selected for the Canterbury University Under-19 rugby team coached by Sir Ron Scott. It was a good team and hard to get into but despite this, when my schoolmate Tim said, "I'm heading to Oz, wanna come?" I replied, "I'm in."

A week later we were gone. After drinking piss in Sydney for a couple of weeks we absconded from our hotel, forgetting to pay our bill, and jumped on the Indian Pacific train for Perth. In Western Australia we both scored jobs driving tractors on a twenty-six-thousand-acre farm in Dowerin, a hundred and fifty kilometres north of Perth. The town's claim to fame is that it hosts the largest annual agricultural field days in Australia.

After a few months on the farm the novelty began to wear thin and I headed back to New Zealand with zero prospects. I camped at home with my parents. The old man had not been impressed with recent developments, particularly my dropping out of varsity. He raised the possibility of joining the police. It was probably a little more forcefully than just raising it.

I had immense respect for my father and still do. He had come from the Netherlands after the war as a nineteen-year-old seeking a better life for his future family. He and three mates were to board the Holland-America line ship in Rotterdam and emigrate, but on the day of the sailing none of the mates showed. Dad came anyway. (Interestingly, in light of my later career, his job before leaving Holland was as a researcher at a private investigation company.)

Dad worked assiduously when he arrived to get himself established. He dug ditches on hydro schemes, worked on farms and finally got into shearing where decent money could be earned. Only doing twenty sheep on his first day in the shearing shed could be considered a setback for some, but not a Dutch immigrant like Dad. He persevered until he reached two hundred a day.

Seven years' toil in shearing sheds allowed him the resources to purchase the lease on the Castlepoint Hotel in the Wairarapa. We lived there for around four years before we returned to mid-Canterbury when Dad became the manager of the Somerset Hotel in Ashburton.

Dad arranged for me to meet a sergeant in Ashburton called Wally Porter. Reluctantly I turned up at the police station and met Sergeant Porter. He gave me a rundown on policing and over the course of our chat my interest was piqued. That interest spiked further when Wally said, "Come with me. I want to show you something."

He took me to a commercial building on East Street not far from the police station. I followed him up a fire-escape ladder to the roof. We wended our way across the roof until we reached a jagged hole cut through the tin. Looking down through the hole I saw a rope, which was affixed to a roof beam, snaking towards the floor.

"Burglars came in through the roof last night and knocked this place over," said Wally.

As I looked at the scene of this crime it seemed a door opened, revealing an unexplored curiosity corridor of my mind. I was mesmerised by what I saw and determined I would give the police a go.

The three months I spent training at Trentham were a riot. I met some great people, learned plenty, trained hard physically and had a heap of fun. My sectional instructor, Sergeant Brian Oliver, was superb. We were his first section and he almost adopted us as part of his family. Albeit we were the drunken, older and out-of-control offspring.

Academically I didn't find the exams too testing and the unarmed combat and PT was fun for someone like me who enjoyed that type of contact and challenge. The partying was constant, with the college bar a continual nest of raucousness.

When I graduated I was posted to Dunedin. In 1978 the city had a population of just over a hundred thousand and a quarter of them were students. Hence the policing issues were not significant, and primarily related to disorder-type offending engaged in by students. For a new uniform cop working on the streets of Dunedin, this was a boon. With little actual police work to be done, the minds of the sectional cops collectively turned to having fun.

On a night shift which spanned from 9pm to 5am there were usually two uniform cars, a crime car and a dog van. When it was quiet, say around 2am, a predetermined code might be broadcast over the radio. If there was any reference to fishing in what was said, that meant a rendezvous at the quarry. All the cars working would converge on the quarry.

The highly trained New Zealand police officer has considerable foresight, so earlier in the day bottles of Dunedin's finest ale would be secreted in the shingle of the quarry, the innovative police officers having established that the shingle acted efficiently as a cooler. Parked in a semi-circle backed in against the shingle piles we would sit on the bonnets of the cars and, while enjoying a cool beer, watch the entertainment unfold. If you were inclined towards a grandstand seat you could sit on the roof between the lights.

The entertainment involved firing up your police vehicle of choice and moving on to the scarf flat area in front of the shingle piles. This was a natural amphitheatre we believed had been crafted specifically for our use. All forms of doughnuts, power slides and other mechanical manoeuvres were encouraged. The very best were met with cheers from Dunedin's constabulary. Once the beer had run out and if it was still quiet, we might turn to further frivolity involving the shooting of rats and rabbits.

My digs in Dunedin were a unit at 108 Forbury Road in St Clair. I flatted there with my mate Gringo. We were both on the same section, but Gringo had more seniority than me. For the things that mattered though, such as chasing girls and drinking beer, we were on the same page. Through a fortuitous architectural turn, our flat was elevated from the road with steps leading to the door. This allowed a commanding view of the road but also allowed us to watch new girlfriends arrive and make assessments as they ascended the stairs.

Our local pub was the Robbie Burns in George Street. The landlord of this fine establishment was Brian Stewart. Brian was of Irish descent, hence his natural affinity with partying. The synergies between us and Brian were immediate; the fact that he ran a drinking establishment prominently positioned in Dunedin's main street was beyond magnificent. The bar was shaped like a horseshoe. There was a perfect spot at the bar in the corner furthest from the George Street entrance. Like feral animals, Gringo and I claimed this as our exclusive lair. It was unfortunate for unwitting patrons who foolishly transgressed on our territory.

Tending the bar was the inimitable Fiona. A blonde vision of loveliness, her maths wasn't very good and we were only charged for every fourth or fifth drink. Fiona went out with Detective Sergeant John Dhyrberg, another mate of ours. Hence she was part of the crew.

Brian had an arrangement with Contiki Tours whereby the tour members would turn up at the Robbie for a bout of partying. Contiki targeted youth from around the world with an emphasis on having a good time. The tours traditionally had a high volume of good-looking chicks from overseas. The tours normally touched down at the Robbie once every couple of weeks, on a Friday about midnight. Being a man who spread goodwill freely, Brian would kindly call our flat and advise us when the tour had arrived. If we weren't working, we would immediately scramble and head into the Robbie to sample the tour's talent.

Gringo was a member of the Armed Offenders Squad. This could be handy in redressing wrongs. One of his girlfriends made the unfortunate error of going out with someone else. She was unfamiliar with the rule that Gringo could go out with other people, but she couldn't. To sort the issue Gringo chose to kick down the unfortunate girlfriend's door in full AOS gear and then patiently advise her and her beau that their liaison was not appropriate.

One of my girlfriends we called the pig farmer's wife, because, yes, she was married to a pig farmer. The pig farmer was a bit of a crook. He had convictions for converting cars and assault, and regarded himself as a bit of a tough guy. Most tough guys, however, are not cuckolded by their wives. I met her at the Prince of Wales hotel. She was drinking there with her mates at a hen party. She was cute. Petite and cheeky, she dressed in a hippie-chic style. During the course of the night our paths crossed and we hit it off. After a bout of sweet talking, she joined me back at Forbury Road. After that night she used to visit on a regular basis, until the pig farmer got wind of something untoward occurring.

The pig farmer's wife used to turn up in a late-model Holden Statesman. It was a nice car, a top-spec V8 in blue. It was also her husband's pride and joy. The day our relationship ended was a Wednesday. She came to visit about 6pm. Just after she arrived we were having a couple of beers in the lounge. Gringo was there with a fine specimen of womanhood also from the Prince of Wales. That day, the pig farmer's wife had parked the Statesman further up Forbury Road instead of right outside the flat as she normally did. As we began to settle in she was surveying the street from the flat window. "Fuck, there's my husband!" she blurted.

Four sets of eyes scanned the street. About five addresses up towards the city, a well-built man wearing a rough leather jacket and jeans was prowling around the footpath. He carried a baseball bat in his right hand. Using the parked Statesman as a point of reference he was checking the closest houses for his wife. The best guess was he had carried out surveillance, but had fortunately not pinpointed the exact property his wife had entered.

A shrill "What'll we do now?" came from the pig farmer's wife.

"Nothing," I said. "It's cool. He obviously doesn't know anything or he'd be at the door."

Our drinking entertainment for the next twenty minutes comprised watching the poor pig farmer frantically combing the reaches of Forbury Road.

I am an avowed petrol head. I inherited this disease from my parents. My children have inherited it from me. At eighteen my mother was riding an AJS motorcycle around the South Island's dirt roads. When she hooked up with Dad he had a Triumph Bonneville 650. For a slight girl, kick-starting those bikes without a decompression switch was no mean feat.

In Dunedin I drove a 1975 V8 Holden Ute with mags and a sports exhaust system. The Ute concept is the manifestation of mechanical greatness and the best thing the Aussies have given the world. It was stupendous thinking to have a huge V8 up front, a cab with car comfort and a deck for motorcycles and sleeping. Gringo had an RX3 Mazda.

As both Gringo and I used to drive north to see family, me to Ashburton and him to Christchurch, it seemed only proper that we should race each other from Dunedin to Ashburton. The best time to conduct these Down Under gumball rallies was immediately after night shift at 5am. The roads were clear, with no public interfering in the craziness.

Gringo and I did that race about four times with the honours evenly shared. There was a bad section of road at Pareora south of Timaru that has now been straightened. The reasons why that section of road needed to be changed were blindingly apparent when we went through it at a hundred and forty kilometres per hour. I was chasing Gringo and about four car lengths behind. He went through the slight left okay but the right at that speed was ambitious.

The RX3 went sideways, crossed the centreline and into the gravel on the other side of the road. It was still early so there was no oncoming traffic, which was lucky for Gringo. His RX3 fishtailed in the shingle and went end for end, before coming to a halt in front of a farm fence strainer post. Of those trips, that was the only brush with disaster.

We still carried on racing — at nineteen your risk modulator is permanently set on "low". The record for the two hundred and seventy-five-kilometre trip was two hours four minutes.

You see plenty of dead bodies in the police. Most people, I think, remember their first one. Mine was a young motorcyclist (ironic, considering the petrol-head gene). He had been travelling towards Dunedin, heading south along State Highway One. Speed looked like a contributor and he had left the road just south of the Kilmog Hill. The bike was down a bank, but the rider was not far off the road face down in the grass. There wasn't much blood and no really visible injuries, but he was obviously dead. He was about the same age as me, but what remained imprinted on my mind were his boots. They were a cowboy style, the type I liked. A tan colour and worn-in just the right amount. The image of those boots lingered for ages; I can still see them. The young dead rider would never again walk in those boots.

The next first I experienced was a serious traffic accident. Four teenagers were in a sports car that hit a bridge over the Leith stream. The driver was alongside his mate in the front. Their girlfriends were in the back seat. The impact seriously injured the driver and his front-seat passenger. It was the girls that affected me most. They were both moderately injured with a large amount of blood splattered around the back seat and on their clothes. Both were pretty blondes, around eighteen, dressed in their best finery. The incongruity of it: pink clutch purse spotted with blood, finely textured stockings seeping blood, a cut above a perfectly made-up eye.

"Are you okay?" was met with a whimper like a wounded puppy's. Crushed beauty. The sense of helplessness was palpable. The practicalities of the accident scene were dealt with, but all I felt was an over-riding sadness.

Walking the beat in Dunedin held no appeal. I was required to walk up Lower Stuart Street to the Octagon and cover Princes and George streets, the main shopping precinct. Despite being in uniform, I wanted to remain as inconspicuous as possible. I didn't want to be asked any questions: I didn't know anything about Dunedin. I certainly didn't want to arrest anyone.

Being as comfortable as a crime fighter should, I adopted the habit of slouching, having my hands in my pockets and my shirt hanging out. Not everyone was impressed with the new style of beat cop presentation — specifically, the district commander, whose Friday morning was shattered by the sight of his staff member in George Street, eyes to the ground, unshaven, shirt tail gently flapping, hands buried, slowly wending his way along the footpath. This episode earned a formal rebuke, but I didn't consider the senior officer's attack sufficient to make style changes.

There were three favourite stops I had on the beat. My first was the Regent movie theatre in the Octagon. I had a deal with management where I could sneak in a back door. By slipping through a curtain I had access to a couple of seats at the rear of the cinema. Perched there, I had a commanding view of the latest movie offerings. I had to remember to turn my radio volume right down or switch it off. Failing to do this on one occasion meant a shoplifter call from Ops splintering the Dolby sound of the afternoon matinee. A few good movies were watched from my secret vantage point, including the first *Superman* film.

My second port of call was the BNZ in Princes Street. I had a fox of a girlfriend who worked there. Considerable fuss was generated by her and her equally foxy colleagues when the local police visited. I was whisked through to the staff room and there plied with tea and biscuits.

From the bank I would slouch further down Princes Street to Max's Men's Shoes. Max was pro-police and a good bloke. Many a fine discussion was held with him while resting comfortably in the La-Z-Boy out the back of his shop.

Night-shift beat in Dunedin was a battle against the elements. No imaginative bobby should get wet or cold. By scouring the South Island rural-supply companies I sourced a pair of black boots with sheepskin lining. Perfect for the below-zero conditions often experienced. When I started at 9pm I would be visible until around midnight, then head towards my refuge downtown. A multi-storey building was being constructed on the corner of the Octagon and George Street. On the top was my fortress. It took the form of the construction office Portacom. The builders kindly had a kettle and tea, presumably for police use. Extreme comfort and protection from the elements was afforded by a three-bar heater and a bench peppered with cushions. A perfect nest and site of repose for the protector of the city.

Across the country detectives working in crime cars have uniform drivers. The crime cars act in a patrol capacity and are the first attenders at instances of serious crime such as murder, serious assaults, robbery and rape. The uniform drivers are seconded from section and dressed in suits. With crime cars attending first, trained investigators can secure the scene and conduct first-instance inquiries. The first steps taken immediately a crime occurs can determine whether or not a case is solved. The scene must be preserved to prevent contamination of evidence.

Setting the scene perimeters is important. First steps to locate the perpetrator need to be directed and timely, as this is the closest you will be to them. Witnesses may disappear, so they need to be assembled and their details taken forthwith. Their recollection will never be better than at that time. Investigative and scene considerations, however, will always be secondary to preserving life. In a shooting, stabbing or serious assault the first priority is to try to save the victim. If this means the scene is somewhat compromised, so be it.

In Dunedin my first crime-driver experience was with a detective who had a reputation for an uncompromising approach to solving crime. After line-up, at the commencement of night shift, he said, "Let's fuck off out there and terrorise some cunts."

It was early in the week, so it was quiet and we didn't get any jobs. We cruised the city and around midnight the detective said, "Let's head over Saddle Hill. There's normally a bit of prey up there."

Saddle Hill was an alternative route from the city to Mosgiel. Nefarious activities occurred up there, including the dumping of stolen cars. As we reached the top of Saddle Hill, our headlights played on a car parked on the side of the road. It was a new 351 Ford Falcon coupé, a desirable and expensive muscle car.

"Hah, that car belongs to the Mason boys," the detective shouted. "Every one of those brothers is a bad motherfucker. I'll fix them. Stop here." A constant stream of expletives was followed by, "Pop the boot."

At that, he jumped from the passenger's seat and disappeared around the rear of the car. As I got out he emerged with a wheel brace. He stalked to the front of the Falcon.

"Shine your torch on there," he ordered, indicating the bonnet. With a swift wrench the bonnet popped open. "In the engine bay," he said, indicating a further need for light. He then grabbed and ripped every piece of exposed wiring he could reach. The result was a bristling nest of wiring, casting tiny shadows in the torchlight. For good measure the distributor and its leads were flung deep into the bush bordering the road.

"Our work here is done," said the detective happily. "Let's fuck off back to the city and get a burger."

After considerable deliberation at the Robbie, Gringo and I devised our own system of dispensing justice. We called it Rule 108. This extra-judicial process was first implemented about 8pm in Crawford Street, on the one-way system. We spotted three students acting suspiciously on the side of the street. Undetected by the students, who were frantically unbolting a street sign from its frame, we cruised to a halt beside them.

"Nice evening for a spot of thievery," said Gringo through the driver's window.

"Fuck!" the three students bleated out, almost in unison.

We both got out of the car and spoke to them. The two males were each holding an end of the sign. Their logistical support, in the form of a girl, had screwdrivers and a hammer in her back pack.

Our shift was to end at nine and the theft of a street sign is not the Great Train Robbery. Hell, I had souvenired road signs myself at varsity and proudly displayed them at Chester Hall in Christchurch. The reality in these circumstances was that if students were arrested and put before the courts they would more than likely be discharged without conviction.

"Right, you little shitbags," said Gringo to the students, who weren't much younger than us. "You've got two options. You get arrested and locked up downtown, or you can opt for Rule 108."

"What's Rule 108?" said the pragmatic female.

"It involves swimming," I said.

"I'm a law student and have never heard of that," said one of the blokes. "What statute is it?"

Gringo replied, "The Fish and Chip Act. It's a new initiative."

The group quickly formed the view that Rule 108 was their preferred option. Upon consensus reigning, we loaded the three into the car and headed for the wharf. The Rule 108 jetty was about five feet above the water. One by one, the students were ordered to jump off, like walking the plank. We waited until the thrashing around had ceased and they had emerged from the harbour.

"Right, don't let us see you pulling that shit again," said Gringo in a very pious tone. We drove back to the station, planning the night's festivities as we went.

After over a year in Dunedin, I had not become any further enamoured with wearing a uniform. So I was receptive to options when approached by Detective Sergeant Tom Lewis. I was in the muster room with the other sectional cops about to start a late shift at 1pm.

Around line-up on this shift, Tom Lewis appeared in the muster room. It was unusual to see a member of the CIB there, let alone a detective sergeant. He asked to speak with me and we adjourned to an interview room adjoining the muster room.

"Had enough of being in uniform?" he asked me. Very perceptive, I thought.

"We think you're the type of joker who would suit working undercover. No controls, out there doing deals and drinking piss." And that was it; two weeks later I was gone.

I never contemplated turning it down. There was no cautionary sage advice from Tom about potential downsides, but even if there had been I would have ignored it. When you agree to enter the undercover programme you can never comprehend how you will be affected. You have changed the course of your life. It is impossibly uninformed consent.

One regretful aspect at the time was rugby-related. About a week before the Lewis approach I had played in a trial for the Alhambra Club senior team. Otago rugby was strong then and club rugby was the backbone of the province. Gringo had suggested that we go and play in the trials. We hadn't done any pre-season training with the club and I had no prior links at all with Alhambra.

I could always play rugby. I played in Mid-Canterbury age group representative teams. I captained the Mid-Canterbury Under-18 South Island tournament team and was selected to play in the trials for the South Island team. My opponent at second five eighth was Steve Pokere, who went on to become an All Black. Also playing in that tournament was Steve Hansen, who became the All Blacks coach.

The Alhambra trials were played on the Southern rugby club grounds for some reason. This was convenient, as the ground was closer to the flat than the Alhambra field in the city. Maybe it was because I was relaxed and had no expectations about making the team, but everything I did in that trial game turned to gold. Gaps in the defence the size of yawning chasms appeared when I had the ball, chip kicks bounced perfectly to hand, covering tackles were copybook, every dummy was sold and sidesteps bamboozled the defenders.

When I was moved to centre, the golden opportunities shifted out a position. I played the full game and finished with three tries. That night I was named in the team. Over the next couple of days I was approached by New Zealand Combined Services Colts selectors about playing for them on a pending tour to Fiji.

At the first Alhambra training, I had to advise the coach that I wouldn't be able to play as I was moving from Dunedin due to work commitments. I have often wondered what would have happened if I had remained in Dunedin and focused on rugby.

◄ FOUR ►

"You need to come clean, son, or things could go badly."

WANA WAS STILL CONTEMPLATING HIS beer. I had finished my first bottle and just started the second. I figured by the time I had finished the second I could leave the Schooner, having been there sufficient time to show my face and hopefully allay suspicions.

I surreptitiously kept scanning the bar and particularly the door to see who was arriving. Luckily I still hadn't seen any of my hard-core associates who could be backing up Wana. I particularly didn't want to see Charlie Shelford or Waha Saifiti. Waha was a notorious criminal who was primarily involved in drugs. A strongly built Polynesian in his early thirties, he looked mean and he was mean. Years later, he would become a major player in methamphetamine manufacture and distribution. Waha was cool, I liked him, but he was the sort of dude you didn't cross and narks were not his favourite category of associate. I had done a couple of stolen-property deals with him on TVs and a cocaine transaction. That would mean little if Waha had solid information that I had assisted the coppers.

Waha was cunning and would likely consider that if I had willingly assisted the homicide team, maybe I was actually something more, like an undercover. Should that hypothesis be correct, then he was fucked and so was everyone associated with me. They would all be facing major prison time unless the source of the problem was removed. If either of these guys turned up, my position would become even more precarious.

"Rick's screaming from jail that you narked him off," said Wana.

"Fuck, you know Rick, man, he's always screaming and dirty about something. You know how tight him and I are. I ain't gonna take out a brother like that. He's in there coz of the crazy fucken shit he did, wasting Paula."

A lump rose in my throat as I thought of the switchblade.

I almost croaked out, "And what about the time we tried to run that pig down!"

The period I had been in the Schooner seemed interminable. Talking face to face with Wana was assisting my cause, but I just wanted to get out of there.

The incident with the cop I was referring to happened one night after we had been on the piss in the Lion. I was there with Rick, Wana and Joe. We had been there pretty much all day, so were well liquored up and out of it when the bouncers kicked us out.

The Mitsi was parked in Queen Street. When we got to the car, Wana and Joe tipped themselves into the back seat. Rick sat in the passenger's seat. After leaving the park relatively sedately, I accelerated through the left turn into Fort Street, the tyres squealing. When the car straightened I could see before us down the road a tall cop in uniform standing on the footpath. I kept accelerating along Fort Street.

As we got closer, the cop began walking out on to the road. About now Rick began screaming, "Run that motherfucker down, kill the fucker!"

A chorus sprang up from the back seat: "Waste the fucker, take him out!"

This was a good opportunity to cement my rep, I thought. I kept accelerating. There's no way he's going to walk right in front of me, I figured. It was a high-stakes game of chicken.

As we got closer, the cop was in the middle of the road waving his torch and shouting. The screaming in the car intensified; by now it was a cacophony. I maintained my line and speed, which was well in excess of the limit. When the Mitsi was about to hit the cop, he athletically did a pirouette and rolled across the driver's-side front guard. I was grateful, for without that manoeuvre he would have been flattened.

This was greeted with extreme merriment by my passengers. "Hah! Fucken superb, Marcus," yelled Rick. "That'll fix the dog, trying to stop us."

General hilarity prevailed all the way out to Cleopatra's, where we stayed for a couple of hours. Wana and Joe cracked on to a couple of birds, so Rick and I left them and ventured back towards the city.

The Police Department and specifically the Wharf station did not share our amusement about what had happened. Rick and I got halfway back to the city when we passed a police car going in the opposite direction.

I guessed something was up when the car braked suddenly and did a U-turn. My car registration number was hot data in the city. In the rear-view mirror I could see the cop car approaching quickly. Its blue lights came on and "Police! Pull over and stop!" boomed out.

"Fuck," Rick said. "Can we outrun them?" Before I could reply, I saw a second cop car appear behind the first.

"I don't think so, mate," I said. "I think they've been looking for us."

As I pulled over to stop, a dog van screeched to a halt on the other side of the road joining the fray. One of the patrol cars nosed in front of us and the other stayed behind. The Mitsi was in a police sandwich, with a dog van on the side. A further side turned up shortly after in the form of a crime car.

As cops approached the Mitsi, Rick said, "Fucken big reception party of fleas. Tell the pricks nothing."

"Yeah, I know, mate. Fuck them."

Two cops came to each side of the car and asked us to step out. "Munro, is it?" asked one. "Might be," I replied.

"Well, we know your mate Rick here," said the D. He drew his weapon from a shoulder holster, a snub-nosed .38 revolver, and walked cautiously around to Rick. "Causing shit again, Goodin?"

"Fuck you, weak little prick," was the venomous reply.

"Were you driving the car earlier tonight?" the detective asked me.

"I'm saying fucking nothing," I replied.

"Okay, smart arse. Hands on the roof, both of you."

Rick and I leaned on the car with our legs spread while we were searched. Luckily, neither of us were carrying weapons or drugs. There was nothing in my car either. I'd done a jewellery buy earlier in the day, but had dumped the gear behind the bar at the Schooner. The demon handcuffed Rick and his crime driver did the honours on me.

"In the fucken cars," said the D, gesturing with his .38. I was put in the back of one of the uniform cars and Rick in the back of the crime car. Even though I was a cop it was an intimidating scenario. On the way back to town I said nothing, but was wondering how this might unfold. The cars travelled in convoy back to the Wharf police station, just along the road from the Schooner.

Rick and I were escorted into the station and deposited in separate interview rooms. I could hear Rick yelling, "Tell these fucken pigs nothing, Marcus! They can all go fuck themselves, fucken bastard pigs!"

A detective I hadn't seen before entered my interview room. He must have been working on another city crime car and had been called over to deal with what the police considered a serious matter. There was a big fish in the net too, in the form of Rick.

"You can call me sir," the detective said. I later found out his name was McDonald.

"Are you Mark Munro?" he asked.

"Yeah."

"You've been on our radar for a while. You and that dangerous reprobate Goodin. You've fucked up this time, though, trying to run down a cop."

"Don't know what you're talking about," I said.

"Were you driving your car earlier tonight?"

"I'd like to help you, detective, but I'm following my legal advice which is to say nothing. I'd like a phone call, though, before you go any further."

This didn't go down too well with the detective, who jumped up from where he was sitting in front of me and ventured around behind me. I braced myself for a cuff across the head but it never came. "Fucken phone call, I don't think so," he sneered. "You need to come clean, son, or things could go badly for you."

I started to become concerned about the way this was going. I couldn't blow my cover and tell him I was a cop; that was out of the question. I had to talk to Roo. The last thing I needed was to be arrested, charged and put in the cells. This would cause problems for the operation and no doubt Rick would be locked up with me. With his history, he wouldn't get bail and I needed him out on the streets.

"Look," I said, "It may be that I can co-operate with you. If I can make a phone call and my lawyer says that it might be best to assist, then I will."

This seemed to placate him somewhat and he sat down again across from me. "You know that talking is the only way you're gonna get out of this and I know you have plenty to say, not just on tonight's shit."

"Maybe," I said. "Give me the call and we'll see."

It was a stalemate. Both the detective and I knew it.

Police always want admissions; that is the way most people are convicted. If a deal can be done which solves other crimes and implicates multiple offenders, then that's always an option. As this was unfolding, I had to be careful how it would present to Rick.

Eventually McDonald said, "Okay, you've got your call."

I was relieved: thus far I hadn't been beaten up, was not in the cells and my cover was intact.

I made the phone call to Roo and got him out of bed. I gave him a quick briefing and he turned up half an hour later, which must have been a quick trip from out west. In the meantime, I was detained in the interview room, as was Rick. His rantings had ceased not long after my interview started.

When Roo arrived, he spoke with McDonald and other ranking cops. He played the line that I was his informant who was assisting him on a major operation and to avoid compromise this situation could not go any further. It is not unusual for this sort of thing to happen. Informants play a crucial role in solving crime. Roo did not divulge that I was a police undercover agent and he was my operator.

The fact that CIB detectives were involved in our apprehension now proved a benefit, as no questions about the informant role were asked. They were experienced investigators and knew how the system worked. Uniform police were often more difficult to deal with in these situations. Roo came into the interview room and told me the line he'd run. I was glad to see his face appear in the depths of the Wharf station.

There was one further loose end to sort. How was this resolution going to be sold to Rick? Being a nark was just as bad as being an agent. Roo and I discussed it and decided that warnings only could be given. This would be on the basis that neither Rick nor I had made any admissions and therefore the police were unable to prove I was driving. This was fed back to the cops dealing with Rick and we were released.

On the steps of the station Rick laughed, slapped me on the back and said, "They've gotta be way fucken better than that to catch us."

"Too fucken true, brother, too true," I replied.

The irony was palpable; I could almost feel it tickling my skin like some huge coarse blanket.

This incident became folklore in the scene and made my cover almost bulletproof: the night Marcus tried to kill a pig.

◄ FIVE ►

"We're all on a fishing trip in the Sounds."

I FLEW TO WELLINGTON AND saw the police shrink. He asked some weird questions, but deemed an hour's session sufficient to declare me psychologically fit to be deployed as an undercover agent. The following week I was standing on the jetty in Picton waiting to be picked up by a sea plane. With me were other prospective agents, including Gringo. He had joined the programme as well, so it was good to have a mate there while venturing into the unknown.

"We're all on a fishing trip in the Sounds," said the programme liaison detective.

We were flown into a resort accessible only by sea. When the plane swooped over the remote bush and gently splashed into a landing in the bay, it began to dawn on me what was happening. I had arrived at my undercover training seminar. Seminars cover ten days and the attendees comprise prospective agents and operators plus agent coaches and experienced operators. Also there are senior police, sometimes ranking as highly as the commissioner.

Ten prospective agents are tested, screened and trained with a view to being paired up with operators to undertake particular operations. You can be deployed as a long-term or short-term agent. Only the best candidates would be deployed long-term, which covers periods up to a year; short-term usually would be only a matter of weeks, maximum. Everyone wants to be deployed long-term.

From the minute you arrive at the seminar venue you are being assessed. The agent coaches are the big dogs of the seminars. They have been out there and done the business. They can do whatever they like and in the seminar environment, because of their reputations, are senior to everyone. Like the other new agents, I was in awe of them, their demeanour, experience and knowledge. (I was later to become a coach on two seminars.)

Roo was a prospective operator. In his mid-thirties, of average height and build, he was cool. You can't teach cool — you either are or you aren't. Roo was.

Like me, he was of Dutch descent but his parents came from Indonesia rather than the Netherlands. Genial, laid-back, humorous and well-liked, Roo was attached to Auckland CIS and his was to be a long-term operation. That's the job I wanted and he was the operator I wanted.

One of the agent coaches was Brent "Ash" Ashley, whom Gringo knew from Dunedin. Ash was laconic in the extreme. He had just come out of a successful long-term operation. Nothing worried Ash, but his freewheeling style belied a razor-sharp mind: his operator told me that, when asked about banking details, Ash regurgitated his three account numbers off the top of his head. His calm, easy persona meant he could readily secure the confidence of targets. Ash became a good mate and we spent time together years later in Christchurch when I was studying for my law degree.

Two other new agents were Crunchie and Oyster. Both ended up being deployed long-term at the same time as me in Wellington and Auckland. We also all ended up together on the same detective-qualifying course. Oyster hailed from Bluff, hence his nickname.

Crunchie acquired his nickname when he was in the CIB in Auckland. He had to be admired for somehow sourcing the most garish, brightly coloured ties that had ever been secured around a neck — so he was named Crunchie, after the clown. We became good friends and remain so. Among all his fine qualities, Crunchie stood head and shoulders above all other men at picking up chicks. It was a wonder to behold. While on our D course, the usual competition was run as to who could pick up the most birds in a seven-day period. The wealth of female finery that returned to the Porirua Police College in Crunchie's company was almost embarrassing. Crunchie won that competition hands down — there was daylight between him and the rest of us.

The activities on the seminar highlighted the gulf between what I knew and what I might need to know to survive as an agent. Although I learned a lot on the seminar, nothing can prepare you for being plummeted into a criminal underworld with mores diametrically opposed to your own.

◄ SIX ►

"It's a secret message, man."

"AND WHAT ABOUT SHAR, MATE?" I said to Wana. "She thinks everything's cool. That chick could sniff out a nark from the other side of the city."

Shar was Wana's girlfriend. At twenty-four she was some ten years younger than him. She had blonde hair and a delightful body. At five foot ten she was a little taller than most women.

Her shoulder-length hair framed striking features and amber eyes. I connected with her in a sisterly fashion.

Wana was very proprietorial around her and was influenced by her views. Wana's fearsome presence wrapped him like a cloak. You would think Shar being on his arm would soften the image, but somehow the reverse was true. She was another compartment of a very dangerous package.

"Yeah, man, she likes you," said Wana. "And you did that camera deal with her that was pretty sweet. She split the money between gear and shoes. I tell you what, though, Marcus, she ever fucks around on me she'll end up brown bread like Paula."

I had virtually drained my second bottle. It was now or never. Consuming the last couple of mouthfuls from the bottle, I said in my most measured tone, "I'd better fuck off, mate. You want me to get you another one before I go?"

I scanned his face, monitoring for a flare of hostility or resistance. Peripherally I was still trying to take in if anyone was around.

"Nah, I'm cool," he said.

"What's say we catch up tomorrow morning?" I asked.

"Yeah, sweet."

Casually, I slipped off my stool, clasped his hand in a street handshake and turned my back. I felt like running, but I ambled from the bar into the daylight. That was the last time I saw Wana until I faced him in an interview room at the Auckland Central police station.

I caught up with Roo later that day for a debrief. The following day I was on a plane to the South Island. My time in the scene was over. Termination day was to come and I wasn't looking forward to that.

Ruby was a hooker who lived in Ponsonby. I met her about three months into the operation at the Lion. I was drinking with Pete "Fingers" Moore, who introduced me to her. Fingers was a "tank man", a safe-blowing and cracking expert. He was different from the other boys in the scene as he was not violently inclined. You could probably characterise him as timid. His criminal focus was upon the technical aspects relating to safes and security systems.

He was an old-school head and did not favour the younger breed of upstart crim who wouldn't hesitate to rob an old lady. Fingers was a burglary master and respected in the scene. If you had an inside man in a good commercial building with cash stashed in a safe, you needed Fingers. But with the advent of better security systems, the instances of Fingers hovering over tanks in the darkness practising his art were in decline. The cracking of safes had given way to drilling. Skilled burglars drilled out the pins of safes enabling them to be opened. Brutal processes such as the use of a thermic lance to physically burn through the steel were favoured by some, although the logistical challenges of this approach were significant. Fingers adopted drilling as part of his repertoire.

Older than most of my associates, he was in his late thirties. He was Maori, bordering on skinny with tight, curly hair flecked with grey. His wise, elderly demeanour made him somewhat of a father figure. He certainly adopted this role with Ruby. One of his roles in life was to be Ruby's protector. Although he had no family relationship to her, Fingers had decided he was the one to map her course through the criminal world. His devotion was endearing.

Ruby didn't need a protector. She indulged Fingers, though, as it didn't hurt to have a respected senior criminal figure in her camp. At twenty-four she was older than me. When Fingers introduced us I didn't hear anything he was saying. I was transfixed by her striking green eyes and her physical presence. Ruby was not much shorter than me and wore tight leather pants and a cropped leather jacket. Her porcelain face, accentuated by dark gothic makeup, was framed by dark ringlets reaching her shoulders. That night I ended up back at her place. She lived with another hooker in a quaint villa just off Ponsonby Road. I was surprised at the tasteful bohemian decor. There was art on the wall in a Mexican Day of the Dead style. We maintained a relationship during the course of the operation. She was a fascinating creature. Her income was derived from prostitution and dealing small amounts of cannabis to other parlour girls.

Ruby's view was that hooking afforded her the lifestyle she wanted to live and didn't mean she was being taken advantage of by men. On the contrary, she considered the power lay in her hands. This view, expressed by a beautiful woman over six foot in her heels, was somewhat intimidating.

"What about threats to your safety?" I asked not long after we met.

"The pricks can look forward to a Thai haircut," she replied, referring to the hooker colloquialism for severing a penis. She showed me what looked like a pen, but it split in half and folded down to reveal a blade. She had bought this on a holiday in the Philippines.

Ruby always commanded attention when we swept into bars with my backstops. She never worked on those nights and didn't cultivate tricks. She liked having a good time and sometimes focused commitment was required to keep up with her.

With her flatmate, Ruby worked out of a massage parlour at the top of Symonds Street. It was owned by Cookie, who had made enough from drugs and fencing hot gear in the old days to invest in the parlour. Cookie was pretty much retired from crime except for running whores. Despite this I managed to buy stolen jewellery off him, so he went in the book too.

Short, squat and bald, Cookie didn't have many endearing features but his was a tight ship and he looked after the girls. I hung around the parlour a bit. I liked mixing with the girls and playing pool. The girls plied my associates with piss. As a quid pro quo, if any fleas turned up causing shit we would sort them out. If any of the girls wanted to deliver up extra benefits by way of further appreciation, these were accepted in the spirit they were offered.

Prostitution was illegal then, but later, in a rare moment of extreme clarity, Parliament moved to legalise the industry in 2003. This brilliantly practical piece of law-making immediately removed the criminal cornerstone upon which the industry stood. Prostitution, while part of the criminal sphere, attracted organised crime, predominantly the gangs. Hence brothels were run by the gangs and used as a base for other activities such as drug-dealing. The working girls suffered collateral damage, often becoming involved in serious crime by default.

One Sunday afternoon after Ruby had stayed overnight at my flat in Sandringham there was a knock at the door. I opened it and standing before me was Kim. I had picked Kim up at the Potter's Wheel Tavern in Avondale. She was straight and worked in a bank. Petite, nineteen, with short black page-boy hair, she was pert in all the right places. I used to crash through her window in the early hours of the morning after a night on the piss. She was always welcoming and her complete absence of any criminal links was refreshing.

This was before the magic of smartphones. Kim didn't visit my place that often, so I got a bit of a surprise to see her. I invited her in. Ruby came out of the kitchen and half-circled Kim like some feral animal. I introduced them and Kim extended a reluctant hand. Ruby took it and offered a perfunctory greeting. The temperature in the room slid down.

My surprise turned to something approaching shock when less than five minutes later there was another knock on the door. It was Charlie Shelford's cousin — she had come around only once before. How could this happen? Was the god of undercover agents punishing me for some bad deal? I invited my third guest in.

Now there were three wary creatures circling each other. After the next introduction I made some inane small talk that quickly vanished like water down a drain. Not one further utterance would come. I was exceedingly glib doing big deals with the country's most hardened criminals, but in my flat that afternoon any semblance of sensible conversation deserted me.

Ruby then established herself as the queen of the girlfriend pecking order: "Time for you bitches to fuck off."

Earnestly Rick said, "It's about drug-dealing."

"What's about drug-dealing?" I replied. I hadn't really been listening to what Rick had been saying. I had a splitting headache and was hungover after a big night out. An unidentifiable concoction of liquor and pills had served to populate my brain with miniature explosive devices that had been going off in sequence since I rose at 11.45am.

Rick was sitting on the couch in his flat looking at me intently. His piercing black eyes could adopt a fierce intensity, even early in the day when intimidation was not a requirement.

"That song *The Gambler* by Kenny Rogers," said Rick. "Most people don't know, but it's about drug-dealing.

"It's a secret message, man. That's what he meant when he wrote it. Fucken drug deals, but it was disguised as gambling. The giveaway is the line about hoping to die in your sleep. That's it right there. We know that, you keep doing deals and the chances of getting whacked go up," Rick stated philosophically.

"Yeah, mate, I see what you mean," I replied.

I found Rick's comments intriguing. Crime wasn't some folly to be indulged in for a couple of years like an opportunistic fraudster — it was Rick's life. The interpretation of the gambler personified his life view. Maybe the song *was* about drug-dealing.

Rick's contemplative mood broke suddenly. "Where the fuck's that belt?" he shouted at Paula. In front of him on the coffee table was the "outfit", the paraphernalia of hard-drug use: syringe, needle (aka "pick" or "spike"), bent spoon, water, matches and a folded packet of glossy paper.

A belt was presented to Rick by his five-year-old son who had found it after crawling under the couch. "Good one, son," said Rick, patting the boy on the head.

Rick bent over the table and, with the deft touches of a master jeweller, carefully unwrapped the small packet of heroin. White powder rested in the folds of the shiny paper. A *Playboy* centrefold had been sacrificed to provide the sachet. It was good for one, or perhaps two tastes at a pinch. That's what fifty bucks bought you. I scored smack as well, another Class A offender in the book.

The powder was mixed with water in the spoon. A match under the spoon heated the liquid. Exhibiting the deliberate care and familiarity of a theatre nurse, Paula assisted in the process. The pick was placed into the fluid which was drawn up into the syringe.

The belt, conveniently already threaded through the buckle, was placed around Rick's left arm. He tightened it with his teeth. His bite on the belt created fresh tooth-marks joining those already present, testament to prior and frequent use. Biting on the belt, his lips turned back and his eyes lit with anticipation, Rick presented like some macabre wolf.

Paula patted and squeezed Rick's arm, massaging for a vein. Once found, the pick was inserted and a little blood drawn back through the needle into the syringe. Then the plunger was depressed, delivering the smack directly into the vein. With his head tilting back slowly, Rick said dreamily, "She's coming up. I can feel it coming through, right up there flooding into my brain, man. Fucken God that's good."

His eyelids drooped and his head began a slow almost imperceptible circling motion. Every movement he made was slow and telescoped, as if he was trying to move through honey. When Rick came down he asked, "How long have I been out of it?"

"About an hour," I replied.

"Fuck, that's a short freak-out. That ping must have been cut with glucose."

About six weeks into the scene I had scored my first buy. This was a momentous step forward as I ceased being a pretender. The first buy builds confidence and somehow unlocks the key to further transactions. It was a colourful character who delivered up the stolen TV for purchase.

His name was Kenny Edwards. A Maori aged about forty, Kenny had a face that looked as though it had been slept in. His smile revealed a gap in his teeth so wide it looked like the entrance to some Egyptian tomb. The speckles on his deteriorating teeth could have passed for the pharaoh's cartouche.

Kenny had two predominant skill sets: as a burglar and a card shark. His burglary skills had netted the TV I was about to load into my boot. What he could do with cards bordered on sorcery. Many an unwitting punter had lost bets to Kenny wagering against the impossible feats he could conjure with cards.

Televisions in the late Seventies were big-ticket items, a lot more expensive than they are now. They were attractive to steal and easy to sell. Many burglars specialised in them and made a nice living. The TV I bought from Kenny retailed at around a thousand dollars and I paid him two hundred and fifty. At twenty-five per cent of its value, the price was right.

Once I'd done the deal and left the city heading west, I was embraced by a feeling of euphoria. It was dizzying to take the first step in achieving what I had set out to do. To do a deal meant you were regarded as a criminal. It is different from just being an observer and gathering intelligence. The person you have dealt with accepts your standing within the underworld and regards you well enough to expose themselves, despite the potential risk. I was to do many more deals, but none were more satisfying than conjuring up a prosecution for the card shark.

As with most buys, I headed to Roo's place in Massey with my exhibit. Every time I headed to my operator's address, I conducted counter-surveillance. I used different techniques and took a different route each time. Crashing red lights ensured you could drop a tail.

Going around roundabouts without exiting meant you could get a good look at vehicles around you. Rapidly moving across lanes on the motorway from the fast lane to an exit is also effective. If I was unsure whether I had picked up any interest, I would do a big loop before touching down at my destination.

When I reached Roo's place he wasn't there, but his wife Chris was. I really liked Chris. She symbolised normality to me. She was kind, patient and considerate. At times it must have been difficult for her, particularly as my life as a criminal became more successful. That meant my turning up more frequently with stolen gear and drugs. Success translated to more demands on her husband's time.

After doing a deal, or when operational issues demanded it, Roo and I would chew the fat for hours over a few drinks. Often I would be half-wasted when I arrived from the depths of some inner-city dive. Chris remained stoic and completely supportive, even with a young family to contend with, toddler Trent and baby Kristin. It was only later when I had my own children that I began to grasp the challenges she must have faced.

I turned up at Roo's place and Chris shared in the enthusiasm of my first buy. I sat at the breakfast bar and commenced writing my first offender statement. Roo turned up shortly afterwards and guided me through the statement. This was to become a ritual for every deal I completed.

To assist with recall and for evidential purposes, I sometimes made notes on a piece of paper or something like a drinks coaster. This was helpful as an aide-mémoire for car-registration and street numbers. Otherwise, I had to consign the details to memory. If a piece of scrap paper had been used for notes it would be affixed to the statement, which needed to be made contemporaneously with the deal. In some instances when I did a big deal, police surveillance agents would be in place to photograph the transaction and the participants.

Surveillance was also used extensively towards the end of the operation to photograph my associates and targets for identification purposes. Rick and I were photographed meandering across Quay Street headed for the Schooner. This shot was taken by Detective John Purkis who was secreted in a van parked on the street.

Roo and I had different places where we would meet. We needed to hook up so I could provide him with my daily notes and to pick up cash. Aside from major buys, I was spending about five grand a week. One of our favoured meetings was the Wintergarden in the domain. This was a large, glass, Victorian-style building housing exotic and tropical plants. It was always very quiet, so was a good location. Amid the lush surroundings and heady perfumes our secret business was conducted. The incongruity of talking about the underworld in such beautiful surroundings was inescapable.

Another favoured meeting spot was the Auckland public library. The most sparsely populated area was among the technical journals, so after circling the general body of the building, that was where Roo and I would come together. These locations were safe, as the gardens and the library were not high on the list of places to be visited by burglars, thieves and drug dealers.

Still, we would both be highly vigilant and conduct counter-surveillance en route to meetings. As an agent, being sprung meeting a D would take some explaining; the discovery of your handwritten daily notes, or being seen offloading a recent purchase, could be literally fatal.

The chemist was one of our primary targets. He was the main supplier of Tuinal to the streets and was flooding the market. Casualties were high with junkies overdosing and the scene awash with pills. I had a chance encounter with the chemist at the upstairs bar of the Exchange Tavern in Parnell. Rick and I had dropped in there for a drink on our way downtown. This was the sort of trendier place where the chemist felt comfortable. He was a most unlikely looking criminal, with glasses and a shirt and tie. His thin and insipid countenance of a shy, retiring accountant belied his cunning and greed.

Rick was sourcing pills from the chemist but I didn't know the nature of the arrangement. Rick was keeping it to himself and didn't want me tapping his supply. When we came across the chemist sitting at a table with another bloke, there was only the most cursory of greetings. Rick intentionally omitted the introductions. However, the chemist had seen me with Rick and that was enough. I could now contact him directly.

I left it about a week and began to frequent the Exchange at the times I thought he might turn up. I didn't like him and was intent on taking him down. Unlike most of my street associates, he came from a privileged background. He was an educated man with a desirable profession. Avarice, coupled with an absence of morals, had driven him to drug-dealing. Of all the offenders I took down, he was the most deserving of a decent prison sentence.

My visits bore fruit on about the fourth day. I was standing at the bar when the weasel-featured chemist arrived in the company of a pharmacy assistant. They cornered one of the remaining tables and the girl sat down. The chemist headed towards the bar where I was standing. As he approached, recognition dawned on his face.

"How's it going, mate?" I asked cheerily.

"Good, thanks. How about you?" he replied.

"Yep, good. Time for a nice relaxing drink after a hard day?"

"Yeah, you can say that again."

"Here, let me get those," I offered.

I knew the chemist was intimidated by Rick. As an associate of his, my criminal credibility would be unquestioned in his eyes. The weasel was not part of the underworld and he remained wary around those who were.

As the bartender was getting the drinks I made a suggestion. "Actually, I wouldn't mind having a chat about a bit of bizzo if you've got a chance."

His eyes narrowed, not with suspicion but anticipation. "Yep, okay. Let me have a bit of a talk to my bird and I'll come back."

I sank another pint of lager at the bar and began to frame up what I would say. About ten minutes later the chemist joined me back at the bar.

"All cool? She's not a bad-looking bird," I said.

"Yep. I've had a lot worse," he replied. "What's on your mind?"

"Look, I know you've got some deal going with Rick and that's sweet, but I've got a pressing need to hook up some brothers down the line. These boys are serious players and things are pretty dry down there. Smack has evaporated and they need sorting."

"Okay…"

"I'm gonna need the gear pretty quick, so there'd be no problem with a premium. If it all goes sweet there could be some decent orders down the track."

On drug deals, offering a premium based on some perceived need was always a good idea, as it could cut out rivals trying to source product. The promise of future bigger deals meant you could get your hands on cash, which activated the greed. I needed to do whatever it took to land the weasel.

"How many you looking for?"

That was it, he was on the hook.

"Five thousand as a kick-off," I replied.

The chemist looked down at his drink. "Shouldn't be a problem."

"What's it gonna set me back?"

"Dollar a pill."

The deal was done. I took delivery a couple of days later and paid five grand in hundred-dollar bills. Sometimes with drug deals you could get an oral arrangement, but the transaction would not proceed because the supplier wouldn't turn up, either because he had run out of gear or someone had been snapped by the cops. That was the nature of dealing with criminals. The chemist was different — he brought business nous to his nefarious dealings.

I did one further five thousand-pill deal with him and then set up a twenty thousand-pill deal just before termination. The idea was for him to be holding a decent amount when his place was crunched by police executing a search warrant. To gain further evidence, I made a phone call to the chemist that was recorded (bugging operations were not used widely then, but are now a central plank of covert operations). With two previous deals conducted without problems, the chemist was disarmed and readily agreed to the next one. Organising the deal for close to termination day meant we could snap him for the pills but not have to pay for them.

It worked perfectly. On termination day he was holding twenty thousand Tuinal tablets at his home address. The chemist was interviewed by Detective Sergeant Tony Lynch and despite making admissions and an early guilty plea, was given a fourteen-year prison sentence. Other than Rick's sentence of life imprisonment for the murder, it was the longest prison sentence I secured.

◀ SEVEN ▶

"We've got some shit going on with the Angels."

ONE FRIDAY NIGHT I WAS on my way to the Exchange Tavern with Joe when a threat to my cover arose. It was getting late — upstairs normally started to rock at around midnight. We had been circulating around the city bars and wanted to top the night off by mixing with a few good-looking chicks. There was a dance floor upstairs that could always be guaranteed to spawn at least a couple of honeys. I bounded up the stairs with Joe behind me.

At the top of the stairs I took one step into the bar and walked straight into a girl from Akaroa. Cindy and I had spent a few days in the quaint little French-influenced town. She knew I had been recruited and was joining the police. Ignoring her or pretending it wasn't me wasn't an option — I was close enough to smell her perfume. It was hard to ignore Cindy anyway. She was a very attractive blonde with a fresh, Californian-sporty look.

Events started to blur. At the very moment Cindy's face lit up in a smile I felt Joe bump me in the back as he arrived at the top of the stairs. Instinctively I moved in front of Joe so he couldn't see Cindy. That tactic proved futile, as he kept moving sideways to get a look at the blonde.

"Hey," I stammered. Cindy's smile diluted into a look of perplexity.

An entirely different being presented before Cindy than the last time I had seen her on the domain in Akaroa. Now I had a ponytail and earring and was dressed in a rough black leather coat, ripped jeans and scuffed, tan cowboy boots. My associate also wore leather, a well-worn brown jacket he had scored in a burglary. Joe's unshaven face and afro haircut completed the look.

Cindy's head moved from me to Joe, her quizzical inspection

continuing. As much as I was pleased to see Cindy, nothing good was happening.

I decided to take the initiative. "Good to see you, baby," I said, giving her a kiss on the cheek. "I can't hang around, sorry. We're late for a date."

I grabbed Joe's arm and pushed him into the throng of people. "What the fuck was that all about?" he said.

"Seriously, mate, that cunt's mad. She tried to stick me one night with a blade. Fucken black widow, the bitch. Don't want to be anywhere near her."

Joe and I managed to slip out later without seeing Cindy. I felt sad the rest of that night and the next day. It was impossible, but I wanted to spend time with her. It hurt to dismiss her so callously. Thoughts of a gentle, sensible conversation with a kind, honest, considerate girl kept swimming into my mind.

There was one other girl I often thought about. When I moved into my digs in Corunna Avenue, my sanctuary when fleeing from the traffic snake, she lived next door. I never spoke to her properly, but as we were living in close proximity we exchanged pleasantries. She was in one flat in the old villa and I was in the other. She was pretty with, appropriately, a "girl next door" look. I bounced down the three steps from my flat one afternoon to find her hunched over the rear of her 1960s VW bug parked close to the Mitsi. The rear-engine cover was up and she was peering at the motor. She was obviously having mechanical difficulties but I just offered a greeting before driving off. A most uncharacteristic move.

I thought I couldn't really talk to my neighbour because she wasn't a hooker, stripper or junkie. Her decency was a threat. I had turned the key in the lock of my previous life.

After I hadn't seen her for a few days I ran into my landlady and asked where my co-tenant was. "Oh, she went back to New Plymouth. She was so lonely here in Auckland." I often thought of that girl and what became of her.

Less than a week after seeing Cindy I saw someone else from my earlier life. It was also in Parnell, but in the Alex pub just up the road from the Exchange. It was in the afternoon, in the bar which fronted the street.

I was with Rick and Paula. We were sitting at a table when I noticed a guy on the other side of the bar taking an interest in me. Wherever you moved in the scene, vigilance was your constant ally.

There was a mirror on the far wall, so I swivelled my chair around so I could see the observer's reflection without making it obvious. After a second look, I recognised him and was flooded with anxiety. It was Paul Carter. We had been at school together in Ashburton. He was a small-time beagle boy who had been involved in petty thefts and car-knocking. I wondered why he was in Auckland and if he had graduated to something more.

European, taller than average with tight, curly black hair, Paul was a martial-arts practitioner. I didn't recognise his male companion from the scene, which was a relief. Although curious, my clandestine observations gave me some comfort. Paul was now focused on talking to his mate. Neither Rick nor Paula paid the pair any attention. My mind had by now reached top gear in processing everything I could recall about Paul Carter. The big questions were: had he positively identified me and did he know I'd joined the police?

Rick and Paula were deep in conversation about a potential cocaine score. My thinking fell into two halves. First, I didn't know Paul that well, as most of my mates played rugby and he had been focused on karate. Second, if he knew anything it was probably that I'd headed to university after school. I was ruminating on the risk when Paul got up and walked out of the bar with his mate. He didn't give us a sideways look. Apprehension trailed in his wake. I had to talk to Roo.

Rick, Paula and I left the Alex about an hour later. I made an excuse about having to do something and dropped them at the Lion. I phoned Roo and gave him a briefing.

"No way that prick's gonna cause problems for us," said Roo. "Might have to pay him a visit. Can't cause any shit if he's locked up." I'm not sure what happened to Paul. Roo never told me, but I never saw him again.

Going to parties with Rick posed unique challenges. Parties were fertile ground for me as they brought criminals together in one place. There were always seriously bad dudes there and the character of the attendees meant violence could be triggered without warning.

As a kingpin, Rick was ready for such eventualities. The most essential component of his party dress was a motorcycle chain he wore draped over his shoulder under his shirt. When we arrived he was fond of saying, "Chained up, Marcus, just in case any of these egg motherfuckers get out of line."

One party we attended where Rick definitely needed to be chained up was at the Grim Reapers Outlaw Motorcycle Club pad in St Lukes. At the time the Reapers were a dominant force in the bikie-gang scene. There was constant rivalry with the Hell's Angels over territory. The Reapers were involved in dealing heroin and I knew there were a couple of members that Rick scored from. The gang became defunct in the Eighties, buckling under pressure from the Angels and heavy drug use by members.

The Reapers' pad was a fortress. There was a fence on all sides topped with barbed wire; a gate in the front was guarded by a gang member. Rick knocked on the gate when we arrived. It creaked open and a heavily tattooed face appeared through the partial opening. The face grunted acknowledgement to Rick and we were permitted entry.

The house that formed the clubhouse proper had steel bars on the windows. A heavy steel mesh covered the front door which led onto a covered veranda with motorcycles parked on it, Triumphs and early Harleys. They all had ape-hanger bars and were painted various shades of black. Closest to the door was a chopper with extended forks and a king and queen seat. We ventured around the back to a steel door that was the only entry and exit. It was open, with a club member leaning against the doorway talking to a good-looking bird dressed in leather.

We passed into the living room which was decked out as a bar. Heavy-metal music blared out. It was dark inside, with different-coloured lights providing murky illumination. The bar extended the length of the room with a commercial fridge behind it and an array of spirits on shelves. Above the shelves was a huge flag bearing the image of a Grim Reaper. There were about twenty patched gang members scattered around the room, standing at the bar or lounging on the numerous couches. It seemed as though for every member there were two good-looking chicks. That surprised me and I wondered what attracted them to this life.

The sergeant at arms, who knew Rick, sauntered over. "We've got some shit going on with the Angels so we might have to pull the plug quick on the piss-up."

"Yeah, no problem," said Rick.

"Have a drink. Those motherfuckers did a drive-by shooting here last night. Didn't hit any of us, though. They'll pay if we can corner one of the fuckers on his own. They know we're all here together, so those low dogs might attack tonight."

Rick nodded.

Most of the time in the scene you experience some level of fear. The adrenalin keeps you sharp. My fear levels were up a couple of notches in the Grim Reapers' clubhouse. I didn't like the fact that there was no escape route. If things went bad you weren't going anywhere. The fear levels went up a further notch when I noticed the sergeant at arms talking animatedly to a couple of patched members in the corner and glancing in our direction.

Rick, who was calm when we entered, was now exhibiting signs of apprehension. After his falling out with the Angels, he had gravitated towards the Reapers. Not all the Reaper members were apparently in favour of interaction. Once an Angel, always an Angel: the only good one was a dead one. If this was the issue that had provoked the fervent corner discussion, I hoped it wasn't going to be settled in the clubhouse.

The sergeant at arms returned to the bar and said, "Look, mate, you're gonna have to go now. We've got a war on and some of the boys are not too happy you're here. Anyone with any link to the Angels is filth as far as they're concerned."

"No problem," said Rick. "Can you guarantee we'll get out without being jumped?"

"Yep, I can."

Under the glare of hostile eyes from the corner, we left.

Seeking solace from the rigours of the scene, I would often go to the movies during the day. Enveloped by darkness, I would immerse myself in the latest release. Something action-packed with exotic locales was preferable. The cinema afforded an escape from the necessarily heightened state of awareness, which was all-pervading.

Among the sparsely dotted darkened figures it was safe to think of home and a calmer life. The enforced split personality takes a toll. The visible manifestations are keenly identified by your close friends and family. At the time you battle the immediacy of the issues; it is only later the resulting personality vicissitudes become apparent.

Your operator is your only link to the real world. When you are out there in the scene you are completely alone. Any familiar links, people or places are absent. Before I was deployed I had never been to Auckland. There is a total divide between your previous life and the criminal being you have adopted. No contact is made with anyone from your former life until periods of R&R. Periodically it was difficult, but I found I could cope with the isolation and loneliness. I often wondered why.

The probable answer lay with when I was young. When the olds ran the pub in the Wairarapa I was aged between eight and eleven. It's a busy life being a publican so I spent inordinate amounts of time roaming the paddocks and beaches of the Castlepoint area. It would not be uncommon for me to trek from the pub at Whakataki to the Castlepoint township and back along the coast, a ten-kilometre trip.

I loved rolling down the sandhills, dancing across the seashore boulders and examining rock pools for life. Sometimes I ventured further, heading up the Mataikona Road and back, covering twenty kilometres and being away all day. On my way there was a derelict Maori pa set on the side of a bush-covered hill. It was one of my favourite spots, quiet, yet its previous long-dead visitors spoke to me silently.

I attended the local Castlepoint School. It was tiny with a total roll of eleven. My claim to fame was that I produced a very rudimentary school rag which was circulated in the community. The featured serial, which unfolded through each edition, was called *The Hand*. It was about a severed hand from an ancient Egyptian murderer, which was continuing on its own to commit killings in modern times. From when my sister and I were very young, our mother would speak to us at a level that extended our comprehension. This fostered in me an interest in language and the meaning of words which has had a lifelong tenure.

For the sake of my education, when I turned eleven I was sent to boarding school in Masterton; St Joseph's College, run by the Marist Brothers. As I was at Form One level and boarders only started from Form Three, dispensation had to be sought from the school in order for me to board. I lived in a dorm with fifty other boys. The problem was they were all two years ahead of me, aged at least thirteen.

Being so much younger, I was at the very bottom of the pecking order. The dorm was open-plan with bunks around the outside and beds in the middle. To further foster vilification I talked in my sleep and was often woken by a rain of pillows and abuse.

At the beginning it was a very difficult and challenging environment: it felt like me against the world. My ability at rugby helped me immensely as the boarders used to have informal games after school. I could elude and take down the very boys who were bullying me.

A seminal event happened on the steps of the dorm one night after dinner. One boy, Neil McKay, was my nemesis. He made it his primary mission in life to terrorise me, a boy two years his junior. I was small then, even for my age, so McKay was bigger than me. As I went to enter the dorm he stood in front of me blocking the door.

"Where are you going, turd?" he asked.

"Just in here," I replied.

"Don't think so," he said, extending his arm towards my chest.

A few of the other boys were lingering around the steps providing an audience. Among them was Scruff. He was called Scruff due to an innate ability to wear his uniform in a manner that looked splendidly rough. It was an ability I applauded. Scruff was in the fourth form; he was respected by the boys and held sway.

As I moved forward, McKay grabbed my shirt at the throat with his left hand and cocked his right hand ready to punch. I knew this was a pivotal moment. I had never been in a proper fight before. I struck at his exposed midriff, punching him in the stomach. His head came down but he rained blows on me, catching each side of my head. I instinctively charged him which reduced his height advantage, flailing with my own punches. There was a babble from the audience which was indistinct but growing louder.

Amid the fracas, instead of roundhouse wild punches I somehow delivered and connected with an uppercut. It was a lucky punch and caught McKay square under the jaw. He peeled away in an arc, like fabric from a zip. Staggering backwards, he hit the side of the dorm and slid to the ground.

McKay's head was tilted forward and nuggets of blood spilled from his mouth. I stood there shocked and puffing, but uninjured. Scruff approached, slapped me on the back and said, "You okay?"

"Yeah, yeah," I croaked.

That one gesture from Scruff could not have been topped by the awarding of a Purple Heart. From that day on, I had no more trouble from the boys at boarding school.

Perhaps my earlier family history was a factor too. Dad was the youngest of seven children and born in 1932. He grew up in Rotterdam in the Netherlands and lived through occupation by the Nazis during World War II. The family's home was a second-floor apartment at Westvarkenoodsweg 357a, across from railway yards. The railway was a prime target for bombers.

On 10 May 1940, Dad and Joop, his older brother by three years, watched in amazement as German paratroopers filled the sky like cotton buds. The occupation had begun. Dad's home was sequestered by the Germans for a time, with the soldiers sleeping in the beds and the family on the floor.

Food was scarce, as was fuel for cooking and heating. Dad and Joop used to sneak out after the strict 7pm military curfew and forage for coal on the railroad tracks. They stole timber from among hedges and levered pieces of timber off bridges.

One afternoon, when Dad was ten, there was a commotion on the corner of the street, just along from the apartment. Dad and Joop saw a Jewish family, the parents and three children, lined up against the wall and machine-gunned by German troops. At night, railway carriages filled with Jews being shipped to concentration camps were stationed at the siding outside the apartment. The pitiful sobbing of the occupants wafted through my father's home.

With food in short supply and the dangers from Allied bombing of the railway increasing, my grandparents decided that Dad and Joop must leave. With their older brother Ton taking the lead, the three siblings began their journey to Akersloot in the north of the country. There were no trains or buses so they had to make the hundred-kilometre trip through occupied territory the best way they could. Ton had an old pushbike with solid rubber tyres made out of garden hose and filled with straw. Ideal to ferry belongings. The boys slept where they could or turned up and cadged board at convents and Catholic churches.

Dad's older sister, my Aunty Ans, was with the Dutch Resistance. At twenty she was a link in the communications system between the Resistance and the Allied armies. Employed in an umbrella shop as her cover, she secreted written messages in umbrellas, which were then dispatched around the country, co-ordinating operations. My grandparents were continually worried about her. If caught she would have been shot.

Halfway through the war, Dad's oldest brother Gerard left Rotterdam and joined the Partisans fighting in Yugoslavia. They were regarded as the most effective guerrillas in Europe, inflicting the highest number of German losses to Resistance fighters. After the war he never returned to Rotterdam and settled in the quiet town of Blijswijk in the north of Holland.

With such DNA, the path I followed was hardly a coincidence.

◄ EIGHT ►

"Fuck with the bull and you'll get the horn."

THE CRYPT WAS A NIGHTCLUB halfway up Queen Street. It was aptly named, as many a plot to bury someone was concocted in its dark recesses. Every head and assorted criminal would turn up there at some stage during the week. It was rough and so was its clientele. Being inky dark, it was actually a difficult place to do drug deals. Overlay this with the fact that most attendees arrived in the early hours and were suitably wasted, and it was a place to slouch with your chick and observe what you could. Ruby liked it and accordingly, so did I.

Another establishment that was a good burglar haunt was the public bar of the White Horse in Pakuranga. Geographically it was perfect because it was frequented by crooks from south of the city. It was a reasonably well-appointed pub, but for some reason it was a burglars' lair. I did a number of deals on stereos and TVs. There was no local pub fence, so I picked up good bizzo easily. I had cracked the pub through city burglars who had spread the word to their southern brothers.

The Mainstreet nightclub was at the top of Queen Street just down from Karangahape Road. It hosted some good bands and was usually the platform for a good night out. Ruby and I ventured there on the first of July 1979. I had scored a woman's black fur coat and jewellery from a young Tongan burglar who usually delivered up good gear. Draped around Ruby, the coat looked good in the stark club strobe lights. A glistening diamond teardrop earring swung from her left ear, booty from the same burglar, its mate either hastily left in its jewellery box or dropped in the darkness by the hyped burglar.

We had a few on board from earlier in the day so only stayed a couple of hours. The Uncles Burger Bar on Great North Road beckoned. We headed there and did a transaction on cheeseburgers and thick shakes. Sated, we cruised back down Great North on to K Road.

"Shit, something's going on," said Ruby as we approached the Queen Street intersection.

A crowd congregated on the Queen Street footpath fanning out and up onto K Road. Three police cars, lights flashing, were parked on the road outside Mainstreet. Black-clad Armed Offenders Squad members stood on the corner. Shit to this degree warranted scarcity, I thought, skirting the Mitsi around the crowd and heading away towards Grafton Bridge and Parnell.

A murderer was at large. Disgruntled Mainstreet patron and known criminal Brian McDonald, affronted at being ejected from the club, had returned armed with a rifle intending to kill the bouncer. From across Queen Street McDonald lifted his rifle and took aim at the bouncer. When he pulled the trigger his aim was off. The .22 calibre bullet missed the bouncer but struck eighteen-year-old innocent Margaret Bell. She was killed instantly, slumping to the cold central-city footpath.

Such a senseless killing stirred media attention and calls were out for action. The calls were answered; McDonald was quickly arrested, prosecuted and convicted of murder. Mainstreet never featured again as a hangout.

Aside from the Schooner, the most fearsome pub I visited was the Star in Otahuhu. It was exclusively a Maori and Islander hang-out. If your face was white, you weren't welcome. The Black Power gang favoured the place and could wear patches in the bar. The first time I went there was with Joe and Charlie. I could pass for part-Maori and Joe's Black Power links would always open doors.

When we arrived, the bar was packed with a sea of evil faces. It was about three in the afternoon and it seemed every eye in the joint swung in our direction. After ordering drinks from the barman, who was the antithesis of a service professional, the personification of evil approached us. Unpatched, wearing a scruffy leather vest over a Harley T-shirt, he stood six foot five. Even with the assembled badness in that bar, he stood out. His face bore a full moko punctuated with boob spots. A scar crept down from above his right eye to his cheek. A milky texture to the white of the right eye betrayed damage from violence. I had never seen him before and was beginning to wish I still hadn't. He walked past Joe up to me and with his head tilted back and his jaw extended said, "Who the fuck are you?"

Staring unblinkingly into the milky eye, I replied, "Who the fuck are *you*?"

At this his face creased into a smile. This softened his evil mien to just plain bad. He extended a tattooed hand, clasped mine and said, "Good one, bro. Welcome to hell."

"How's it going, Hector?" said Joe, embracing my new acquaintance.

Even with a staunch contact in the Star, I was wary of the place and only went a few times. I didn't see Hector again until close to the end of the operation. He came into the Schooner and we did a deal on cameras he had stolen in a robbery.

I had paid a spot (a hundred dollars) for a rucksack full of silverware. The rucksack, conveniently supplied by my burglar, was canvas with a cord that secured the top. It was like those used by sailors. I swung it onto my back ready to make the short walk from the car park, where the deal was done, to the Schooner. The valuable contents rattled in a way only expensive silver can. The plates, candelabras, goblets and cutlery were loved family heirlooms. The collection was destined for handling in the underworld stolen-property scene. Without my intervention through doing a buy, it would likely have been lost forever. Like many others, the items were reunited with their owners after the operation. Difficulties were sometimes encountered in matching the property I had bought with burglary complainants. Considering the wealth of stolen items I bought, it was a huge task completed diligently by Roo and CIS detectives.

As I left the car park and emerged onto the street, booty slung across my back, I must have presented like the classic cartoon thief, minus the eye mask. As I was clanking towards the Schooner in the full glare of Auckland's foreshore sunlight, a beat cop in uniform also joined the footpath. He had come from the Wharf police station just along the road and was walking towards me.

Now, realistically, the suspicion attaching to me could not be greater. It was the afternoon on a week day; most of the real world were at work. I was dressed in my favoured leather coat and ripped jeans. I was outside the city's most notorious criminal downtown hangout, well known for its burglar, thief and drug-dealer constituency. The huge rucksack on my back could not be wished away, nor the melodic jangling of its contents.

The beat cop and I came together at about the door to the Schooner. Surely he'll stop me, I thought. His asking to look in my bag would cause problems. A glitch with the filth immediately outside the pub where I was the fence would not be helpful to business. The beat cop and I exchanged glances. He was junior, younger than me.

I veered right into the Schooner and the cop disappeared over my left shoulder continuing on his way. Slowly shaking my head with relief, I entered the gloom of my place of business. I didn't actually blame him for not doing his job. No cops tread the dangerous carpets of the Schooner.

As was my usual practice I went through the room, nodding to familiar faces, and placed the stolen silverware on the bar. Willie the barman gave me a wink and lifted the section of the bar that allowed access to the serving area. I went through, swept up the rucksack and stored it in a cupboard in the bowels of the pub. I had an arrangement with Willie whereby I could store hot gear there until I was ready to move it.

Willie was an elder statesman of crime. Bordering on ancient, being in his mid-fifties, he had been involved in stealing for more than forty years. As a by-product, he'd done a couple of lags for receiving but "rock college" stints didn't worry him; he just made more contacts.

His long, dark, grey-streaked shoulder-length hair and black eyes gave him a Rasputin-like bearing. With his hands spread on the middle of the bar, he held court over the assembled rabble. Willie hated police. He would assist in any criminal enterprise being formulated in the bar, just to get back at the Old Bill. A slide to him wasn't necessary; he would help just for the pleasure of fostering further crime. Economical with words under normal circumstances, he would not utter a sound to a cop. When he did speak to patrons, it was to educate with sayings like, "Fuck with the bull and you'll get the horn."

The trust Willie placed in me was his downfall. Due to his helping with numerous buys through storing gear, he was charged as a party to all those deals. He pleaded not guilty and went to trial, but was convicted on all charges and weighed off with a decent prison sentence.

CIS had received intelligence that the chemist was not the only regular supplier of Tuinal. Although the amounts being moved were a lot less, they were consistent, unlike the chemist-shop burglars. The only further information available indicated that the suspect was European, in his mid-twenties and operating in central Auckland. As luck would have it, I encountered the potential dealer about a week later.

I was in the Lion with Wana and Shar. It was about 10pm and we'd just had a feed together. Following an incident earlier in the afternoon, I was shaken up and had come out tooled up, carrying my shotgun.

It had all started out as just a regular deal I was going to do on a couple of cameras. I was to meet the seller at the Alexandra pub. Not the one in Parnell but another establishment by the same name downtown in Federal Street. The bar is right on the street and I was strategically positioned by a window allowing a view of the footpath.

When I'd entered there were a couple of patched Hell's Angels members standing at the bar, but they didn't draw a lot of attention. My seller was late. Criminals are notoriously late. The reasons for this tardiness could cover a wide spectrum: I got wasted, I had no gas, I had a fight with my chick, I had to do another deal, the cops snapped me, I thought you said tomorrow, I was asleep, I forgot, or the sky fell in.

After waiting about half an hour, I heard the distinctive sound of unbaffled Harley motorcycles roaring up the street. City high-rises served to bounce and amplify the V-twin chorus. Three bikes rumbled to a stop on the footpath outside the bar. All three riders wore Hell's Angels gang patches stitched on vests. Underneath the distinctive winged skull symbol appeared a rocker bearing the name Auckland. The front bike had ape-hangers, drag pipes and a bedroll tied around the sissy bar. The rider kicked down his stand and took off a matt-black open-face helmet. He loosened a black bandana tied around the bottom half of his face, cowboy style. European, aged about thirty, he looked vaguely familiar.

The three newcomers came into the bar and joined their mates. After a few minutes the lead rider began to pay me more scrutiny than was necessary. Something wasn't right. Did I know that Angel and if so, from where? Apprehension surged through my system. I looked out the window and assessed my escape route. The sash window was half-open, so if necessary it was a good option.

When I swung my gaze back to the bar, the lead rider was walking towards me with a gang member at each shoulder. They collectively exuded menace. This wasn't going to be a convivial chat about Auckland's traffic woes.

"Are you a mate of Rick Goodin's?" the lead rider spat out accusingly.

"I know him," I replied.

"Well, we've got a major problem with that fucker."

"Hey, that's not my issue, man."

"Well, he's a fucken dog and an enemy. If you're running with him, then you're a fucken enemy too."

This wasn't playing out too well but I sensed these bikies didn't know the exact extent of my relationship with Rick. The window was looking inviting, but I hoped I could talk my way out the door. "Look, I've done some bizzo with Rick and that's about it. I don't know what your beef is with him but we all know he's a mad, unpredictable motherfucker."

At this the lead rider's shoulders dropped slightly, which I took as a sign of tension dissipating.

"Maybe, but I tell you what," he barked. "If we see you hanging round with him in future, you're going down too."

"Fair enough," I replied, accepting the warning. It wouldn't have been just a warning if they'd known I'd been in the Grim Reapers' pad a couple of weeks before.

Still, I took the threat seriously and hence was protecting myself. Wana often carried a handgun so that night we had more than enough firepower. Shar was sitting with some friends and Wana and I were standing at the bar. I noticed Shar was joined at her table by a very straight-looking European guy who was about twenty-five. Shar was attractive so there were a lot of guys hanging around. This was a bit different, as it didn't look like he was hitting on her.

Curious, I said to Wana, "Let's sit down," and we wandered over to Shar's table. When we reached the table she was deep in conversation with the new guy. Wana wasn't interested and just ignored him. I slumped in my chair and kept an ear on Shar's conversation. At one point I heard "batch" and "chewies" in the same sentence. I wondered if perchance this new guy might be the unidentified chewie source. When Wana and I had finished our drinks, I stood up, leaned over to Shar and asked if she wanted a drink.

"Oh, Marcus, this is Harry," she said.

"Hey, man," I said shaking hands. "Want something?"

"No, I'm still good," said Harry.

On my return from the bar I made a point of sitting so my coat was slightly open and Harry could see the butt of my sawn-off. A little intimidation could do wonders in facilitating deals.

Harry was seriously out of his depth. The bottoms of his black business trousers were a considerable distance from his brown scuffed shoes. His large-collared striped shirt was directly from 1960 and nicely offset his heavy black-rimmed glasses. This was not the regular ensemble of a Lion Tavern client. Harry was a moth flying too close to the flame.

Shar left for the bathroom with a couple of friends so I took the opportunity to drop into the seat beside Harry. "How's the night going, mate?" I asked.

"Pretty good, actually," he replied.

"I heard the topic of chewies raised with Shar. My favourite subject."

"Yeah, we were talking pills."

It was falling together: Shar was always flush with pills and Harry looked like the key. I needed to confirm if he was her supplier and if so, get a deal done with him. Even better still, he could be the subject of the CIS intel.

"Always on the sniff for a good line on gear, bro," I stated directly.

"Well I might be able to help," he replied.

The flames were licking around Harry's feet.

"I can probably take as much as you can get your hands on."

"Oh, okay," Harry said, sitting forward in his chair.

"Tell you what, drop by the Schooner tomorrow arvo and we'll hook something up."

"Sweet. No worries," he replied.

The next day Harry fronted in the Schooner. It transpired he *was* the second chewie source. He worked in a pharmaceutical warehouse as a storeman. The arrangement was simple. Harry filled a fictitious order for Tuinal and I sent in Ruby dressed as a chemist-shop assistant to uplift the product. I did three deals with Harry, one for five hundred pills and two for a thousand. The justice system burned Harry badly. He was sent down for a five-year prison lag.

I had to put the brakes on with Harry at only three transactions. This was not unusual and sometimes difficult. The objective was to snare as many offenders as possible. Shifting from one source to another when you were already getting good service could become strategically challenging. It was a difficult situation, as it made sense to stay with a limited number of sellers to reduce your risk as a criminal. Much of the time crooks were unaware you were dealing with their associates. When they were acquainted with the situation, it could take some thoughtful advocacy to explain why you had shifted your business elsewhere.

After a huge day drinking around the traps, Rick and I finally touched down at his flat in Locarno Avenue, Sandringham, about one in the morning. To complete my departure from conscious thought, we spotted hash on knives heated up on the stovetop element. I had to drive as I couldn't walk. Finding the driver's door was a challenge surmounted only by trying to find where to insert the ignition key. The journey from Rick's flat to my place in Parnell was about seven kilometres. I made it out of Locarno Avenue but was met by challenges in Fowlds Avenue.

As I attempted to turn right into Fowlds, spatial recognition departed.

The traffic island splitting the road sat mockingly before me, daring me to navigate around it. As I bore down upon it, the island suddenly grew longer and higher. Inevitably the Mitsi's right-front wheel connected heavily with the concrete shapeshifter. Despite the impact and mounting of the obstacle, forward momentum continued. Encouraged by movement, my brain made a hazy call to keep going.

The trip itself was a blur. The Mitsi literally ground to a halt at home in Parnell. Fingers of blue smoke crept up to meet me when I opened the door. The oblong wheel was circled by loose rings of smoking shredded rubber and wires. It looked bad that night, but in the morning it looked as if some huge creature had chewed on the wheel.

After a successful night drug-dealing and drinking to excess, I was driving to Kingsland to Joe's digs. Rick and Joe were in the car. It was about 3am. Not far from Joe's we saw a girl crossing the road in front of us, hugging something to her chest.

"Hey, I know that chick," said Rick.

"What's her name?" said Joe.

"Fucked if I know, I just know the bitch. Pull up by her, Marcus."

I kerbed the Mitsi alongside her and Rick opened the passenger's door, leaning out.

"Hey, Rick," said the girl in a friendly fashion. She was about my age, cute, Maori, wearing tight jeans and a top with one shoulder exposed. "What are you guys up to?"

"Fucken just about to continue partying up the road," said Rick. "Wanna join us?"

"Might do," said the girl.

"What's your name?" asked Joe.

"Candy," replied the girl.

"Come on," said Joe. "It'll be a riot."

Candy looked at the ground, made a couple of circles with her foot then said, "Okay." Joe flipped open the door and she slipped into the back seat beside him.

I could see that the item Candy was hugging was a portable record player. As we headed off down the road Rick turned to her and said, "Giss a look at that," pointing to the record player. Without question Candy passed it through the gap between the seats. Rick snorted, wound down the passenger's window, "You won't be needing this," and threw it out the window. At the fifty kilometres an hour we were travelling, the player hit the road and smashed into pieces. It was a strange and unpleasant thing to do, but that's the sort of shit Rick did.

The four of us arrived at Joe's flat. "We're cool coz the missus isn't here," said Joe, opening the fridge. The only form of sustenance inside it was beer. Handing Candy a beer, he winked. "Unless you want something harder?"

"Maybe," said Candy coyly.

We sat around on Joe's couches drinking and chewing the fat. Joe produced a bottle of tequila, which led to a series of shots.

I watched Candy on the couch beside Joe and wondered if she might be a hooker or stripper. Perhaps she was both? Maybe she worked in a bank? The delicately tattooed butterfly on her left cheek probably eliminated institutional employment.

"I'm gonna fuck her first," said Rick.

I watched for a reaction from Candy but she remained impassive.

"That's cool," said Joe. I just shrugged.

Rick looked at Candy and gestured towards the open bedroom door. "You right, then?"

"Okay," she said cheerily. She looked as though she was enjoying herself. Irrespective, I wasn't going to partake in the bedroom activities.

Craig Smith ghosted up to our leaner in the Schooner. Conspiratorially he said, "Too many ears here. Let's sit over there." He nodded to a table in the far corner of the bar.

Stationed with me at the leaner were Rick, Waha, Wana and Charlie. Happy to oblige, we all followed him to the table. Craig was well known in the scene as a clever and cunning criminal. He never touched drugs. His physique was a testament to regular gym training. At six foot four with sun-bleached blond hair and matching moustache, he was an impressive physical specimen. Craig was suave and a favourite with the ladies.

High-end burglaries were Craig's forte. He focused on industrial premises and had a penchant for stealing jewellery. Twelve months previously he had been the prime suspect in the robbery of a jewellery store in Parnell. Nothing more than suspicion attached to him, but those in the scene were convinced he'd done the job. Speculation abounded as to the proceeds. Various amounts between fifty and two hundred grand were bandied about.

"Glad you guys were all together," Craig said once we were seated at the table and drinks refreshed. "I got a job I want to float."

"We're listening," said Rick, establishing himself as our spokesman.

"It's a while since an armoured car's been hit," Craig said, pausing for a response that never came. "I've been monitoring Securitas patrols for about two months now. Neighbourhood drops after major bank pickups are particularly interesting. The security is a fucken joke and they just don't believe they'll be taken. I've got more planning to do but I need a team. A team that is trustworthy and won't fuck around. What do you think?"

"Well, business is business, mate," said Rick.

"Yeah, fucken oath," said Waha.

Nods were delivered by me, Wana and Charlie.

"What do you reckon the payday would be?" queried Rick.

"I dunno. Need to do a bit more on that. Could be up to three hundred grand. I'm cultivating a guy on the inside. Fucken fat pig who works for the security mob but he's a greedy fucker and is easily freaked so he can be kept in line."

"He'd better stay in line or the fucker will end up buried in the Riverhead Forest," said Wana.

Cutting to the chase Rick said, "Whaddya need?"

"Three to do the job plus me, a van, a wheel man and at least two gats to put the frighteners on."

Rick in his role as spokesman said, "You know you got the team here, man, Wana's the gat man. Probably sawn-off shotties, right?"

Craig nodded.

"Marcus can be the wheel man. He can drive the wheels off anything."

Rick looked at Waha speculatively. "Mate, you got links with that chop shop, so can lift a van no problem, aye."

"Yep, be sweet," said Waha.

"Why don't you give us the word when you got more shit on this, specially on that inside flea," said Rick.

"Yeah," said Craig. "And… this conversation never happened."

Everyone at the table understood that. It didn't need to be said.

Roo and I traversed the angles on the phone that night. Whatever happened, there was no way I could participate in an armoured-car robbery like the one being proposed. Time was on my side. Craig still had planning to do, which would push the job back closer to termination. We settled on a plan to let the lead-up progress and then find reasons to delay if necessary. As it transpired the job never went down before I terminated, but the evidence was such that the participants ended up being charged with conspiracy to commit robbery.

Ironically, Waha did rob an armoured car about four years later. It was a good score, bagging around a quarter of a million dollars. As a result of being caught and convicted, he did a decent lag of six years in prison. The spoils of the robbery were to kick off a drug-manufacturing business which was stalled by the conviction. Not a man to be deterred, Waha persevered after being released from prison and became a major drug kingpin involved in the manufacture of methamphetamine.

◀ NINE ▶

"If you sit by the river long enough, the bodies of your enemies will float by."

AFTER SEEING WANA I KEPT my head down in the South Island for the two weeks leading up to termination day. This was set for a Wednesday. I flew back to Auckland the day before and stayed at Roo's that night. We had our customary few drinks in the lounge chewing the fat about the operation. This night was different.

Roo cast a pensive look towards me and wryly asked, "You all set for tomorrow, mate?"

"No," I replied. "I don't really know what to expect."

If uncertainty was a river, it was about to burst its banks. My rum reflected in the glass of the coffee table. It too seemed to be seeking answers, querying my resolve.

"We can't do any more," said Roo. "Everything's set, all the files are done, addresses checked, it's in the hands of the gods. We're just gonna have to wait and see how it rolls, who's at the addresses when the doors are kicked down and what they say in interview."

None of this calmed my turbulent waters.

Baby Kristin cried that night but it didn't disturb me, I was awake. Staring at the darkened ceiling I thought the wail might be a prelude to the next day's anguish.

The knock on my door came at 4am. I was greeted in the kitchen by Chris cooking bacon and eggs. It was considerate of her to get up and prepare breakfast, a small but valuable contribution to the big day.

There was virtually no traffic as we cruised down the North-Western motorway towards the city. The orange motorway lights of the sleeping city blinked in the early morning dew. We pulled in and parked on the top deck of the Central police station. Standing like a sentinel at the bottom of town, Central rises nine storeys. Its austere grey concrete exterior and flat windows hark back to the Cold War era. Straddling the corner of Vincent and Cook streets, it is essentially a fortress. The Vincent Street entrance serves as access to the watch house where prisoners are processed. Solid doors retract, allowing police vehicle access.

Roo exchanged pleasantries with different detectives as he led me through to the line-up room behind the watch house. This was unfamiliar territory. The surroundings and faces were foreign. I felt uncomfortable and estranged. To the criminal persona of Mark Munro, which I had carefully cultivated over the last year, this was enemy territory.

The line-up room was a big long rectangle. Rows of seats had been unfolded in anticipation down the brightly lit room. A mixture of uniforms, plainclothes cops and detectives milled around the seats. A steady stream of personnel drifted in. The briefing was set for 5am and by then every seat was populated. Counting the Armed Offenders Squad members and dog handlers standing at the back, there were more than one hundred and twenty cops at the briefing. It was an intimidating sight and swallowing failed to keep the lump in my throat at bay.

At the front of the room was a stage with a lectern set in the middle. I later found out this stage was used to parade prisoners from the cells in front of detectives: this was termed CIB line-up and allowed detectives to familiarise themselves with crooks who had been arrested the previous day. As each prisoner was produced from the cells and faced the blaring lights screening his unseen observers, the detective inspector would provide a rundown on his history and detail the circumstances of his arrest.

Detective Superintendent Barry Smith, the officer in charge of the Auckland Police District, kicked off the Operation Emu briefing with a rundown on what had transpired. Hearing what I had engineered in such secrecy being shared in such a public way was like leveraging the roof from a hidden bat cave.

"Today at six am we will be executing fifty-two search warrants around the city and nationally, seeking over one hundred offenders for a variety of serious crimes," he said. "This is down to the superb work carried out by our undercover agent in dangerous and trying circumstances. He is to be commended and I present him to you now."

At this, I was ushered to the stage and unsteadily stood behind the lectern. Looking into the lights I could see about ten rows back. All eyes in those rows were surveying me curiously. I felt like some rare wild animal lured into captivity. Luckily I didn't have to speak, as I'm not sure my vocal cords would have functioned. My misery was short lived and I was directed to sit down again beside Roo.

The briefing continued for thirty minutes with Roo and CIS bosses addressing the assembled throng. Files had been distributed previously to the various teams who had been allocated offenders and addresses. Search warrants had been secured from the Magistrates Court previously. Aside from the original Summary Proceedings Act search warrant, each file comprised a full background on the offender, copies of my statements, notes and photographs of exhibits, being drugs or stolen property. Inside the front cover of each file was a photo of me, which the interviewers could show suspects to confirm who I was.

The search warrants were to be executed simultaneously at 6am. Doing them early meant offenders could be caught at home and usually in bed. Each team consisted of a detective and two uniform cops. Armed Offenders Squad members or dogs would also be deployed depending on the target.

Due to the number of warrants and targets, the teams would have two files each but would complete the most important first. After the briefing the room emptied like water down a sink. Hyped up and ready to hit their targets, the teams headed for their vehicles and fanned out all across the city. Roo and I went to the CIB offices on the sixth floor to wait for the action.

I needed to compose myself after the briefing and sought sanctuary in the men's room. Alone, I caught my reflection in the mirror. Unrestrained emotions surged through my mind. I felt bereft of any identity. Was I cop or criminal? Or some twisted gargoyle hybrid? Despite being in a building full of people, I was overcome by a crippling loneliness.

The men's room was my willow tree, just like the one to which the possums I hunted as a teenager fled. My feet, reacting to the emotional turmoil, were adhered to the floor. The willow tree was protection I didn't want to leave.

Either through chance or design, John Purkis entered the men's room, walked to the urinal and cheerily said, "How's it going, Marcus?" lifting my emotional canopy.

"Yeah, yeah, good," I replied shakily.

Purkey's was a familiar face. He had been involved in the operation and I had seen him at CIS piss-ups. About three times during my operation I got together with other agents and operators who were deployed around the country at the same time as me. The secret parties were valuable for support and sharing experiences. I knew the other boys from our shared undercover seminar. It was good to catch up. I saw none of the hints of suspicion on Purkey's face that I had seen flickering on the countenance of some of my colleagues. I was to see that look many times in the future.

I reluctantly took leave of my sanctuary and found Roo sitting with his feet on a desk, drinking coffee. "Won't be long now, mate, and your pals will be turning up here with their day completely fucked up," he mused.

We heard radio chatter over an RT base set, reporting on developments at the different addresses. Due to the violent nature of most of my criminal associates, no quarter was given in the execution of the search warrants.

The gap between announcing "Police!" and kicking the door in was minimal. Handguns drawn and waved somewhere around the head ensured compliance. "Hands against the wall!" was being shouted simultaneously all around the city and further afield.

Not all the targets brought into Central needed to see me, but some of them did. When interviewed, many wouldn't believe I was cop, even when they were shown my photo. In these circumstances I was wheeled in to confront my erstwhile friend. It was a difficult task to perform. Betrayal in its most brutal and raw form.

Joe refused to believe I was a cop. The interviewing detective came to see me and explained the position. Apprehensively I followed him to the interview room. Stark and clinical, the room had only a desk and two chairs as furniture. A uniform cop stood in the corner with his arms folded. Joe sat in front of the desk with his back to the wall. He was rocking backwards and forwards on his chair. The file open at my photo sat alongside an A4 hard-covered notebook.

"Joe," I said quietly.

"Marcus, I don't believe this. Is it true? Are you a cop? How could you do this? I thought we were brothers, man."

"I was doing my job, mate. That's the way it is."

"Yeah, but what about all the shit we did together?"

"All part of the plan, Joe."

"Fuck me, I don't want to go back to jail."

"You do the crime, you do the time, mate," I said pensively.

"Yep." He dropped his head and looked at the floor. "I don't want to talk to you anymore," he added resignedly.

Next up was Charlie. Despite being roused from his bed, Charlie was as well dressed as usual. He sat rigidly in his chair. "So, fucken stinking undercover nark, are you?"

"Yes, I'm a police officer."

"Fucken low dog. I trusted you. I introduced you to my family, for fuck's sake. I suppose they're going down too."

"I'm sorry, Charlie, but that's the way it goes."

With narrowed eyes he replied, "If you sit by the river long enough, the bodies of your enemies will float by."

The interviewing detective shuffled in his chair and said, "Is that a threat?"

Charlie sat resolutely and said nothing.

I left the interview room and trudged back to the sixth-floor offices. Continual radio chatter spewed from the base set. Repeated calls were made for QPs (Query Person) and QVRs (Query Vehicle Registration). These checks were as a result of other criminals being located at the addresses. They could have outstanding arrest warrants or been found in possession of drugs or stolen property. The operation collaterally snared these crooks, cranking up the arrest tally.

I grabbed a cup of weak tea and slumped in a chair opposite Roo.

He was discussing tactics on secondary targets with a couple of Ds and their uniform support. I heard a voice from behind me say, "Mr Munro, we finally meet properly."

I swung around in my chair and was faced by Detective Sergeant John Hughes. He stood ramrod straight. His buzz-cut hair, perfectly trussed tie and slim, wiry physique combined to exude a military bearing.

"Yes. A pleasure, Mr Hughes," I replied.

"I knew there was something up with you, but I didn't think you were UC. You did a number on me too."

"Well, you certainly put the heat on me out there. Not quite good enough to pin anything on me though," I grinned.

"Yep. Great job. You knocked a big hole in the hard-core criminal scene. Speaking of hard-core heads, I'm dealing with Wana. He's been pretty measured, but not co-operating. It might assist if you were to front him."

"Yep, no problem." I swallowed the last of my tea and followed Hughesy to the interview room, unconsciously walking a little straighter than normal. Wana was sitting with his ankles crossed and his hands clasped behind his neck. He was a career criminal who wasn't fazed by a police interview or the fact he was facing a decent prison lag.

"So it was you who nailed Rick on the murder," Wana said casually.

"Afraid so, mate," I replied.

"That thing we talked about last time we had a rave?"

"Yeah," I said, recalling the fast talking I'd done in the Schooner.

"Fuck that was fifty-fifty man, it was set to go. Only the history between us put the brakes on."

"Well, that's good then."

Wana uncrossed his legs and settled in his chair. "Fair cop, though, Marcus. I'm still fucken spewing and I wouldn't say it outside of here, but you took us down fair and square."

"Okay, cool," I replied.

"That don't change nothing, though. You'd better watch your back. I ain't saying a word, either. I'll see you in court. That's if you make it," said Wana.

"There's only one cunt in here with problems, arsehole, and it isn't our agent," said a bristling Hughesy, rearing up over the sitting Wana.

I figured this was an appropriate juncture to take my leave.

Galloping through the range of human emotions, I was paraded through seven further interview rooms. One was occupied by Fingers, the old-school safecracker. He just gave me a smile and a wink, saying nothing. (Later on when I was a detective, Fingers became one of my best fizzes. As an informant, his bully was always accurate. Fingers had his finger on what was happening with property crime. He usually had a steer on who was involved in any big burglary or safe job.)

In the early afternoon, the teams caught up with Ruby. She wasn't at home in the morning, having stayed at the Mt Eden parlour overnight after a party with the girls. Later in the day she walked into another party, a welcome home from members of the Auckland CIB.

Ruby refused to believe I was a cop and demanded to see me. Like a hunted animal she sat in the corner of the interview room. She was rocking, her heels up on the edge of the chair, her arms clasped tightly around her knees. Her eyes, full of fear and anger, swept over me. Smudged mascara crept down her face.

About a month before termination, I had raised the issue of Ruby with Roo. I said tentatively, "You know Ruby?"

"Yeah, I know Ruby," he replied facetiously.

"Do you reckon we could leave her out of the book and maybe use her as a witness?"

After a pause Roo said calmly but firmly, "Just coz you were rooting her doesn't mean she gets any special favours."

Capitulating, with the words drifting away, I replied, "Yeah, I know, I just thought…"

Now I took a seat in a spare chair to the right of Detective Brown, who was conducting the interview. Ruby was opposite us. Just as I opened my mouth to speak, Ruby sprang from her seat, launching her lithe body headlong towards me.

Detective Brown, no stranger to martial arts, reacted immediately and caught the flying figure mid-air. A perfectly manicured talon clawed the air, sweeping in front of my face. Screaming, "You fucken bastard, you fucken bastard!" Ruby slumped to the floor. Her attack collapsed into a sequence of sobs punctuated by the word "bastard".

Gratefully, I heard Detective Brown say, "Nothing more you can do here, mate."

Ruby had paid the price of straying from hooking into dealing drugs.

◀ TEN ▶

"I didn't do it. I don't believe she's dead."

IN THE WAKE OF THE termination, intelligence confirmed that there remained a bounty on my head. It was simple: I was the evidence. If I didn't make it to trial, convictions would not hold up. I disappeared to a safe house in the South Island foothills. Clear skies, clean air and verdant countryside were my buffers. For six months, aside from returning to Auckland for trials, I left the house only to go for a run and get the newspaper. It was a time for reflection and massaging a tortured mind. Police psychological support was not forthcoming. This situation was remedied in later years, but then it wasn't considered important.

The first time I gave evidence was at Rick's murder trial. Even though I had been in the police in Dunedin for fifteen months and made a number of arrests, none of those had gone to defended hearings. With considerable trepidation I left Christchurch for Rick's trial.

I was met at Auckland airport by Roo and armed members of the VIP Protection Squad. The high levels of protection didn't help my levels of disquiet. I was spirited to the Supreme Court where Roo and I met with Crown prosecution lawyers. I had previously been provided with my brief of evidence which I had committed to memory.

The Auckland Supreme Court is an imposing temple of truth straddling the inner-city block between Parliament Street and Anzac Avenue. The trial began on 11 February 1980 before Justice Speight and a jury in the Number One Court, the building's pièce de résistance. The stone vaulted ceiling of the entrance hall gives visitors an initial taste of austerity and formality. As you move on into the body of the court, it's impossible not to be impressed. The raised ornate judge's bench, prominent witness box and heavy wooden jury benches dominated by towering marble pillars complete the intellectual intimidation. (The courthouse also acts as a repository for historical criminal and legal case files and holds the original roll of Barristers & Solicitors which is signed by every lawyer admitted to the bar. My signature and subsequently that of my daughter would years later be added to the roll.)

Rick had pleaded not guilty to Paula's murder. His legal counsel, Eb Leary, had devised a provocation defence. Although not a complete defence to the charge, the strategy was in effect to run an extended plea in mitigation, with the objective of escaping with a conviction on the lesser charge of manslaughter. This would change Rick's sentence: manslaughter would attract years but murder meant life in prison.

The provocation advanced was that in the lead-up to the killing Paula had denigrated Rick by casting aspersions upon his manhood and taunting him with being sexually inadequate. The comments had been so outrageous and humiliating that they had driven Rick to breaking point. The success of this approach depended on the fact there would be no contrary prosecution evidence as to events immediately before the murder. My evidence would be critical in contradicting the claim of provocation and supporting premeditation. Although I was unaware at the time, while I was standing in the witness box Armed Offenders Squad snipers were positioned on the roof above me, affording me protection.

My evidence was that Rick was affronted at Paula being so out of it on Tuinal that she was unable even to sit on a stool. And furthermore, that his rage was born from the ignominy of being beaten by Joe and losing his leg in the scuffle. Also telling against provocation was my evidence regarding the murder weapon, the switchblade. Rick had got the blade off me *before* the alleged goading by Paula. In addition to the murder there were numerous other crimes with which Rick was charged: conspiracy, wounding with intent, dealing controlled drugs, burglary, receiving stolen property, threatening to kill and carrying offensive weapons.

As with any defence counsel faced with evidence from a police undercover agent, Eb tried to discredit me. He tried the same tactic with other offenders from the operation he represented. The whole of the operation was under attack: structure, approach, tactics and my conduct in particular were fair game. Typical questions defence asked were variations on:

"Constable, you don't even know what name you're using before this court. You live by deception. We already know you're a liar — how can we expect you to tell the truth today?"

"You've spent a year telling lies. You don't know what the truth is any more."

"You're as much a street criminal as the man being tried here today."

"You acted as an agent provocateur. This man wouldn't have committed any of the crimes with which he's charged unless induced to do so by you."

"It is the defence's contention that you dealt in drugs yourself."

"You had a sexual relationship with this woman, didn't you. You used and abused her."

Joe was summonsed as a prosecution witness but he had gone to ground and a warrant was issued for his arrest. There was no way he was going to give evidence against Rick.

John Sullivan had been the barman that fateful night. He gave evidence about our group being present at the Station Hotel and that Rick was well known as an Auckland criminal kingpin. He described how he had seen Rick slap and punch Paula:

"I was behind the bar and I went over and told Ricki that he would have to cut it out. It quietened down but the next thing the Maori guy and Ricki were fighting. During the fight Ricki lost his artificial leg. The Maori guy definitely got the better of Ricki. After the fight Ricki produced a knife which he waved in the air. The next words I recall was the girl saying, 'You wouldn't have enough guts to do that'."

Sullivan then recounted how there was a scuffle between Rick and Paula with their both going outside. He detailed what he saw:

"There is a little rock garden just outside the entrance. The girl was sitting on the footpath. Ricki was leaning against the wall. She opened her blouse and said, 'Look what you've done, you bastard.' She had blood around her breast, but the two of them were still arguing. I went back inside briefly and when I came back the girl was lying down on the footpath and the colouring in her face was bad. I said to her there was an ambulance coming. She was still, I could still talk to her, and then there was no reply."

Asked about his feelings when the knife appeared, Sullivan said he was frightened by it and kept his distance from Rick. He confirmed that Paula had clawed at Rick's face and tried to punch him but Rick's retaliatory blows were much more effective. Poignantly he recalled something specific he witnessed when the two were outside and Paula was dying:

"There was one thing, when the girl was lying there and by now unresponsive. Ricki was sitting up against the wall. He gently nudged her legs with his foot as if to check she was okay."

In a heightened state of nervousness I entered the Number One Court to give evidence. As I walked to the witness box I saw Rick sitting beside Eb at defence counsel's table. He had obviously been given leave to sit there instead of standing in the dock. Stoically looking straight ahead he wore a black collarless top, his long black hair resting on his shoulders.

I gave evidence in my cover name, Mark Munro. I introduced myself as a police constable attached to the Criminal Intelligence Section and deployed to Auckland as an undercover agent. I specified my role as being to identify major crime figures and gather evidence against them.

As is usual I was required to identify the accused, Ricki Goodin, by pointing to and describing him. When I did so Ricki remained unmoved, deliberately ignoring me. Although the man was a hardened criminal and vicious killer, I felt a pang of regret. We had been friends; he completely trusted me and unquestionably would have protected me to the death.

A young, recently graduated policewoman, Ainsley Bisset, and her partner had been the first police to arrive at the scene. By this time Paula was dead.

The pathologist, Dr Dryson, gave evidence that the nature of the wound, a blade through the heart, meant she could have lived for only two to three minutes.

The attending ambulance officer said that Rick kept repeatedly asking him, "Is she dead, is she dead?"

Detective Owen Mitchell gave evidence that police searching the scene in Anzac Avenue outside the hotel had difficulties finding the murder weapon. Army personnel using mine detectors were called. They found the switchblade buried in a garden by the Harbour Lights Bar entry.

Detective Gordon Webb dealt with Rick following the murder and gave evidence of what Rick said to him: "I didn't do it, I didn't do it. I don't believe she is dead. You're lying to me. I don't believe she is dead. She's going to walk in here any minute and then we're both going home."

Unusually, at Rick's request Detective Webb took him to the mortuary to see Paula's body. When Rick saw the body he broke down crying and kissed her on the face. While in the charge room back at Central Rick said to Detective Webb, "I believe you now. She's dead."

Rick gave evidence in his own defence. He described a difficult home life growing up and how he had lost his lower leg in a motorcycle accident. He had fathered two children with Paula, whom he had been with since she was sixteen and he twenty-six. He gave details of Paula's drug and alcohol dependency and that she failed to look after his son properly.

When asked about his feelings towards Paula, he replied firmly that he loved her.

Regarding their sex life, he recounted how Paula humiliated him by saying that sex was no good with him and he was washed up as a man. Additionally, she used to call him a black bastard.

Asked why he would take all this from her, he replied, "It was simple. I loved her."

Rick confirmed that he often slapped Paula to get some sense into her.

When he challenged her about taking barbiturates she would say, "If I have, it has nothing to do with you anyway."

Ironically, although Joe had defended Paula from Rick's treatment, during his evidence Rick repeated what she had said to him after he lost the fight: "Why don't you do something about it? You're all washed up, no good at all. If you think I'm coming home with you tonight you must be joking. I'm going to find me a real man."

I had to smile when Rick gave evidence that he had not been in employment since he had been with Paula. He said his source of income was from gambling. This gambling being betting on horses and playing pool for money. His revenue stream as a pool shark, he said, had started when he was fourteen. Rick, of course, was a major crime figure. All his income was from drug-dealing, burglaries, receiving stolen property and intimidation. Now he could add murderer to his résumé.

◄ ELEVEN ►

"Run it up the flagpole and see who salutes."

DEBATE ABOUT MY FUTURE DIRECTION in the police didn't last long. During one of the many long waits outside the Auckland courts, I said to Roo, "Dog section might be quite good. I love dogs."

Impassively Roo replied, "Nah, you've got too much skill. CIB is the only option. You need to become a detective."

That was it. I was fast-tracked into the CIB. With the success of the operation, I could do whatever I wanted in the police. Except handling a specialist drug dog or subsequent attachment to the Drug Squad — too much risk, was the decree from above. Part of the reasoning was the hangover from former agent Wayne Haussemann.

Wayne had worked undercover in a heavy drug scene before entering the CIB in Christchurch. After qualifying as a detective, he was attached to the Drug Squad there. He decided to use his training and considerable drug-dealing capabilities for his own benefit. He had unfortunately picked up a drug habit while deployed and was using heroin. At the undercover seminars I attended there was one absolute and incontrovertible rule: you never main-lined drugs. Breaching that rule was a guaranteed route to despair, as Wayne sadly discovered. His drug habit was so strong that he was shooting up heroin in the toilets of the Drug Squad office. He arranged to import two kilos of heroin from Thailand. Suspicions that had been circling around him led to an internal covert operation that intercepted his shipment. He was charged with serious drug importation and dealing.

The destruction of Wayne's life through service to the Crown was completed with a sentence of sixteen years in prison. On appeal that was reduced to eight years and he ended up serving four and a half. Wayne's conviction placed in stark relief the risks and realities of undercover policing.

I was scheduled to attend the next CIB induction course in four months. At that time, to qualify as a detective you needed to complete the month-long induction course and, two years later, a detective-qualifying course. During the two-year period you completed a series of twenty units on a monthly basis. These units covered the law and investigation techniques. They were monitored and marked by in-service training instructors.

I had the privilege of having Detective Sergeant Wally Walden as my instructor at the induction course and also back in Auckland. Wally was a real character with a wide collection of entertaining expressions. His favourite was: "Let's run it up the flagpole and see who salutes."

He would also say, with gusto and almost always out of context: "There's only three things a detective has to do — drink beer, tell lies and skite."

My other instructor, who took over from Wally, was Detective Sergeant Kevin Gee. KG, as he was known, was a top bloke. He knew the criminal law inside out. He wasn't a bush lawyer; he was a forest-canopy lawyer. He had never formally studied law, which he could have done easily, but took great joy in feasting on the complexities of intent, conspiracy, parties and colour of right. Correctly answering papers he was marking was not enough; KG wanted to interrogate the legal principle founded in some obscure Court of Appeal decision. The intellectual sparring was enjoyable. When I sailed into stormy waters with the police, KG unreservedly supported me.

Qualifying as a detective wasn't easy. As a detective constable, the rank obtained following the induction course, your case load could be high. In this two-year period you moved around the various CIB squads to gain experience. I worked on Robbery, Crime, Cars, Break and Fraud squads. As a DC you were expected to work long hours and get results. When working on major investigations such as homicides, long hours were the norm. As I flatted with another DC we were regularly called out if something big went down. Completing the CIB units had to be shuffled down the priority list.

On the qualifying course participants were extended not only academically but also with practical exercises. The Police College in Porirua has a crime-scene room which is used for scene examinations. For a DC trying to pass the course, it is a daunting prospect entering that room, trying to establish what has happened and then taking the right steps. Discerning instructors and senior detectives watch smugly from seats stationed above the open-top room. Sometimes, uniform recruits in training will also observe; the increased audience heightens your apprehension.

My first time in that room was not entirely successful. I was so intent on trying to establish what had happened and not disturbing the scene that I made a major error. I assumed the victim was dead and failed to check for vital signs. It is all very well to manage a copybook scene, but all of that is secondary if a life can be saved.

The most terrifying ordeal on the D course was the final major crime-scene investigation exercise, which took place at the end. It was notorious among trainee detectives. Stories spiced with exaggeration circulated from previous courses. It involved a major crime scene being set up at an undisclosed location, usually with multiple victims, a shooting or stabbing, numerous witnesses to be found and interviewed plus murder weapons to be located.

One trainee detective constable is appointed to be the officer in charge (O/C). It is this person's job, essentially, to solve the crime. The O/C appoints their subordinates and needs to bring the case together, culminating in a final briefing. No one wants to be the O/C. The role is an investigative poisoned chalice. The course instructors revel in making the case difficult and it is rarely solved completely.

Our exercise was set up in Queen Elizabeth Park out of Wellington, which meant a thirty-minute bus ride during which all thirty course members were silently awaiting the decree from Wally Walden as to who among our number was to be the hapless O/C. Wally wasn't about to put us out of our misery early.

He was tight-lipped as the bus pulled away from the Police College. For the next twenty-five minutes, like some medieval torturer, he paced up and down the aisle of the bus. Periodically, for effect, he would stop alongside seats and stare at the downturned heads before moving further along the bus. Incantations of "Please not me" or some hurried prayer were murmured at each cessation of footsteps.

I was sitting beside Crunchie, who was in a particular state of turmoil, so when Wally stopped alongside our row five minutes out from our destination I think Crunchie started trembling. I'm not completely sure as my mind had gone blank and my breathing stopped. When Wally extended his arm, pointed at Crunchie and said, "Detective Constable," two things happened. My faculties rebooted and Crunchie became cadaverously pale.

Crunchie did his best as the O/C but it didn't go that well. There were multiple bodies and unfortunately the cordon was set in a manner where one of the bodies and the murder weapon, a rifle, were outside the boundary. Anyway, whatever deficiencies there may have been were rectified that night in the Police College bar and the exercise became another chapter of CIB folklore.

Months later, as a qualified detective attached to Crime Squad, I was dispatched to a suspected homicide along with my uniform driver. At 2am we arrived at the scene, a dilapidated weatherboard house in West Auckland. A long driveway bordered the house, providing access to the rear garage. From the open side door a corridor of light fell across the driveway, swathing the body. She was sitting stapled, her back against the fence, her neck snapped, her head hung forward like a wilted flower.

Protruding from below her sternum, nudging through her blood-stained blouse, was a kitchen-knife handle. She was obviously dead, but I checked anyway. The pathologist later told me the ten-inch blade had been driven into her midriff with such force it had broken her neck, killing her instantly.

We searched the house for the offender or any other occupants. It was empty. A uniform car was stationed across the drive to initially control the scene. They had arrived first and we had been called as the closest crime car. The key in this initial stage is to freeze the scene to preserve evidence.

A critical part of this process is setting the cordon. It needs to be wide enough to capture all evidence relating to the crime but not so wide as to be unmanageable. It's easy to get it wrong, as happened on the qualifying course. Once the cordon is set, uniform staff guard it to prevent contamination.

Securing witnesses at this time is critical. This is the only opportunity you will have to speak to them in the immediate aftermath of the crime. It is then their recollections will be fresh about what happened and who was responsible.

All crime scenes are interesting. Homicide scenes where a victim has been recently killed have their own aura, a macabre dominion of palpable violence. There is almost always blood; only the volume changes. The musky redolence of violently spilled blood is unmistakable.

I was O/C Body (officer in charge of the body) at a homicide scene in South Auckland during the height of summer. The female victim had been stabbed by her partner in the kitchen of their home. She had survived the first two stab wounds to her stomach and made her way down the hall towards her bedroom. Blood-splatter patterns at waist height on the walls spoke of a weaving gait.

She made it to the bed but her killer ended her life there, cutting her throat from behind. Face down on the bed, her remaining blood was expelled under her, creating a jelly-like pad in which she was suspended. That's how we found her. The pathologist's view was that eighty per cent of her blood had coagulated beneath her.

As O/C Body you stay at the scene until the body's removal and you also attend the post-mortem. Complications in examining the scene meant I was in the house for over two days. Temperatures of over thirty degrees made the place uncomfortably pungent. Returning home at night provided no respite from the olfactory overload.

The Springbok Tour of 1981 was a tumultuous time. The country was firmly split between pro- and anti-tour factions. The objectors argued that the tour should not proceed, as dealing with South Africa in rugby tacitly provided support for their apartheid regime. It's not an exaggeration to state that rugby is a de facto religion in New Zealand, so the societal divisions were fierce.

Tour protesters were well organised and supported. Their objective was to halt the games and gain international attention for their cause. Protests at games escalated until cops armed with batons and wearing riot gear were in violent confrontation with protesters in motorbike helmets and armed with batons and missiles such as bricks. It was a simple issue for the majority of cops: they loved rugby and wanted the games to proceed. The opportunity to be deployed against protesters, with the possibility of swiftly delivering justice to those disrupting our national game, was a bonus.

Given my undercover experience, I was attached to a plainclothes target squad made up of three detectives and a sergeant. Our instructions were to establish where the protesters were meeting before each game and gather intelligence by mingling with the marchers. In addition, we were to identify anyone who was committing the offence of inciting a riot. The leader of our team was Sergeant Dave Scott. Scotty liked getting the job done but he also liked to have a good time doing it. At our first briefing he clarified our role: "We're gonna sort these fucken pricks out." Our "targets" included John Minto, the figurehead of an organisation called HART (Halt All Racist Tours), Trevor Richards, Hone Harawira and Donna Awatere.

For the first few protest marches we were able to mix freely within the protesters without exposure. As the numbers of protests increased and the violence around the country escalated, we learned that the protesters were conducting counter-surveillance. At times we became actively involved in arrests; not an ideal situation.

Physical apprehension normally took place at the end of a protest, once evidence of riotous comments had been gathered. On about our third march Minto had made statements sufficient to meet the evidential threshold for inciting a riot and we moved to arrest him. We waited until the march had dispersed and followed him to an alley off Fort Street. Apart from a young female he was alone.

While shadowing the pair one of our boys said, "Let's deal to that fucker right here, aye?"

Scotty was the voice of reason. "Nah, let's get the business done, get him off the streets and down to Central. But don't hold back if the prick resists."

With repeated arrests and through counter-surveillance we started to become known. We weren't fully aware of the extent of the protesters' knowledge but we found out during a motorway protest when about five thousand protesters successfully occupied the North-Western motorway, paralysing one of the city's main arterial routes.

We were participating in the march which wended its way along the motorway. Our squad stayed close together, at least to the extent that we had visual contact with one another. The march was joined by criminal elements, including a sprinkling of patched gang members. This was a disturbing trend as the tour progressed: certain people took part in protests solely to engage in conflicts with police.

By this time, tensions were elevated because the Hamilton match had been cancelled for security reasons. Protesters had torn down fences and stormed the pitch, preventing the game from proceeding. The police riot squad, termed Red Squad, had been confined under the grandstand and not let loose on the protesters. Police Commissioner Bob Walton had made the call, which was met with derision by almost all police. The feeling was, despite the merits or otherwise of the tour, we had been unable to uphold the rule of law.

Tactics changed after Hamilton. There was a resolve that no further games would be halted. If this meant dealing brutally with front-line protesters, then that's what would happen. And it did. Clashes in the future were bloody. Long PR-24 batons used in martial arts were wielded destructively by the Red Squad. The protesters' full-face helmets offered no protection. The batons made short work of smashing visors and the facial structures behind them. Police suffered too, with one Red Squad member having both shoulders broken.

Agitation was the prevailing mood of the march this day. There was an edge to the atmosphere which had previously been absent. Chants of "Amandla" and "We don't want no racist tours" were shouted in unison by the assembled throng. Baseball bats, sticks and bricks were brandished.

As we approached the first motorway overbridge, we could see protesters standing on the section of road above us. At this point the behaviour of the people around us changed. The march stopped. Like a cog in a mammoth machine the throng moved around us. "Pig! Pig! Pig!" became the new hostile chant. We later learned that earlier that day our photos had been posted at the HART HQ.

There was no way out. We were at the mercy of the fifty-person-deep crowd. Venom exuding from such a mass of humanity acting in unison was frightening. If the horde ventured into violence, we didn't stand a chance. Maybe because of our vulnerability, four people among hundreds, the mood of the mass shifted again. It moderated. With the march lumbering forward again, we were ejected from the side of the snaking human train, rolling out like pebbles from a rug.

"We're gonna have to flog a door from somewhere," Scotty said as he scrutinised the significant passenger's door dent on our unmarked Holden HQ police car.

"Central's top parking deck's our best bet," he muttered, examining the crumpled metal. Tinges of red paint scoured the rippled steel of the grey finish. "The door needs to be the same colour. We'll just swap them over. No one will know a thing."

"Fuck off, Scotty," replied one of the squad. "You think the boys in the car that ends up with our fucked door aren't gonna notice it?"

The accident had happened that night. We had been on a march and finished up about 7pm. Led by Scotty, the squad's usual modus operandi was to roll into drinking piss. Our leader's firm directive was that such entertainment was a necessary requirement in relieving stress. None of the squad could conceive of any counter argument to our O/C's position. After sampling a number of the downtown bars, the call was made to head to Parnell. Scotty was driving and occasionally he would get slightly exuberant behind the wheel. That night was one of those occasions.

We were travelling down Fort Street in the central city. Gore Street approached and its entry required a left-hand turn. It was now about 11.30pm and the road wore a slight coat of dampness from a recent shower. Even if it had been perfect daylight conditions, Scotty was travelling too fast for the corner. He lost control and the car spun. The Holden circled end for end before slamming into a parked car. The passenger's door took the brunt of the impact as we jarred to a halt.

The door was crushed against the parked car on the wrong side of the road but at least we were facing the right way. In unison the cry went up, "Let's get the fuck out of here!" With the engine still running Scotty stomped on the gas and in seconds we were gone. Getting caught there with all of us drunk and the car damaged would not have advanced our career prospects.

"Let's at least look and see if there's any other grey cars on the deck," implored Scotty.

"Nah, look, I've got an idea," said Trev, a twenty-year veteran of the CIB. "I've got a mate who's a panel-beater. I reckon he could fix the thing overnight."

Anything was preferable to completing the voluminous paperwork required for a police vehicle accident. No damage would mean it wasn't our car in Gore Street either.

An hour later the Holden and our squad were concealed behind the doors of a Grafton panel-beater's. Luckily the boot still held a decent quantity of beer. By the early hours of the morning, tainted by the pungency of paint fumes, the beer was finished as was the car. Circulating the next day as if nothing had happened, we didn't realise that this was only the beginning of the issues with the Holden.

The Springboks were scheduled to play the NZ Maoris on 25 August in Napier. This eleventh tour game was significant because the Springbok opposition was an indigenous team. At this stage of the tour, radical opposition took a sinister turn.

Credible intelligence had been received that one of the Springbok team would be shot. As a result, personal protection measures for team members were elevated considerably. I was shifted from the target squad to a team-protection role in Napier. Along with other Auckland cops covering the game, I travelled to Napier on a Hercules military transport aircraft. Aside from transport, the military provided superb support to the police. Cops are notorious tooth-men and love a good feed, especially if it's free. Army cooks fed the throngs of cops deployed at the various games. The nose bags dished up were excellent — so good that diners needed three helpings to be sated.

I was deployed in a venue-security role at the Springboks' hotel. The comings and goings at night were engrossing. Over the six days the team was in residence, a posse of local women maintained a permanent vigil. These women wanted to hook up with a player and positioned themselves wherever they thought they could achieve their objective.

One night at about 7pm a brand new Mercedes coupé glided to a halt in front of the hotel. Behind the wheel sat a stunning blonde who could have just driven from some slick French Riviera cafe. She gracefully extended a perfectly manicured hand and flipped open her passenger door. Approaching the car was a lumbering member of the Springboks front row. This giant forward appeared wider than he was tall. Short prickles of hair covered his huge dome head. What passed for ears — scrum-ravaged gristle — hung from each side of his skull. This possible movie monster dropped into the expensive sports car to be greeted with a model smile. The Merc growled away from the hotel entrance followed by the envious eyes of security.

Cops are one demographic who don't miss an opportunity. There were more women hanging around the hotel than there were players. It seemed natural that the void should be filled by bodyguards, which is what happened. We were the grateful recipients of the players' leftovers. As far as the women were concerned, sufficient celebrity attached to us. A typical ruse was to offer a tour of the locked-down hotel.

The final game of the tour was the third test at Auckland's Eden Park on Saturday 12 September. By then, a lot of blood had been spilled on the country's streets. We as a squad spoke about it; there was a whiff of Armageddon in the air.

We were back on the target squad but no longer took part in the marches. The exposure we had received made it too dangerous. The day of the test we travelled to Eden Park. I was driving and after negotiating the police-manned checkpoints, steered the Holden into a parking spot in Onslow Road.

From early morning, the area around the ground looked prepped for war. Rolls of barbed wire ringed the venue. The fences were all topped with razor wire. Shipping containers formed barricades in the streets. On every ridge and vantage point uniform police in riot gear and carrying long batons stood as sentinels. More than two thousand cops suited up that day. For New Zealand, a safe, harmonious country at the bottom of the world, this was a new chapter.

Our squad's role was to be inside the ground and target any hard-core troublemakers we could identify. During the course of our intelligence role we had become entirely familiar with the faces of those creating turmoil.

The predicted violence came to pass, worse than anticipated. There were running battles in the streets around Eden Park. The protesters came well prepared. In addition to their helmets they wore body armour and had fashioned wooden shields for protection against police batons. Their missiles, hurled at police lines, were bottles, rocks, pipes and Molotov cocktails. At some points around the ground protesters tried to prevent spectators from getting to the game. Fierce fights between the pro- and anti-lobby ensued.

Inside the ground the game kicked off — followed by a change in the protesters' tactics. An attack came from the air. A Cessna aircraft had been hired from Dairy Flat airfield north of Auckland. Piloted by Marx Jones, it buzzed Eden Park many times, dropping over the grandstand and swooping down low over the pitch. Passenger Grant Cole dropped flour bombs and flares on to the field.

Our squad was positioned near where the Springboks reserves were seated. It was disconcerting watching the Cessna make its passes — there was an inescapable fear that the plane might, mistakenly or otherwise, fly into the crowd. It was so low that it loomed large within the stadium. With each pass the bombing became more accurate. One flour bomb hit All Black prop Gary Knight on the back of the head, felling him. The game stopped briefly and team members gathered around him as he groggily regained his feet.

Despite the bombardment the game continued, albeit with numerous stoppages. In the event the All Blacks won with an injury-time penalty kicked by Allan Hewson. The win gave New Zealand a series victory, in a small way providing some vindication for the tumultuous tour. After the game our squad ventured into the streets around the park. Mayhem abounded. Bleeding and wounded protesters lay on kerbs and footpaths. The roads, littered with placards, rocks, paint and flour, provided evidence of the street battles. Police milled about, uniforms plastered with paint and flour. Some were seated with helmets off, heads hung, licking blood from their mouths. Limping constables were helped by their colleagues, hobbling away from the battle zone.

This carnage unfolded as we picked our way to Onslow Road. Emerging through flare smoke I caught my first glimpse of the Holden. Windows smashed out, it sat upturned on its roof. Unthinkingly I felt in my pocket for the useless keys.

◄ TWELVE ►

"You're not in the Schooner anymore."

I WAS WORKING WITH DETECTIVE Wayne McDonald on early-shift city crime car. Cruising down Queen Street, the objective was to hit as many red lights as possible. This allowed us to watch the lunchtime throngs of office girls crossing the intersections. Hitting all six lights down the main drag was a major score.

Wayne was piloting the car as we came to a stop at the bottom of Queen Street. The Walk sign activated and pedestrians streamed across in multiple directions. Although we were in an unmarked vehicle it is not difficult to pick a D car. An obnoxious young male accompanied by three females did just that. As he reached the front of our car he stopped, turned towards us and made outlandish masturbation gestures. The appropriate response to that would be to smile and laugh it off or tell him to fuck off and stop being so stupid.

Not, however, when you have recently terminated from a long-term undercover operation. In the scene such disrespect calls for immediate retribution, no matter the consequences. An automatic response born of a year living by a street code drove me from the car. My attack corridor led directly to the punk's throat. A blow sent him down to the tarmac. I straddled him, my hands around his throat. His female associates took exception. Blows from handbags rained around my head and back. Meanwhile my dismayed partner sat stranded at what was now a green light, with traffic behind him.

Next, Wayne was there dragging me off the punk. "What the fuck are you doing?" he hissed. "We're gonna have to lock this prick up now."

We travelled back to the Central with the punk in handcuffs in the back seat. When we arrived I went up to the sixth floor to face the music from KG, our D sergeant.

"Are you fucking mad?" he shouted, looking simultaneously perplexed and worried. "You know I got disciplined for calling some jerk a goose, and you attack someone in the middle of the busiest intersection in Auckland!"

"But he deserved it, KG. You can't pull acts like that and get away with it."

"Fuck off, Marcus. You're not in the Schooner anymore."

KG stood up from behind his desk and folded his arms. He looked out the windows, a view that included Queen Street, the scene of the ruckus. He turned to me and said, "Stay in here and keep your head down. I'll see what I can do."

"Okay, no problem," I murmured, and slumped down in the chair opposite his desk. Somehow, KG sorted the issue out after a long roundtable with the punk and his female sidekicks. No complaints were forthcoming and no charges were laid.

The accepted undercover psychological paradigm of the time was that pre-deployment screening was necessary, but post-termination debriefings weren't. Sure, you were given the contact details of the police psychologist, but reaching out then was still stigmatised. There was little emphasis upon the effects on the agents of undercover policing. Post-traumatic stress disorder existed in their conceptual world but not their real world. Attributing aberrant behaviour by former agents to previous deployments was nonsensical.

Former agents were supposed to seamlessly integrate back into police thinking in the collective police manner. Zero account was taken of the fact that agents had been trained to act individually, survive on their wits, trust no one and often act extremely.

The modern undercover programme is completely different. Legal action by disgruntled agents facilitated change. The very nature of undercover policing is such that it carries physical and psychological risk. Undercover operations are always hazardous: an approach based on mitigating risk would compromise operational outcomes.

The police were subjected to a raft of claims from former agents claiming drug addiction resulting from their deployment. A further target was the Accident Compensation Corporation, the no-fault scheme for employment accidents. The scope of the scheme meant it could include claims by the agents, drug addiction being one cause of action along with post-traumatic stress disorder. Personally, I don't think drugs were the primary issue — it was violence. Drugs could be sidestepped in a street scene but violence couldn't. The street parallels the wild. Kill or be killed.

I graduated on 3 December 1982. At twenty-three, I was the youngest constable in the New Zealand Police to qualify as a detective.

The first day I joined the Break Squad I was greeted with, "We'll tie these bastards up so tight their arses won't pucker. When we come to interview them there'll be nowhere to turn."

Speaking was Detective Sergeant Morrie Raskin. A true individual, Morrie became one of my best mates. Wiry, with ginger hair and freckles, he stood about five foot ten. Always ready with a smile that almost separated his face, Morrie was a man of many parts. Anything physical ranked highly: running, swimming, rugby, windsurfing, gym, diving, carting hay, play-fighting and anything else that required exerting energy.

Morrie's comment in the Break Squad office was in reference to a burglary ring. Significant evidence had already been gathered but Morrie, as was his custom, wanted the case watertight. I learned a lot from him about structuring inquiries and attention to detail. He had a prodigious ability to present an entire investigation diagrammatically, distilling it down to digestible components.

Despite not having a drop of Maori blood running through his veins, Morrie was a devotee of the culture. He studied Maori at Auckland University and was an adept speaker of the language. He was also an exponent of the taiaha, the traditional close-quarters weapon. He trained young Maori in its use, helping to keep Maori weaponry and martial arts alive.

Morrie lived at 16 Rodney Road, Northcote. I flatted there for about a year. We had a lot of fun there; it was a happy house. A fatigued brown

1970s Ford Escort station-wagon always sat in the drive. The car held a warm place in Morrie's heart. Comments even resembling criticism of that Ford were met with stern resistance.

It transported us on some great adventures, one of which was a trip to Russell in the Bay of Islands. Playing continuously was *Waylon & Willie*, a CD by Waylon Jennings and Willie Nelson. We picked up a couple of English girls at the Duke of Marlborough pub. Saturated with sun, sand, music and beer, we hung out with those chicks for two days. Warmed at night by a driftwood fire, we slept inside and alongside the trusty Escort.

Superseding the car in Morrie's affections was his Dobermann, Denby. The dog was slightly unhinged, something his owner found appealing. Denby would allow visitors to come through the gate and get to the back door before choosing whether or not to act. A visiting girl got to the back door before Denby sprang and ripped the arm from her expensive puffer jacket. Morrie found it highly amusing. A raft of complaints flowed through to the police about the dog at number sixteen. Mysteriously, none were actioned.

The first thing Morrie, an ardent environmentalist, did after purchasing a bare block of land in Papakura was to fence off the wetlands for preservation. He built a house on the block for his mother. As if in some melancholic line in one of the country songs he loved so much, one fateful spring day Morrie's luck ran out. While he was cutting firewood for his mother's home, a tree fell on him, breaking his pelvis. Following surgery, a blood clot stopped his heart, killing him on 30 September 2000. He was forty-seven. My indefatigable, exuberant, cheeky, irreverent, loyal friend was gone.

Such was his mana within Maoridom that Morrie was farewelled with a tangi and designated an honorary chief of the Tuhoe iwi. Following the tangi a full formal police funeral was held, attended by hundreds. The police helicopter Eagle flew above the casket as it was carried to the hearse. Even as a pallbearer I never saw it.

◀ THIRTEEN ▶

"Shoot to kill."

IT GOT TO A POINT where after six months attached to Fraud Squad I was sick of holding files. I wanted to get back on the street. My chosen option was the Crime Control Unit (CCU). The squad was plainclothes and a mixture of uniform cops and detectives. The idea was to act like a consorting unit, roaming the city streets, visiting pubs and placing direct pressure on criminals through tip-outs and executing search warrants.

The squad's other role was VIP Protection, providing bodyguard services to politicians and overseas dignitaries. Plenty of variety and no files. My transfer from Fraud Squad went through in less than a month. I saw the roster of who would be on my section: Detective Wayne Wright whom I knew, Sergeant Neil Morris whom I had heard of, and Constable Ainsley Bisset, who was a mystery.

I had in fact seen her a couple of months before in the ninth-floor canteen. Fetching, in her uniform of baby-blue blouse and navy skirt, she had her back to me as I came in. She sat alone with a homemade lunch before her. Shiny blonde curly hair settled on her shoulders and down her back, accentuating her slender form through the fitting blouse. As I passed by her table, I smiled at the individual touch of sleeves carefully folded over twice. She was a picture of femininity and I wondered who she was. All was revealed on my first day with CCU: there she was, the policewoman attached to the squad.

About a week later Ainsley and I were sitting together in the CCU office. For some reason we were the only ones working that afternoon. Wayne and Neil were absent. I wanted to learn more about this intriguing woman. "Let's get out of here and head over to the Poe," I suggested, grabbing the car keys from the desk. The Poenamu was a popular

Takapuna pub and not the sort of place where any crap might go down necessitating our involvement. We cruised over the harbour bridge and settled in the Poe's garden bar.

Ainsley wore tight blue jeans and a tight T-shirt. Traces of her perfume wafted across our shared table. She was simply sexy. Small talk flowed easily and we were immediately comfortable with each other. I learned early that she was from the South Island, a shared heritage.

Her glacial blue eyes danced with enthusiasm with each new topic. We spoke of travel and specifically Phuket Island in Thailand's south. We had both been there within the last twelve months. This was unusual then, as Thailand was not the tourist destination it is now. It was reserved for only the quirkier intrepid traveller. On the Thai theme Ainsley said, "The first time I saw you I think you had just come back from Thailand. We drove down the ramp opposite the watch house and you leaned in the back to speak to Wayne. You had on Buddhist prayer beads and a white muslin shirt. I thought you looked like a hippie, not a cop. You were brown and your hair was bleached, shaggy and long. Wayne said you were pretty wild but very smart."

"Gee, I don't know about that," I replied self-consciously.

"Joe from the other section said whenever you went out you always had good-looking birds with you. The boys also said you had worked UC. They actually spoke about you with awe. They were a bit wary of you, but most cops are like that with former agents."

I didn't like to talk much about my operation, but felt comfortable with her. "The operation got tricky when my running mate killed his missus," I said solemnly.

"I remember that murder. I was first on the scene."

"No!" I was surprised. Our paths crossing in that manner was uncanny. There are coincidences and then there was this revelation which on a languid North Shore afternoon was almost too big to comprehend. There was an uncomfortable gap in my knowledge that I needed filled. As I was a witness at the trial I didn't hear the other prosecution evidence so was unaware what transpired in the aftermath of the killing.

"Can you tell me what it was like?" I asked intently.

"I'd been in the job for just over a year. When we got the call from Control it came through as a fight, a disturbance involving patrons."

"So you had no idea how serious it was?" I queried, wanting to know more.

"No, it was just a regular call, but we were close and got there quickly, within two minutes. When we arrived there was no one else there. My most vivid memory was the body of a female who was dead or very close to death. I remember she looked very peaceful. It didn't look like any violence was involved."

"How do you mean?"

"She appeared to be resting as if at any moment she might awaken. I remember her top was open and skewed to one side. That was the only sign of something out of the ordinary. I checked her for vital signs but couldn't feel a pulse. She appeared fragile and looked out of place, like somehow she had become the victim of a set of circumstances over which she had no control."

"It's strange that you say that coz I think that's right. She had a pretty tough life and didn't deserve to die like that."

"Yes, it was very sad, and because of that I remember it vividly. Information kept coming through in a disjointed way from staff and other patrons. It was to the effect that she had been stabbed by her partner. The information wasn't in any sort of chronology and happened over about five minutes. But I knew by then it certainly wasn't a random attack."

"What was the story with Rick; did you know what was going on with him?" I asked.

"Well, retrospectively, you realise that when the victim is beyond help your focus automatically shifts to the killer. The assumption at that point was that the offender's location was unknown and that he was mobile. Our information then was the offender was a high-profile criminal named Ricki Goodin."

"Did you know who he was at the time?"

"Yes, I was well aware of him. He was known as the godfather of organised crime, violent and unpredictable. We had to assume he was still armed with the murder weapon and would use it if approached."

"Did you know about his leg?"

"Yes, we all knew he had an artificial leg, which would have made getting away difficult. Our initial thoughts were he had left the scene in a vehicle. The scene was chaotic. Some of the patrons weren't even aware of what had happened. We knew the victim had been stabbed, so we began a search for the knife along the footpath each side of the pub entry but didn't find anything."

"What was the feeling at the scene? I mean, there'd been a lot of drama and fighting leading up to what happened."

"It wasn't your typical murder scene. There was no blood and at first glance I expected the victim would just wake up. On closer inspection it was obvious this wasn't going to happen. She looked so vulnerable and although it went against all my training I just wanted to hold her, to protect her and comfort her during her final moments."

I was silent – and grateful to Ainsley for her thoughtful reflections.

In our VIP Protection role we were required to protect the prime minister when he was in Auckland. In Wellington, he was covered by the Diplomatic Protection Squad. Affectionately called Piggy, Robert Muldoon was the incumbent at the time. A brash, uncompromising politician, for some reason he took a shine to me. The feeling was mutual.

The first time I was on a protection detail with Piggy was when he attended the gallops at Ellerslie Racecourse. I was to learn he had two great loves aside from his wife Thea and his country. They were horse racing and gin. On this detail Ainsley and Joe were Piggy's personal escorts and I was in a venue-security role.

Personal escorts maintain close protection of the principal. They will be physically around the principal when on foot and will maintain line of sight at a function or meal. When mobile in cars, politicians use dedicated Crown drivers and the escorts travel in a car immediately behind the principal. Driving an escort car requires aggression and precision. There should never be more than three or four metres between the escort car and the principal's vehicle. At speed this can be challenging.

The role of venue security was to secure the proposed route and buildings where the principal would arrive. Prior reconnaissance was necessary. Venue security would advise the protection members when arrival points were clear of threats. Aside from physical searches and the use of explosives dogs, venue security would cover such aspects as the closest hospital to where the principal was at any given time and ensuring that the principal's blood type was available.

We were armed with Smith & Wesson .38 calibre snub-nose six-shot revolvers. These did not provide significant stopping power but could cause significant damage at close range. One benefit of the .38 was that it was small and easy to carry. When our squad had new shoulder holsters made, Ainsley had the leather of hers etched with a flower. Petals and lead. We also had available .223 calibre Ruger rifles.

Firearms training was every month and a requisite standard had to be met each range session. We also undertook regular mock training to hone skills. I was later to work with the US Secret Service on the protection detail of former US President Jimmy Carter. The Secret Service policy was "shoot to kill" if an aggressor came within ten feet of the principal. Our policy wasn't as extreme, but if you weren't prepared to take a life and risk your own in doing your job, you were in the wrong profession.

As the greenhorn of the squad, I was posted at the bottom of the lift leading to the second-floor members' restaurant where Piggy and guests were dining. Ainsley and Joe were seated in the restaurant, able to view their principal. I was still wondering exactly how these protection details worked when the lift opened unexpectedly. Piggy's distinctive features appeared. Ainsley and Joe were not there. Shit, I thought, this isn't right.

Piggy scuttled past me and grunted, "Ha ha, shook them off," followed by a chuckle. He evidently treated losing his bodyguards as some kind of sport. The scuttle continued out the exit to the waiting Crown LTD limo parked immediately outside. Sal, Piggy's regular driver, stood by the open rear passenger door. The escort car was parked behind the LTD. There was still no sign of Ainsley and Joe, who were obviously caught at the lift.

In a state now approaching panic, I raced around to the driver's side of the escort Falcon. Luckily the keys were in it because one of our venue-security team was stationed with the vehicles. Sal, always complicit in Piggy's shenanigans, accelerated away from the racecourse entrance. I followed, minus the designated personal escorts who I saw running through the exit in my rear view mirror.

As per schedule, Sal sped to Piggy's regular hotel, the South Pacific downtown on Customs Street. Both cars came to a halt on the hotel forecourt. As Piggy lurched from his seat, I was already out of my car and ready to escort him into the foyer. Displaying his hooked smirk, the prime minister gave me a wink and together we entered the hotel.

Piggy was notorious for not speaking to his bodyguards but usually reserved a chuckle and a greeting of "Son" for me. The other squad members were not bothered by this, but the bosses could be miffed. They liked to grandstand at functions where dignitaries were present, particularly royalty. For us doing the work, it was just business as usual. Still, there was something about being in the presence of the famous and powerful. Their normality often stood starkly against the public persona.

Piggy liked speed. One particular trip from his holiday house at Hatfields Beach north of Auckland may have endeared me to him. For some reason, on this Sunday morning Sal couldn't make it to take the PM and his wife Thea to a function in Epsom. The call came through with urgency, as by now Piggy was running late. I was instructed to take our Falcon escort car and get to Hatfields as soon as possible. When I arrived at the holiday house, Piggy and Thea were waiting on the doorstep. Once settled in the back seat he said, "City, son, fast as you can." Magic words from the leader of the nation to a speed freak.

With no chatter from the back seat we went through the fifty zone in Orewa at a hundred and twenty. When we reached the harbour bridge we hit a hundred and sixty. For the eighty kilometres per hour bridge this was fast, even without traffic. Thea was compelled to comment, "This is good, just like when we were in Paris."

A chuckle from Piggy's side of the car confirmed his agreement. Epsom arrived promptly. Again came the chuckle and "Good one, son" from the prime minister as I opened his door on arrival.

We were covering the protection of Prime Minister Muldoon as he gave an address to a Catholic Women's gathering in St Heliers. The venue was a primary school prefab. Around a hundred people listened attentively. One side of the room had concertina doors which could be drawn back allowing easy access for pupils. Ainsley and Joe were Piggy's personal escorts and sat about three rows back on each side of an aisle down the middle of the venue. Wayne and I were venue security, standing at the back of the room. Piggy stood at a lectern at the front of the audience, dazzling his faithful with heartfelt oratory.

Around twenty minutes had elapsed when a man in his mid-forties rose from a seat on the aisle twelve rows back from the front, an unusual move in the middle of a speech. He began to advance down the aisle towards the front of the audience. This was cause for alarm.

I looked across at Wayne on the other side of the room and we simultaneously moved forward. I walked quickly down the aisle behind the man. Wayne mirrored me down the side of the hall. In front of me the man walked faster heading directly towards where the prime minister stood. Both his hands were visible, holding no weapons.

To intercept him at the front of the room before the raised lectern, I broke into a jog. Out of the corner of my eye I saw Ainsley rise as I passed row three. At the front of the hall where the first row of the assembly sat, I caught up with my quarry. His head turned back towards me and he tried to duck away as I hit him in the back.

I quickly gained an effective hold and frog-marched him towards the side of the room with the concertina doors. By now there was a stirring of disquiet among the audience. Behind me to my right was a blur of activity which I knew would be Ainsley and Joe securing the PM. I wasn't sure how I was going to get my quarry out of the room without a ruckus. The concertina doors presented as a solid wall but our impetus meant we hit them with some force. Inexplicably, the section of door my quarry's head and shoulder met simply folded back, spilling both of us onto an outside deck. We stumbled across the deck, my hand behind his neck, and I drove him to the ground on a grassed area beyond. Wayne arrived and joined the fray by driving his knee into the man's back, hissing "Fucker!"

Wayne handcuffed him and while he was face down on the grass we searched him. His pockets contained nothing but a wallet and car keys. Slid down the inside of his left cowboy-style boot, however, was a kitchen knife with a four-inch blade. Our prisoner, now identified as John Cooper, was roughly dragged to his feet and taken to the car park by the hall. There he identified his car, a dinged mid-Seventies Holden. After we had relieved him of his car keys, Cooper was delivered into the custody of uniform police for transport to Central.

We searched the car and soon found items of interest. On the passenger's front seat was a brown manila folder containing handwritten plans of the school grounds and buildings. Another diagram was of the wider school precinct, including surrounding streets. In the rear footwell was a black leather bag containing sections of rope, cloth and a bottle of clear fluid, later identified as chloroform.

During interview by Crime Squad detectives back at Central, Cooper admitted he was a zealot. He did not agree with the direction the country was taking and was intending to address the issue by attacking the PM. Intelligence revealed he had mental-health issues and had participated in militant anti-establishment protests. His plan had fallen apart spectacularly — it is not worth contemplating the potential outcome if his planning ability had matched his enthusiasm for carnage.

◀ FOURTEEN ▶

"There's a guy out there who looks exactly like Mark Phillips."

"He's a good prick." High praise indeed from the squad lads when referring to a Pom. It wasn't just any Pom being referred to but none other than Captain Mark Phillips, the former husband of Princess Anne. And how could such a Pom, a member of the Royal Family, be elevated into the realm of "good prick", a decidedly loftier title than Captain?

An accomplished equestrian, Captain Phillips visited New Zealand in 1984 to run show-jumping clinics. As he was a member of the Royal Family, his security was covered by Royal Protection officers. That role fell to us. The captain chose to stay at the Hyatt Hotel in central Auckland. Only two days into his tour, with fellow equestrian Andrew Hoy, he decided to sample the city's entertainment delights.

In the wee small hours, while leaving the Hyatt, he found the forecourt inconveniently stacked with parked cars. Performing leaps, skips and jumps befitting an Olympic equestrian, he migrated across the bonnets and roofs of the cars. The next night, piloting the Rover sedan supplied by the New Zealand importers, he decided that leading his bodyguards on a two hundred and thirty kilometre high-speed chase to Rotorua might be fun.

Wayne was the first to make a proclamation about the captain's activities: "That's fucking awesome, must be a good prick."

Ainsley lived in a flat with three others in Oaklands Road, Mt Eden. Immaculately presented, with an established ambrosial garden and decks, the white two-storey villa was a superb residence. One of Ainsley's many skills was hosting parties. Always embracing a theme, they were famous. One of the best remembered was the French party. Attendance demanded dressing in a French theme. This was pleasant for the male attendees as it involved women adopting fish-net stockings and garters.

I attended this party with my mate Roman, whom I had met at Police College in 1978. Christened Marcus Walcroft, he felt his character matched better with being born earlier in history. The most appropriate period, he felt, was the Roman Empire. Police recruits being an empathetic bunch, we felt his pain and extended the courtesy of nicknaming him Roman.

Distinguished police careers must also be out of step with Roman tendencies, as his was a short and incandescent service. On night shifts, when walking the beat in Auckland, he became easily bored and gravitated to the bright lights of nightclubs, strip joints and massage parlours. The minor impediment of being in full uniform didn't bother him. Roman would imbibe if offered, dance if the music took his fancy and partake in the socialisation afforded by ladies of the night. On more than one occasion when he had gone AWOL, his sectional colleagues were compelled to hunt him out.

For Ainsley's party, to do justice to the fabulous celebration of Francophilia, Roman and I deliberated upon the most appropriate ensemble before settling upon top hat and tails. Although this was not French per se, we reckoned the bedazzling formality would meet Ainsley's expectations. Such formal attire warranted appropriate transport and so we hired a Rolls Royce to deliver us from pre-party city drinks to Oaklands Road.

The French party was a triumph. French champagne, French bakers, French kissing, French letters and Moulin Rouge antics combined to elevate the event into folklore. Months later people were still asking, "Were you at that French party?"

The next party, less than two months later, happened to coincide with Mark Phillips' visit. The captain had taken a shine to Ainsley. They had dined together a couple of times and been to the Club Mirage nightclub. The bodyguards that night reported that he was anxious that they not be seen dancing together. There was a rumour he had turned up at Ainsley's flat at 3am one night but when pressed she adopted the "neither confirm nor deny" line.

The invite specified early evening on the Sunday night. Ainsley's flatmate Sue was religious and maintained that her beliefs prevented her from attending any such festivities on a Sunday. Inevitably, Captain Phillips turned up to the party. About the time he arrived, Sue was preparing to leave the house to avoid participating in any heathen undertakings. Passing the lounge and catching sight of attendees, she returned to the kitchen and sought out Ainsley, saying, "There's a guy out there who looks exactly like Mark Phillips."

Without looking up from a cheese platter, Ainsley said, "It *is* Mark Phillips."

Some twenty minutes later Sue appeared in the lounge wearing a party dress.

"Do you think he's partaken of the odd gin tonight?" Ainsley asked.

"You wouldn't blame him, the crap he has to put up with," I answered.

We were the personal protection for Piggy. It had been a long day, culminating with a dinner address to businessmen in South Auckland. PM Rob Muldoon was not averse to sampling a gin in the rear of a Crown car. Fortification for the maelstrom of politics.

"Now, if you're quick," Ainsley said urgently.

We were approaching the South Pacific travelling along Customs Street towards Queen. Getting to the hotel forecourt required a U-turn. Stopping the Crown car in the street waiting to turn posed a security risk. To prevent this, the escort car was required to move from its staggered position behind the Crown car to a position in front and then dive across to sit sideways on the road blocking the opposing traffic. To execute this manoeuvre well required boldness and timing. At Ainsley's instigation, I powered past the Crown car and turned abruptly across Customs Street, taking advantage of a clear gap in the traffic afforded by the traffic lights. Sal turned the Crown car unimpeded into the hotel entrance.

We met our venue-security colleagues at the door. Ainsley pushed the lift button and together we entered the lift with the PM. As the lift sped to the top floor Piggy said, "I'm pretty tired, son."

"Yes, sir. You must be. It's been a long day," I replied.

The lift glided open and the three of us moved along the corridor to the suite, a walk of some forty metres. Ainsley walked in front of our principal and I walked behind. It was the home straight and I was looking forward to getting our man delivered and the shift finished. The concentration required in being a bodyguard is draining. Not for one second can you drop your guard. That second could be the time an assassin strikes.

It was only metres from the suite door. Movement on our right. The shape of a figure. He had been shielded by a service alcove off the corridor. He stepped towards the PM, who instinctively recoiled. Ainsley pivoted and shouldered her way in front of her principal. In the same movement, from her petalled holster, she drew her revolver.

Fuck, I thought, hasn't venue security checked this area? With Ainsley's weapon pointed at the threat's head, I bustled the PM behind her to the suite door.

"No no no, I only want an autograph," came the strangled cry behind me.

Squad colleague Wayne Wright was, by a wide margin, the most observant person I ever encountered. He was a big man, his size matched only by his personality. His continually happy countenance fronted a prodigious intellect. He was a human Google regarding music. When asked he could accurately identify every genre, every song and every band.

Stand-up-comedian funny, he possessed a sword-sharp wit. Wayne had two permanent accompaniments: his brown vintage flying jacket and equally vintage doctor's bag. No standard detective's briefcase would suffice for Wayne. I often wondered what mysteries were stored in that capacious bag.

It's incredibly difficult to identify someone in a crowd from a photograph. Not for Wayne. We were looking for a bank robbery suspect who had been given up by an informant and we had information that he was drinking at the Potter's Wheel Tavern in Avondale. Two slight impediments were that it was a busy Friday night and all we had for identification was a five-year-old photo. We arrived at about 10.45pm. The place was packed. Undeterred we entered the heaving public bar. We mingled on the fringes of the crowd for about ten minutes before I heard behind me, delivered in a smug monotone, "There he is."

"Where?"

"There, standing by the pool table. He's got a beard now."

"You're pulling my tit."

"No mate, that's him. Come on, let's front him."

I wasn't convinced and was still shaking my head as we moved through the crowd towards the pool table. I was amazed; Wayne had picked the suspect out in a dimly lit bar with hundreds of people and everyone pretty much dressed the same. In black, with lashings of leather. Westies always wear black.

The crowd, previously a problem, now became our friend. If the bar was less full, the suspect would probably have clocked our approach. Confirmation it was our man was provided when he tried to bolt. By then it was too late: he was bounded by a flesh wall shutting off his escape. Back at Central, after three hours of vigorous debate about the philosophical underpinnings of crime and punishment, our suspect coughed to committing the robbery and dobbed in two co-offenders.

I had an excuse the next time Wayne displayed his uncanny prowess. I was sitting in the back seat of the police car. Alongside me was our sergeant, Neil Morris. Wayne was up front with Ainsley who was driving. It was Christmas Eve and there was a concert on at Western Springs. Such events during the festive season attract vermin to the car parks, intent on stealing from the vehicles. The concert was about half an hour old and we were cruising around looking for prey.

"A broken quarter light!" blurted Wayne. "Over there."

When I looked where he pointed, I couldn't even see the car properly, let alone the broken side window. As we changed direction and headed towards the car, a stocky male scampered out from behind the car and began running away. A backpack jiggled and bounced on his back as he ran.

For his retreat he chose to flee down the access road between the cars.

Unfortunately for him he mistakenly assumed Ainsley wouldn't use the car to apprehend and hurt him. As he ran, Ainsley accelerated after him. The ground between the car and our quarry began to rapidly disappear. The car's nose sniffed the bouncing backpack.

Around this time there was a movie called *48 Hours* starring Eddie Murphy as a cop. In one scene a car door is opened and slammed into a fleeing villain. Before my eyes life imitated art.

Knowing he was probably going to be run down the quarry, like some galloping prairie animal, swerved suddenly to his left. The car overshot him. The backpack loomed to the left of the front guard.

Using his foot to assist, Wayne threw open the passenger's door which connected squarely with the backpack. The backpack disappeared, replaced by legs and boots. Cartwheeling to a halt went the quarry. Sideways the car skidded to a stop on the grassy surface. Like a bulldogging cowboy Wayne leapt from the car onto the prone, puffing prey.

The backpack contained children's presents stolen from cars. By finding the damaged vehicles we were able to reunite most of the presents with grateful owners, who could then put them under Christmas trees.

In February 1984, former US President Jimmy Carter and his wife Rosalynn visited New Zealand. As the country's top female bodyguard, Ainsley was seconded to the protection detail. She was Rosalynn Carter's personal escort for the duration of the visit. Like every former US president, Carter was protected by the US Secret Service.

Temporarily authorised to carry weapons in New Zealand, the Secret Service brought elevated firepower. Two bullet-proof limousines were shipped, automatic weapons, shotguns, numerous handguns, anti-aircraft measures and a satellite for communications were on hand. An intelligence unit travelled from the US a week earlier. They traversed proposed venues and routes. Liaison was established with our police, customs and intelligence agencies. I was attached to the detail while the former president was in Auckland.

"Like a camel pissing on a flat rock," commented Moose over a few beers.

Moose was a Secret Service veteran and at thirty-seven the head of the protection detail. He was like a moose, only bigger. I never knew what that saying meant, but its delivery in Moose's Tennessee drawl had a nice ring. Moose had his own language, brewed alongside some backwoods moonshine still. When he saw some less-than-attractive hefty girls in the alcove opposite, he said, "It's the bay of pigs."

When there was a glitch with the protection Moose would dismiss it with, "It's a mystery, like the last kamikaze, Chicken Teriyaki."

Nicknames consign real names to history. None of his subordinates knew Moose's real name, neither did they care. Hailing from Nashville, Moose constantly hummed country songs. I wondered if the pissing-camel line might have been buried in the lyrics of some Tennessee redneck jingle. With a ruddy complexion and face that never smiled, Moose had an uncanny ability to heave raucously with mirth but display nothing on his face.

Jimmy Carter was on a walkabout in the Auckland CBD. As was his custom he had run five miles that morning with his agents. Despite this he still felt like a walk in the sunshine to greet locals. Such unplanned jaunts pose security problems. He had reached Quay Street. There he turned and walked down past the port area. Routine radio traffic streamed. Then, from Moose: "Dancer wants to visit a bar. Entering now. Schooner Tavern, Quay Street."

If blood could stop flowing in your veins, that's what happened to me. I couldn't believe it. Of all the pubs in Auckland, the country or the planet, Jimmy Carter chose to visit the Schooner. It was too late to pass any intel to the Moose. The Schooner was still dark, dingy and carpeted with crooks, but by all accounts the criminal fraternity fronted, displaying a reserved welcome. My old hunting ground was being feted by a former leader of the free world.

The minister of justice does not usually have protection, but Jim McLay, who was also the attorney-general, had been threatened in writing. The specific threat, claiming that McLay would be shot, had been traced to a farmer living in Helensville north of Auckland. Ainsley and I were tasked to visit the letter's author, Bill Upton. He had no previous form and apart from this letter appeared an upstanding citizen. What motivated him to threaten a government minister was a mystery.

A closed, ramshackle wooden gate confronted us at the entrance to Upton's property. When opened, it threatened to collapse completely. A short gravel drive took us to a modest weatherboard house painted an unusual shade of green. Purple window ledges did nothing to enhance the colour scheme. The front door was stripped of varnish and had two opaque glass inserts at the bottom. Ainsley's loud knock was met by shuffling and a figure visible behind the glass.

Another knock brought a terse, "Who is it?"

"Police. We'd like to have a chat."

"The filth, aye? I don't like cops."

"It won't take long," said Ainsley calmly.

The door creaked open and a shaggy sheepdog ran through the gap. Running behind us in a circle the barking mutt scattered stones on the driveway. A man opened the door, leaned between us and bellowed, "Get in behind, Blue, ya silly bastard!"

Blue ignored the command and kept circling. "Mongrel," the man muttered. "It'll get the lead pill one day. Anyway, I'm Bill," he said, turning on his heel and walking back into the house. We followed on the assumption that his movement was an invitation inside.

"Even though you're pigs, you can call me Digger. Got the name many moons ago when I was a fencer."

Digger walked with a slight stoop and looked to be a bit over seventy. He wore a blue and black Swanndri, the classic Kiwi outdoors jacket, and dirty green cotton pants, from the bottom of which extended heavy fluffy woollen socks. Beneath his home-spun wool beanie a thatch of grey curly hair was fighting for release.

The lounge we were led into was adorned with all manner of animal skins. Two black-and-white cattle beast skins on the floor, four goat skins draped across the couch, rabbit touches to two easy chairs, a possum-skin footstool and what appeared to be a skin lightshade. Overlooking the room was a regal sixteen-pointer stag's head.

"How many acres do you have here?" I asked.

"Twenty-five," came the reply.

"So it's more a lifestyle block," I commented innocently.

"No, son," said Digger, his voice up a couple of octaves. "It's as much a proper farm as those big swinging dicks on runs in the South Island," he said emphatically. "I've still got twenty sheep to shear and drench, plus I need to tend to the milking cow every day. That Blue needs to be trained, too. He'll be a good heading dog one day."

Agitated, Digger slumped into an envelope of goat skin. "What's all this about, anyway?"

"There's been a letter received, apparently written by you, threatening to kill Justice Minister Jim McLay," explained Ainsley. "Did you write the letter?"

Digger scratched his silver mop through his beanie.

"Scone anyone?" said a female voice. Just beaten by the smell of cheese scones, Digger's bird-like wife entered the lounge. Before her on a plate were six buttered cheese scones.

"A scone, my dear?" she said, stooping to offer one to Ainsley.

"No thank you," came the reply.

I love cheese scones but when the offer was made to me I reluctantly lied, saying I didn't want one.

"Back to my question, Mr Upton," said Ainsley formally.

"Yeah, actually I did write it. There was no particular reason. I just don't like the prick. He's a faggot and faggots shouldn't be making big decisions. I wouldn't do anything to him."

If eccentricity was a risk factor we'd have Mr William Upton in maximum security. As it was, we didn't expect any further problems from Digger. He was given a formal warning about his conduct, and as a precaution we seized his firearms, an old Lee Enfield .303 rifle and a Sterling .22 rifle.

As we left past the still crazily circling Blue and an old ewe cast in the paddock, Ainsley said, "You meet all sorts in this job."

I just nodded, my thumb comfortingly hooked around my shoulder holster.

Fighting with Che Guevara, being imprisoned in Bolivia in 1967 and writing the definitive textbook on guerrilla warfare were the foundations of Régis Debray's diplomatic career. When he visited New Zealand in 1983, aged forty-three, he was adviser to French President François Mitterrand on foreign affairs. Tensions with the French meant personal protection was required.

We were covering the party at Clichy, a downtown French restaurant. Aside from our principal the French and Australian ambassadors were also present. Ainsley and I sat in a booth directly across from Debray. We were accompanied by a member of the Wellington Diplomatic Protection Squad.

I don't quite know how a senior police officer inveigled himself into a place at the dignitaries' table, given there was no operational requirement for him to be there. Like a giant polar bear charging onto thin ice, this senior officer trod where he shouldn't have, trying to display an aptitude for French dining. Using the tongs to grasp an escargot shell went well enough, but all semblance of technique evaporated when he tried to fork the snail from its shell. In one violent, utensil-clattering manoeuvre the snail leapt from its place, sailed through the air and landed in the middle of the table before the French ambassador.

Before the horror, shock, crippling embarrassment, mirth and bemusement had abated, a commotion erupted at a booth not far from us. A male patron had slumped face down across the table and his female partner was hovering concernedly over him. Restaurant staff attended.

"That's a diversion," said Ainsley urgently.

The DPS member and I agreed and we three rose as one. Swiftly, with hands close to our weapons, we surrounded our principal's table. Anxious eyes swept the room and the apparent medical emergency.

The Australian ambassador tried to stand up for a better view. "Sit down!" hissed Ainsley.

Time hung suspended before the diversion dissolved into legitimacy. Ambulance officers arrived and stretchered the man from the restaurant.

"For God's sake get that guy out of here," said our DPS colleague under his breath.

The night started off like any other. There was no indication the day would end with life-changing events. No black cats or portentous birds; just a quiet meal and a few loud drinks at a Victoria Street pizza parlour. Ainsley was chatty, Liz was complaining about mosquito bites on her legs, Roman and I drank beer.

Liz was Roman's girlfriend, a nurse from Wellington. She was willowy pretty with dark hair and eyes. We decided to shift our entertainment to the bars of Parnell. We all piled into Roman's early-model, powder-blue Mercedes sedan. With Roman driving, we headed away from the city and got to the bottom of Parnell Rise.

Just before the Exchange Tavern we were pulled over by an Auckland City Council traffic officer. This snake's name was David Johnson. He was naturally aggressive and his attitude that night wasn't moderated when he spoke to Roman. The fact that we were police enraged him. Suspected drink-driving was the reason for the stop.

The events of the next few minutes were later aired during two court hearings. What none of us in our car knew was that Johnson was the subject of a police criminal complaint of wounding with intent. The allegation was that he had viciously attacked and kicked an elderly man during a traffic stop. The victim finished up in hospital.

It was not in dispute that Roman was over the legal alcohol limit for driving. What *was* in question was Johnson's statement about what happened. Roman did not respond rapidly when instructed to get out of the car. He also dragged his tail when required to accompany the traffic cop.

Inexplicably, considering the situation, Johnson issued an emergency call to police saying he was under threat. ACC traffic cops had no powers of arrest and always called the police when they wanted assistance. Given the calibre of their staff, this happened often.

I was hanging around in the street where Johnson and Roman were. Two couples dressed as punk rockers, who had been drinking in the Exchange, took an interest. They began to yell abuse at Johnson, which further riled him.

I approached them and said, "Fuck off, you're not helping." An event which apparently never happened, despite later evidence from Ainsley and Liz to the contrary. A crime car driven by Detective Tony Scully arrived in response to the assistance call. I knew Sculls as I had worked with him previously. He spoke to Johnson then came back to me saying, "Marcus, I have to take you back to the station."

"Fuck off, Sculls. What for?"

"Come on, mate. I have to take you back for interview coz of what the traffic cop says."

"What's he saying? Nothing happened. Geez, am I under arrest?"

"No," said Sculls apologetically.

"I'm not going to say anything until I've taken advice. It feels like a fit-up."

"Fair enough."

Following the interview I was suspended from my duties as a detective pending investigation. The knives slid from their sheaths. The O/C of the investigation into my conduct was Inspector Derek Davison. The next day I had to make one of the most difficult phone calls of my life. I called home and spoke to Dad. I knew he would be bitterly disappointed with the besmirching of the family name. Choked with emotion I relayed the situation.

"Well, it was overdue coming," was the response.

Later I came to understand why Dad would make such a comment. He didn't know how to respond or deal with the situation. At the time I felt abandoned. I needed support, but it wasn't forthcoming. The department for which I had put my life on the line was moving against me. One person stood unreservedly beside me: Ainsley, who, merely for being present at the incident and aligned with me, would unfairly suffer at the hands of police administration.

After a week I was summoned to Central by Inspector Davison. "You are going to be charged with assault and obstruction. To make it easier I won't put you in the cells."

Nice — plummet me into purgatory but with a first-class ticket. The Police Association provided me with legal counsel, barrister John Haigh. John was the Police Union's counsel of choice, significantly experienced and from a respected legal family. He would go on to become a Queen's Counsel, a title acknowledging the best within the legal fraternity.

"We need to find those punk rockers," said John after our first briefing.

Detective Superintendent Graham Perry administered my prosecution. In the meantime, due to the seriousness of the complaint, the investigation into Johnson was going ahead. Detective Terry Batchelor had been given the file. Following the assault, Johnson's victim spent four days in hospital with back and head injuries. Despite the compelling evidence, Johnson wasn't charged immediately. The decree came from Perry. "Detective Batchelor, you are not to charge Johnson until he has given evidence against van Leewarden."

Batch, being the good bastard he is, refused. His resistance was such that he exposed himself to disciplinary counselling and damage to his own career. His actions were futile. Perry was intent on removing an unpredictable and violent former undercover agent.

Exhaustive inquiries did not turn up the punk rockers. At my hearing in February 1984, defence evidence was given by Roman, Ainsley, Liz and me. The Magistrates Court was not persuaded. Johnson's evidence, unimpeached by the wounding with intent investigation, was accepted in totality.

Convictions of assault and obstruction were entered. There was a fair bit of media interest. Ainsley and I were photographed by *Truth* photographers leaving court. The shot was featured on the paper's back page. Following a rehearing, I was acquitted some eighteen months later, but the damage had been done.

My conviction led to silent visceral umbrage. My planet slipped from its axis. I was plunged back to being an eleven-year-old boarder fighting the world. I got no credit for anything done previously on behalf of the Queen. Sure, running foul of the system was probably inevitable; the incident at the bottom of Queen Street was an example. But the way Johnson was backed up by the police hierarchy was contemptible. Contrary to what she had been promised, Ainsley was transferred from CCU to answering phones in Control, the equivalent of being banished to Siberia.

People whom I had regarded as good friends fled my sinking ship. Wariness and suspicion became my new companions. Only Ainsley's blue eyes reflected continual solace and support. So one day when Roman and I were sitting on the floor of our flat in Northcote I said to him, "Fuck this, mate. There's nothing left in this country for me. I'm gonna head to Thailand. You on for that?"

"Yep, why not," was the clipped reply.

With that Roman and I jetted out to Bangkok and down to Phuket; Ainsley promised she would come and see me once her situation was sorted.

◄ FIFTEEN ►

"Badness grows like rice in the fields."

My new digs were a bungalow at Thamdee Inn, Patong Beach. Long-term rates were a dollar a day for a bed, toilet and cold shower. The perfect wound-licking base. The complex comprised twelve standalone bungalows circled around a central basic office. Farang (European) guests of the backpacker ilk came and went.

Idyllic by any standard, the beach extended for a kilometre nestled within a bay. Crystal-clear water lapped the golden sands. Set back about five hundred metres, Thamdee Inn sat at the northern end of the beach. Rising late, around midday, we would wander to our favourite stall at the edge of the beach for a breakfast of Thai omelette. It was tart and not to everyone's taste but I loved that culinary oddity.

Shirtless and riding a hired motorcycle through a village, I was stopped by the fattest cop I have ever seen. His bulk, squeezed into a khaki uniform and topped by a bald, scarred head, made him particularly confronting.

"You arrest. No shirt," he stated loudly, pointing at my torso. "Come, follow, police station."

The ferocity of his pointing down the road allowed no resistance. After he had mounted his bike with some difficulty, I followed him. Generous folds of fat sagged down each side of his seat.

The police station was a basic concrete-sided hut surrounded by bush. Wondering where this might be leading, I was greeted by Captain Sun Ustasha. Short, slim, youthful, Sun wore a smart uniform adorned with shoulder pips. He spoke excellent English. In the discussion that followed, he let me know that the indecency charge could be disposed of with the immediate cash payment of five hundred baht. I pleaded that not wearing a shirt anywhere around Patong beach six kilometres away brought no sanctions, but this proved pointless.

Sun became a good friend. Supplementing his police role, he owned a beachfront bar which became one of my haunts. His signature dish was American fried rice, being Thai fried rice topped with two fried eggs. This was usually the primary meal of my day.

The proprietor of Gonzo's bar was Swiss German and hailed from Zurich. He'd been in Patong for about five years and was a known heroin dealer. His girls, like most of the other bar girls, were hookers, but they had the extra distinction of being smack addicts. They were good looking, but most of the time they were wasted.

A vindictive Thai girl can be dangerous, as Steve, an Australian associate of mine, found out. He'd been running with Lek, one of Gonzo's pretty bar girls, for a couple of months. She took a proprietary interest in Steve, probably thinking he was a passport away from a difficult life. During a rigorous night out at the Boogaloo Bar, Steve took an interest in another girl, a recent arrival from Bangkok. The bar Mama San, who ran the girls, facilitated their union. Word among the bar girls spread quickly and Lek soon learned about it. She didn't strike immediately. She waited until Steve had to leave Thailand to renew his visa. (Every three months Thai visitors had to leave the country. Dropping down to Penang in Malaysia was the best way to secure a new visa.) Steve checked in as usual at Phuket airport for the flight to Penang. Based on an apparent tipoff, he was pulled by Thai Customs for scrutiny. A search of his Manly Sea Eagles bag revealed two grams of heroin. Steve might have eaten the odd hash cookie but had never touched smack. Lek had wrought her revenge.

One afternoon I was hanging in Sun's bar. Two Americans turned up and took stools opposite me. They were both in their mid-thirties and, although roughly dressed, had a whiff of the military about them. The bigger of the two was unshaven, wore camo pants and a cap on backwards. The second wore a singlet revealing a well-trained upper body.

It was not unusual to see US military in Phuket. Navy war ships moored there and the sailors took shore leave in Patong. The three days they were ashore was a good time to hole up in the bungalow. Girls poured in from all over Thailand to relieve the military boys of their cash. Liquor, food and accommodation prices doubled.

The bar visitors certainly weren't current military. After a couple of Singha beers, the big Yank stood up and came around to my side of the bar. "How's it going?" he said.

"Not bad," I said. "What about you?"

"Hard to be bad sitting around here, that's for sure."

I nodded in agreement.

"Got a couple of minutes?"

"Depends. What's on your mind?" I asked.

"Well, I hear you might be a resourceful sort of character looking to make a bit of cash."

"Oh yeah? Where'd you hear that?"

"Just around. If I'm talking to the wrong guy, that's cool."

"Tell me the game and I'll see if I wanna play," I said, stringing him along.

"If you looked at the menu you might see AK sandwiches."

"Oh yeah? How many and where?" I asked, mainly out of curiosity.

"Components. One truckload, here to Chiang Mai."

Gun runners were common in Thailand. The place was used for trans-shipment to the world's hotspots. Everyone had a handgun and the murder rate by firearms rivalled the US. Hit men were easy to come by. For fifty US bucks you could have a Bangkok professional killer take out any nominated target. A couple of weeks earlier, I had seen the aftermath of a shooting resulting from a dispute over a bar bill. A drunken German tourist foolishly abused a local bar owner and received two nine-millimetre bullets in his chest as a response. The top-quality Seventh Day Adventist hospital in Phuket saved his life.

These Americans, however, were not like the usual gun runners. The big Yank's oily patter was contrived at best.

"Decent cash?" I asked.

"Yeah. We can talk details later."

"Let me think about it," I said, cutting off the dealing. "Where you staying?"

"Phuket Town."

"The Pearl?"

"Could be," he replied, confirming that they were camped at the best hotel in town.

Later that day I saw Sun at his bar and asked him about my new friends. Watching expectant tourists trail like cows towards the lights of the main strip, I gave him a rundown on what had happened earlier in the day.

"What do you think, mate?" I asked.

"CIA," he replied.

If I had been inclined, I could have taken up any number of opportunities to get involved in gun running and dealing drugs. I'd been paid by the New Zealand police to become a drug-dealing criminal and had done it successfully. I wasn't interested in crime — I had been playing a role and tried to do it to the best of my ability. It was a personal challenge to wear a coat of villainy and yet preserve personal mores of right and wrong. However, I suspected the New Zealand police viewed me as a dangerous rogue agent who was using Thailand as a route into international crime. This belief was confirmed a few months later when Sun found South Thailand intel reports listing my activities as being of interest to the global drug-enforcement agencies. This information only added to my rancour.

The sun sat on its haunches as I loped down the dirt road. I'd been running for about an hour and was heading back to Thamdee down the hill overlooking the beach. Layers of late-afternoon light licked through the lattice of rice paddies below me. Dirt crunched beneath my weathered running shoes and hot beads of sweat crawled down my face. The green carpet of paddies rolled down to the beach and into the glistening blue sea before me. Sometimes, if you're lucky, the threads of life will bind momentarily into one unforgettable special memory knot. This was one of those, a lifelong memory that has never dimmed or departed.

I had moved up into the village with Saia and Toey. Saia epitomised friendliness. Always happy, he had an almost perfectly round face and, unlike most Thais, an almost ruddy complexion. The village was a grouping of around twenty buildings on a dirt road. Saia's place was typical of the dwellings: rudimentary construction with concrete slabs walls and a thatched roof. Both the exterior and interior were without any adornment except for one Buddha figure on the kitchen-area window ledge. Most Thais are Buddhist and my hosts exuded the very best of the religion: kindness without exception.

Cooking was carried out over a small gas cooker on the floor. Pretty and graceful, Toey squatted for hours, deftly preparing fresh, locally grown ingredients. The meals she produced using that small device were amazing. I looked forward to each one of them. Sitting cross-legged on the floor in a circle around the cooker, the three of us discussed our respective cultures.

"Marcus, it sounds like your people gather a lot of things instead of focusing on how they live their lives," said Saia.

"Probably," I said. "It's easier to accumulate things in our world."

"Should that make a difference?"

"No it shouldn't, I suppose."

"Maybe it's getting the things that makes people lose sight."

"Could be, but you have people in Thailand who are not living good lives."

"Yes, badness grows like rice in the fields. This shouldn't change our own way of living, though. It's how we respond to evil. Buddha said people are created to be loved and things to be used. Chaos comes because things are being loved and people being used."

"It's not the things themselves, then, that are the problem," I said.

"That's right. It's not that you shouldn't own things, it's that they shouldn't own you."

Through intellectual acuity and working with tourists, Saia spoke excellent English. Discussions with him were candid and thought-provoking. He taught me the basics of the Thai language, but he was a better teacher than I was a student.

Outside the front of the house was an old but sturdy wooden bench.

It overlooked the road and the dense green bush opposite. For me, the bench became a place of repose and contemplation. I'd been staying in the village for about three weeks and was sitting on the bench on a quiet balmy afternoon looking into the bush. While staring into the mottled greens, I experienced an epiphany. With blinding clarity I suddenly and unerringly knew my future. I must return to New Zealand and complete the law degree I had started as a younger man. A prophetic path.

At last Ainsley arrived to be with me. I had missed her and was counting down the days to her arrival. I picked her up from Phuket airport on an old Honda dirt bike. We holed up together back at Thamdee Inn. The arrival of my love completed the circle of life. Softening of reckless behaviour and proper perspective flowed. She saved me.

There were little balconies at the front of each of the inn's bungalows. Deck chairs could be positioned enabling you to put your feet up on the concrete ledge border. Ainsley and I often sat in the chairs surveying the complex and the dirt driveway leading to the office. One afternoon I saw a figure walking towards the office and said to Ainsley, "That looks like a guy I was in the job with in Dunedin."

"That's funny," she said.

As he came closer, his features got clearer. It was former Detective Sergeant John Dhyrberg.

In the years since I'd last seen him in Dunedin, John had founded a successful national security company in Australia providing plainclothes, armed, cash-escort services. It was a pleasant surprise to see him. I didn't think he knew I was in Thailand. After the obligatory back-slapping we sat down and caught up on what had been happening. At some stage during the discussion he produced a bag of weed and commenced rolling a joint.

"Geez, mate, talk about coals to Newcastle," I said.

"Yeah, but you can't live by bread alone. Just a bit of personal I brought from Perth."

"That's rolling the dice, brother."

"Yep, but here I am."

"I've got a treat for you," I said, "by way of welcome to the Golden Triangle."

With that, I organised some of the finest hash cookies in southern Thailand. There has always been something cool and contradictory about high-quality cannabis oil subsumed within a most innocuous sweet treat. But you had to be careful because the uptake of the drug was slow. Punishing hallucinations could plague the greedy.

Not long after John left, another visitor arrived. I was sitting in Sun's bar with Ainsley about to start my second Singha beer of the day. Straight off the street and into the bar walked Batch, a canvas bag slung over his shoulder. It was unexpected and great to see him. All he'd had to do to find me was ask for Marcus at any of the bars. His query resulted in his being directed to Sun's. He brought tales of the department and fallout from the criminal case. He was tired after arriving from a trip to the United Kingdom. We decided, therefore, that the best remedy for Batch's malaise was a big night out.

Body-building was Batch's thing. Standing just under six foot, he arrived packed with muscle mass from recent competition. A handle-bar moustache magnified his square shoulders and massive biceps. At thirty-five he cut an impressive figure, particularly to the Thai girls who had never seen anyone of his stature. Batch was loquacious and amusing, a slight Pom accent betraying his heritage. He'd been drawn to acting and fed his cultural side by appearing in television commercials and programmes alongside his policing.

There was a nasty underbelly to Phuket in the form of local criminal gangs. Batch and Roman lamentably crossed their path after a night out down the strip. Walking back to Thamdee in the darkness, the revellers got about halfway back before a two-up motorcycle appeared before them. The pillion's weapon was a full whisky bottle. His aim was unerring. The bottle hit Roman squarely on the forehead: he was unconscious before he hit the ground.

After rousing him to a form of sensibility, Batch supported the bleeding Roman back to Thamdee. Batch woke us and told us how four gang members had wrongly claimed he and Roman had shouted them drinks and meals and had insisted they pay. When they refused to pick up the bar tab they were met with unmistakable threats of bodily injury. At least Roman had been dealt to with a bottle, not a bullet like the German tourist.

When I went into Roman's room in the morning to check on him, I was greeted by walls splattered with blood as high as the ceiling. My friend lay on blood-soaked bedding mumbling incoherently.

A hut staffed by one nurse passed as the medical centre in Patong. Batch and I, supporting a staggering Roman, carried him to the one plastic-covered bed. He vomited thick blood into a bowl. The nurse, concerned, hurriedly pressed into service a man sitting outside, peppering him with instructions. He left, returning shortly after with a man driving a Ute. This only served to annoy the nurse, who barked further urgent orders.

A car arrived. "Hospital, Phuket Town, quick," she repeated beseechingly.

During the speedy trip over the hill Roman began to deteriorate. Unable to support himself sitting, he lapsed from scarily delirious into periods of unconsciousness. Halfway through the journey we began to think he might die.

At the hospital a quick preliminary examination spawned a scramble of medical staff. Roman was whisked away on an aluminium gurney with decidedly squeaky wheels. After a long thirty minutes a nurse, apparently of seniority, appeared. In halting English she provided a prognosis. "He very lucky man. He lose a lot of blood. We cannot find blood pressure. He getting blood transfusion now. He may have problem with organs, have to see. You wait any longer coming here, he die."

It was a solemn trip back to Patong. The following day, with a brighter outlook, the three of us turned up to visit Roman. Locating his ward, we found he already had a visitor. Like a sentinel, underneath Roman's scratched and rusted bed frame stood a rooster. We were interlopers on his ward so the feathered guardian watched us with beady-eyed suspicion.

With sun on his back, fresh food and the odd medicinal beer, Roman was soon back on his feet.

Ainsley and I stayed together in Thailand for three months. It was a wonderful time. We frolicked on the beach under crystal-clear skies, ate fresh fruit, watched movies at local bars and talked. We talked about all manner of things — politics, art, music, history, sport, philosophy, fashion, cars and literature. Nights and lazy mornings were spent in our little Thamdee bungalow. I shared with her my epiphany, the sign from the Thai bush. It was a journey I wanted her to come on.

When she arrived in Thailand, Ainsley had plans to travel on to Barranquilla, Colombia. From there she planned to take a three-month overland trip, canoeing the Amazon and visiting Machu Picchu. There was another complication. One of the US Secret Service agents from the Carter protection detail had been sniffing around. He'd gone so far as to send one of his CIA colleagues to Patong with a note inviting her to dinner in Bangkok. She was flattered. I didn't like the intrusive attention.

Jimmy Carter had also personally offered to take Ainsley back to the US and install her as part of the Reagan presidential protection detail. She was the woman I loved and wanted. I wasn't going to let the might of the United States foil my plans. It was time to play the big card. I would ask her to marry me.

Making the call to pop the question was the easy bit. The plumes of terror that surrounded even thinking about the execution were the problem. We were due to drop down to Malaysia to renew our visas. Penang would be the proposal venue. Two weeks later, on a sticky September night, we boarded a rickshaw outside our Georgetown hotel. Following a circuitous route, we absorbed the sounds and sweet tropical smells of the city's colonial section. With a final clank and squeak from the bicycle-powered rickshaw we arrived at the quaint Eden Garden restaurant.

I'd dealt with some of the worst guys criminality could deliver up, but I had never been as scared as I was this night. Why this was I couldn't really fathom — maybe it was the fear of rejection. With a cold pewter mug of Carlsberg in hand I stammered through my proposal. Ainsley said yes and we set a date for February of the next year, back in New Zealand.

"That's a betrayal of the study of law."

This was uttered by one of my lecturers at Canterbury University in Christchurch in 1988 when I had completed my law degree. I couldn't quite believe what he had said. We were at a roundtable where graduating honours students were asked what they proposed to do with their degrees. Most mentioned aspiring to join one of the big law firms like Russell McVeagh, or Meredith Connell who held the Crown warrant. I had entered university at the beginning of 1985 and started a small private-investigation company. We were doing mainly process serving for the local law firms and things started to roll when we secured a contract to serve documents for the Inland Revenue Department.

"I think I'll carry on with investigation. I reckon there's a future in it," had been my response to the question.

Ainsley and I married on 16 February 1985. Pursuing the law and investigation dream was hard. Ainsley initially worked as a hotel receptionist and cleaner to support us while I studied and developed the PI business. She had redeemed me in Thailand and supported me one hundred per cent with the investigation dream. I was convinced the future lay with a combination of a law degree and the experience of having been an undercover agent and detective. That combination could be effectively commercialised with international investigations as the end game.

It was hard for Ainsley but she never flinched. Her status and police career had been stripped because of association with me. In the police I had regarded her as head and shoulders above anyone else as a partner. Although she was an attractive and refined woman, I always wanted her with me in any threat situation, as I knew she would not hesitate to shoot to kill. Something which could not be said of others. I owed her a payback and being successful would silence many doubters within the department.

Our first child, a daughter, was born on 27 November 1988. While enduring the torture of labour Ainsley insisted we name her Charlotte. That's the one time in life you can't argue. Wee Charlotte was a joy to behold. Our family was completed four years later when Charlotte's brother Ben arrived with a bellowing ruckus. He hasn't changed since.

◄ SIXTEEN ►

"You guys will also be killed in the explosion."

"For five thousand dollars we will have every cop in Thailand and Sri Lanka looking for him. We will arrest him, put him in a cell for you, or if you want we will kill him."

Speaking was the 2 IC of the Bangkok Police. Sitting at a table in Patpong, the city's red-light district, he was flanked by two uniform colleagues with automatic weapons resting casually on their hips. Metres away bar girls gyrated to rock music flooding from the strip venues. His eyes narrowed as he looked from me to my colleague and fellow private investigator, Dave "Hoon" Hay, waiting for an answer.

"We won't want him taken out," Hoon told the Bangkok Police 2 IC. "But we are really keen on locating him. If you can find and grab him for us, we'd really appreciate it."

"Okay, no problem," came the reply. The deal done, we stood up and shook hands. I slipped our collaborators an envelope containing five thousand US dollars in hundred dollar bills. As the three Thai police officers moved through a parting crowd of revellers, Hoon looked towards the most raucous bar and said, "Since we're here, might as well have a beer." I led the way.

Hoon and I were working for an Australian-based private investigation company. The subject of our discussion with the police was Vannyasingham Sothirasan. A Malaysian national of Indian Tamil background, he had defrauded the Swiss Bank Corporation (SBC) of twenty million US dollars. Our instructions were to get it back. To perpetrate the fraud Sothirasan, or Sothi for short, had enlisted the help of a distant relative, Basant Singh, an employee of the SBC in Zurich.

The Clearing House Interbank Payments System (CHIPS), based

in New York, processes coded requests for the transfers of hundreds of millions of dollars to beneficiaries worldwide. Singh inserted a forged order into the system resulting in the fraudulent transfer on 7 December 1989 of the twenty million from SBC to the State Bank of New South Wales in Sydney.

Months earlier Sothi had put his scam in train, posing as a merchant banker able to source large loans internationally. He needed a method to get his hands on the cash once it had been fraudulently transferred. He settled on the device of a fictitious loan which would never be delivered. His target was the financially distressed Australian property developer Malcolm Edwards. He presented as Edwards' saviour, able to organise a five hundred million US dollar-loan which would satisfy stretched creditors and bankers.

During the course of negotiations about the loan Sothi was able to extract eight hundred thousand dollars from Edwards as upfront fees required to facilitate the loan. This is a classic fraud technique where all manner of fictitious reasons are advanced to justify payments, such as due diligence inquiries, legals or insurance requirements.

The plan was that Edwards would receive the twenty million in the belief it was the first tranche of the five hundred million loan drawdown. The loan was purportedly to come from the Beyina Merchant Bank of Cameroon, but this entity was no more a legitimate lender than it was a retailer of furniture. Once Edwards had the funds, Sothi would receive ten million by way of further fees and costs for setting up the loan.

Another player in the game was Santiago Laureano, a Filipino who was to launder the ten million by withdrawing large amounts of cash to remove it from the banking system. The scam worked exactly as planned and Sothi got away with the cash. SBC was embarrassed, as was CHIPS, which had experienced a first-ever breach of its system. Sothi was human game — we needed to hunt him down and recover his ill-gotten gains.

Sothi travelled with a Malaysian QC, allowing him immediate legal advice while on the run. It was an unusual situation, as the QC must inevitably have known of Sothi's offending. One benefit for us was that the QC was a conduit to Sothi in our efforts to recover the money.

We knew Sothi was in Bangkok but not exactly which hotel. He had chosen Thailand because it had no extradition treaty with the US. A sweep of the hotels proved fruitless, as we were unaware which of his numerous aliases Sothi was using. Hotel security contacts are very useful in these circumstances. Usually they can activate other hotel contacts to supply information. Guests' records including credit cards, telephone records and CCTV footage can be very helpful in advancing inquiries.

Through airline contacts we had a watch on whether Sothi was trying to leave the country. With a couple of airlines covered, those contacts could usually grease the palms of associates with the other carriers. Sothi, like other fraudsters, would book and pay for flights to different destinations at the same time. This made it difficult to establish which flight he was actually taking. To effectively cover a departure required separate surveillance teams for each flight. (This was a technique we also used to confuse our quarry and as a security measure when dealing with organised crime.)

Sothi had been active and Interpol had an alert on him regarding other fraud matters. We were not concerned with the specifics, but sometimes other offending can become a factor in your own inquiry. Sothi was well aware that we were on his tail. As a result, his QC reached out proposing a meeting. The suggested venue was the Tradewinds Hotel in Penang. This was an interesting development as we had more leverage in Malaysia than we did in Thailand. At one stage we considered using former Special Forces to encourage Sothi to travel across the Thai border into Malaysia where we could better deal with him.

Hoon and I flew from Bangkok to Penang three days before the proposed meeting and scoped the Tradewinds. It was strange being back in Penang. This trip was the antithesis of my last visit when I proposed to Ainsley. The hotel was five-star and we were able to spend time by the oversize pool enjoying a beer and a burger plotting Sothi's downfall.

Just a day before the meeting we received a call from a New York-based FBI agent: "We've received credible intelligence the Japanese mafia are going to move against Sothirasan. He's ripped them off, so a million-dollar contract has been placed on his head. The word is he'll be taken out by a bomb placed in the room where you're to meet. If it goes ahead you guys will also be killed in the explosion."

It didn't take much thought to decide the meeting wasn't a good idea. Ironically, the Yakuza did us a favour. In only two discussions with the QC we reached an agreement that Sothi would travel to Zurich to do a deal with SBC. The deal wasn't quite as Sothi imagined: upon arrival he was met at the airport gate by armed police and arrested. He remained incarcerated, a guest of the Swiss government.

This international fraud case was intriguing and like a dog worrying sheep I had tasted blood. I wanted fraudster blood in my nostrils and needed to find a way to hunt more dishonest humans. I figured fraud is just theft wearing a finely embroidered dress. It makes it look appealing and is difficult to put together.

Distilling an array of dishonest manoeuvrings down to the digestible basics is where the challenges arise. Greed, ego, intelligence, charisma, callousness and duplicity are but some of the constituents that swirl in a fraudster's consciousness. Fear of prison, however, is an overarching weakness. There is a skewed perception that white-collar crime is not the equivalent of, say, a bank robbery, despite the ramifications for victims being the same; or perhaps more significant in the fraudster's case, where retirees may have had their entire life savings stolen. With a psychological perception that their actions are not criminal per se, the fraudster cannot come to terms with serving a prison sentence with "actual" criminals.

Operating internationally provides another level of intricacy. Running a fraud across multiple countries and legal jurisdictions means there will be detection, investigation and prosecution difficulties encountered by those chasing the perpetrators. As there is no global financial crime-enforcement agency, co-ordination of investigations is difficult. Interpol is only an intelligence-sharing body and does not co-ordinate investigation for multi-jurisdictional criminal activity. It is therefore left to the private sector to deal with international fraud investigation and funds recovery.

To accumulate fees, assemble evidence and gather sway, victim groups need to be formed to mount effective challenges against the fraudsters.

Once an effective group is formed worldwide, criminal or civil legal measures can be mounted.

The fraudster's strategy is to house different aspects of their operation in different countries and often to keep amounts stolen from individual targets relatively low, so it is too expensive for each victim to mount recovery steps.

Lucrative returns and low risk make fraud attractive to international organised crime groups, who will use all manner of tactics to protect their operations, including murder. If you are effective at freezing money or creating legal exposure, then you become a target.

◀ SEVENTEEN ▶

The legal mile.

THE REAL OPPORTUNITIES WERE IN Auckland so we moved north in 1989. After working for the Australian PI firm, I was admitted as a Barrister and Solicitor of the High Court of New Zealand in 1992 and set up in practice as a barrister in Shortland Street, the legal mile and premium area for lawyers.

My practice combined investigation work and acting as a criminal defence lawyer. I joined Central Chambers with criminal defence lawyers Mark Edgar, Dave Reece and Graeme Newell. The best word for criminal defence work is "distasteful". It is a tough game and I admire those who dedicate their careers to the field. The stresses are enormous, the responsibility for another's liberty being a heavy burden. Some practitioners are over-run by dirty money, tax problems, drug use and suicide.

It's a fair way on the other side of terrifying to stand in court for the first time as counsel. I chatted about this with former All Black captain and lawyer Jock Hobbs. "You know," he told me, "I can honestly say I was more nervous and scared the first time I appeared in court than I was leading the All Blacks onto Twickenham."

It didn't escape me, either, the first time I appeared, that I had already been in the witness box as a cop, had stood as the defendant and was now counsel. I had only the bench as a judge to go. The chances of that were slim.

The case that tipped the balance for me with criminal defence work was a robbery. The accused was Jono Parker, who was charged with robbery after threatening and taking two hundred bucks back from a hooker he felt didn't deliver properly. Jono was a hard-core criminal with a long list of previous convictions. In the circumstances he had a clear defence to the charges. If he believed he legitimately could recover the money he had a "colour of right" defence to theft and in turn robbery, which is theft accompanied by violence.

When Jono appeared the judge denied bail based on the charge and his previous history of disappearing when facing charges. Down in the cells I met with Jono to discuss the case and his clear defence. Before I could open my mouth, he unleashed a barrage of abuse at me about the bail and the jeopardy he was in. The guy was a dog and didn't have a good word for anyone, hence his previous list. I was there doing my best to represent and help him. I remember thinking, *Here I am, paid for by the government through your legal aid, and all you can do is deliver up abuse. If you were in the Crime Squad office at Auckland Central I'd punch you out of your chair, you fucken idiot.*

I had a brief stint in chambers with my old mate Gringo. He had left the police and done his law degree a couple of years before me. There was a befitting symmetry: we had both been young cops in Dunedin and were coming together as lawyers smack in the middle of Auckland's legal precinct.

To further my experience in civil cases, I joined the commercial law chambers of Phil Grace and John Long. Phil played social rugby at halfback and was a small guy with a huge tenacious heart. He was youthful and well-groomed with dark close-cropped hair. The practice of law meant everything to him. He epitomised the smart, respected, focused, diligent and successful city barrister. His legal drafting was without peer and I learnt a lot from him about evidence on paper. We did a lot of cases together and I appeared with him as counsel in a number of high-profile trials.

My legal investigation practice continued to evolve. I had my first involvement with the US courts in 1992. A Kiwi, Paul Burke, had been arrested in Los Angeles by the federal authorities for running an international wildlife smuggling operation. I flew to LA and met with Paul at the downtown Metropolitan Detention Center where he was jailed. The MDC houses only the worst federal criminals. Getting into the center is an arduous process with multiple doors and levels of security.

A one-hour briefing would take most of the day. "Hey man, don't finish up too late and leave your car downtown," a smiling guard advised. "It'll be either gone, have no wheels or be burnt out."

In his orange overalls Paul presented as lonely, isolated and vulnerable. He smuggled exotic birds and their eggs, yet he'd landed in the midst of serial killers, drug dealers and mafia hitmen. Paul had a lucrative operation going smuggling birds from and to New Zealand through Australia, the Canary Islands and the US. He could command up to twenty thousand dollars for a single parrot. The birds were drugged and transported in plastic tubes: mortality rates could be high. Eggs were moved by couriers with specially adapted vests strapped to their bodies.

Paul's American contact in Orange County was the supposedly staunch Falcon. Falcon, however, was facing his own legal problems with the Feds and sang like a smuggled canary, resulting in an international investigation involving the US Fish & Wildlife Service and the NZ Ministry of Agriculture and Fisheries.

"Yeah, man, we don't have much trouble here with fights, not like in the state prisons. The dudes in here are serious so when it does go bad, it goes real bad and someone usually ends up getting killed. If a dude's facing multiple life sentences he ain't never getting out, so it makes no difference if he takes someone out." Further comforting advice from the smiling guard.

The comments about things going bad made me think of Rick in my undercover days. He could descend quickly into sinister moods. It was like a cloud crossing the sun. A darkness descended. Eyes blackening, brow furrowing, a hunching of the shoulders, a primal bristle. The physical manifestations matching his emotional change were unmistakable.

I recalled one day in particular from the scene, when despite the sunny Parnell afternoon a black mood descended upon Rick in the Alex public bar. There appeared to be no apparent trigger. He'd been using heroin, but not constantly, and when we first met up by arrangement from the previous low-key Friday night, all seemed well with the world.

We were on our second game of pool. After the first couple of balls had been played, he changed. I knew immediately and didn't like it. Before I could even assess where this episode might lead, Rick suddenly raised his pool cue and smashed it across the edge of the table. The tip broke off, leaving a splintered shaft three quarters its original length. He waved it in my direction saying, "Let's do it. Come on, life means fuck-all anyway, let's fight to the death. The loser will probably be going to a better place."

"Come on, mate, we're just having a quiet game of pool," I said in a placatory tone.

It made no difference. He wasn't listening. Eyes blazing, he snorted, "Fuck pool and fuck everyone. One of us will end up brown bread." He smacked the pool cue on the edge of the table for emphasis.

The bar was virtually empty when we arrived, but now it was deserted. "Hey, Rick, calm down, man," I said. "Living's the way to go, brother, we got shit to do."

While speaking, I tightened my grip on the pool cue and grabbed a ball off the table as a further weapon.

Deaf to any reason, Rick hunched over and had the cue extended out to his side. He flipped it so the thick end was away from him, for use like a club. With the table between us, we moved around it like predatory animals. I was watching his artificial leg. That's where I would kick first.

"If we're gonna do this, let's do it another day," I said, hoping it might have an effect but now gearing towards seemingly inevitable violence. I glanced towards the bar but no one was in attendance. The pub crew knew us both and wisely didn't want to be involved.

In street fights your senses focus on your combatant, but your arena can contain a number of different weapons or adversaries who may enter the fray. You not only need to deal with the immediate close conflict, but also have to be aware of these other factors that can rapidly change events. Really good fighters in a traditional sense, through boxing or martial arts, can be undone by a mongrel with a hidden blade and nothing to lose. The influence of alcohol, drugs and women can further bedevil the conflict.

Yet as fast as it happened, it stopped.

"Yeah, fuck it," said Rick, turning away from the table and dropping the cue. He walked to a stool against the wall, exhaled loudly and slowly mounted the seat. I followed him over but stopped outside striking distance.

"I think I need a drink," he said quietly.

The Convention on International Trade in Endangered Species of Wild Fauna and Flora (CITES) is a multi-lateral treaty which has been in force since 1973. Most countries are parties to the agreement, including the US and New Zealand. Its objective is to protect such creatures as exotic birds and it acts as a global framework under which respective domestic laws operate.

Paul was a major player in the smuggling game and had come under the international spotlight. Considering wildlife smuggling is a multi-billion dollar worldwide issue, second only to drug-dealing, the case was being treated seriously. Just how seriously became apparent in my first meeting with FBI and Fish & Wildlife federal agents. They revealed that a significant undercover operation had been undertaken spanning some two years. Two federal undercover agents had travelled to New Zealand posing as musicians with an interest in exotic birds. They ensconced themselves playing in Paul's favourite Auckland bar. His "casual" meeting with the band was anything but. As far as he was concerned no suspicion could attach to the musicians, and when eventually they expressed an interest in smuggling New Zealand native parrots to the US he was happy to oblige. The operation involved establishing a cover bird dealership in Los Angeles.

Bugs had been installed in Falcon's home, capturing phone and personal discussions between him and Paul about the mechanics of the smuggling operation. CCTV installed in Falcon's street produced ID shots and good footage of the smugglers' comings and goings. The operation terminated with search warrants executed in six US states plus in New Zealand and Australia. Hundreds of parrots and macaws were subject to seizure.

Early on it was apparent that the weight of evidence demanded serious consideration of a plea arrangement. Defending smuggling, conspiracy and wire fraud charges in another jurisdiction with the threat of up to twenty years prison if convicted did not hold much upside. Paul was keen to do the best deal possible, even though it would require full co-operation with the authorities about his activities. Over the course of three further meetings with the feds and assistant attorneys we struck a deal where Paul would serve fifteen months in prison — served at the MDC.

In early August 1993 I was approached by a US public relations agency to organise bodyguards for a mystery international businessman. Personal protection was one aspect of wider security services I was offering.

After due diligence checks and a couple of briefings I was formally instructed, we had operation orders completed and were ready for the one-day visit of our principal on 23 August. Donald Trump is an imposing man: taller than you'd expect and with an undeniable presence. He was recently the leader of the free world — in 1993 even he would have thought that was a joke.

Barry Brown's eyes darted when he spoke. With a subject about which he was passionate, the darting became staccato and placed his eyes in peril of damage. The virtues of Donald Trump was one of those subjects. "Man, I've been protecting him for six years now," he said. "He is without a doubt the best employer I've had. After the NYPD and Secret Service I worked for a few of those celebrity movie types, but most of them were a pain in the ass."

High praise indeed as most subjects who warrant protection have some problematic foibles.

"And loyal," Barry went on. "If he likes you guys and you do a good job he'll give you the casino security if he wins the licence. I'm telling you, man, I'll only leave if I'm shot or get too old." Fleeting eyes backed the emphatic statement.

Trump was a fiend for work, with an amazing capacity for output. I found him impossible not to like. It was a short detail, but Trump seemed to be on the go all the time. His schedule was peppered with media interviews, one after the other, in vehicles or even walking to transport. "He's a hard man to keep up with," said Barry. "He tops out at about four hours' sleep a night. I love it, though — plenty of energy."

Ever courteous and polite, the Donald gave me a signed photo when he left. I am not sure if that's the norm, but it was appreciated.

About a week later another celebrity, actress Brooke Shields, flew in to film a shampoo commercial. The filming was to take place in Wellington, so after meeting her in Auckland we flew down together. I had planned her security and assessed that she only needed one bodyguard. A female was considered initially, but I thought it would be cool and did the job myself. Brooke physically presented as she had in film and television, but this was augmented by warmth and charisma.

An arduous two days' filming was spent in the Wellington studios. Brooke's double was an eighteen-year-old model named Kylie Bax. Attractive and tall, with brown shoulder-length hair, she possessed verve and an elemental confidence. During a chat between takes she matter-of-factly opined, "I'm going to be a famous model, then you can protect *me*."

Prophetic words, as she did make it big internationally, joining the supermodel ranks and gracing the covers of *Vogue*, *Maxim* and *Vanity Fair* among others. She also ended up as a consort of Donald Trump. I wondered later if there was some sort of cosmic coupling in train at that time.

I shuddered at the words, "We can play charades after dinner." Not really my scene and I foresaw a fair bit of discomfort on the horizon. "It'll be fun," said Brooke excitedly. Carousel-like, the words *I don't think so* kept circling in my head.

On the second night in Wellington, Brooke had been invited to a dinner party with people she knew in Oriental Bay. She was ensconced in the penthouse suite at the Intercontinental Hotel. I had implemented some extra security measures there, including an electronic beam that detected anyone approaching the suite door.

At the appointed time to leave for dinner I gently knocked on the suite door. It was opened by the American actress who was dressed fashionably in a turquoise cashmere dress over black leggings. Her outfit was completed by black Italian leather boots. Two understated gold rings on her right hand completed the look.

On our way down in the lift a soft "ding" indicated a stop on the third floor. In stepped Sydney barrister Mike Williams and former Australian rugby international Nick Farr-Jones. I knew Mike as we had done a case together in the US. He had formerly practised in Auckland and was famous for one day simply laying down his pen, putting on his jacket and leaving his chambers never to return. A larger-than-life hard case, he subsequently carved out a successful practice from Edmund Barton chambers in Sydney.

"Running around with actresses now, mate?" he said.

"Bit of decorum, thanks, Mike," was my smiling reply.

Upon arrival at the dinner venue, a tasteful villa on the hill, as per protocol I told Brooke I would wait in the car for her. "No, come in, please," she said. "I insist. I won't take no for an answer. You can do a better job protecting me inside."

Not long after, the charades plan was unveiled. I'm not sure how I avoided participating — probably some decidedly thin argument about detracting from my professional responsibility. My reluctant exclusion was a palpable relief, but watching Brooke and her host couple play was enthralling. So this is how the Hollywood elite entertain themselves, I thought, watching Brooke revelling in playing her parts.

The next day we sat side by side on exercycles in the hotel gym. Long, narrow and well appointed, the gym was empty but for us. Brooke turned to me, her face pressed into a pink sweatshirt. Puffing only slightly, she said, "I heard from my friend Michael Jackson. I'm really annoyed at the negative publicity he's getting. He's the most wonderful person and a truly loyal friend. It's terrible the allegations being made against him."

Everyone internationally was aware at the time of the challenges Jackson was having regarding sex offending allegations. Such a heartfelt plea made me think maybe there was another side to the whole sordid situation.

There were hugs all round when Brooke flew out of Auckland airport. Usually at the end of such a task you are relieved to see the principal leave without incident. This time the feeling was replaced with a pang of regret at her departure.

◄ EIGHTEEN ►

"This will change investigation and security forever."

Murray often wore a resigned look, as would a bear watching a river absent of fish, or a cow plodding to milking, or a dog whose master has left the house without him. Benevolence circled Murray like a lazy whirlpool.

Unkempt in a cool way, he was a devotee of the T-shirt. For him only the most unique incarnation of it would suffice: a carefully aged old rock band's Sixties tour shirt, something tie-dyed, or a majestic multi-coloured piece of finery.

Murray was a computer whiz — not in the sense of a startling bright young thing with a bent for computers, or some highly skilled hacker living in the Dark Web. Murray Haszard was the real deal. A computer genius. Single-handedly he developed a disk-cloning programme. He did in four years what hundreds of the best minds beavering within the elite corporates worldwide had failed to do. The sale of his Ghost software to Symantec for twenty-seven-and-a-half million US dollars made him a wealthy man.

"Mark, I've got a bit of a problem," came Murray's voice down the phone line. I had acted for Murray before and knew him pretty well.

"What's up?" I replied.

"I've got a problem. The problem is cash, cash that's gone missing."

"Yep, that's always a problem. Go on."

"I invested a lot with a currency spot-trading operation based in New York. I paid funds into their local bank account here where they were supposed to be secure, but now the bank has been in touch saying the funds have disappeared. Gray and Graeme have also been bitten."

The purported currency-trading operation Murray referred to was

Evergreen International Spot Trading Incorporated, based in New York. Their associated entity was First Equity Enterprises, also New York-based, which apparently securely held investors' funds. Returns on investment were represented as being between fifteen and twenty per cent per annum. Murray, Gray Treadwell and Graeme Lodge had been contacted initially through cold calling, but had subsequently met the operation's front man Justin Fauci, an American, in New Zealand.

I had met Gray and Graeme through Murray. Both technologically savvy and in Murray's circle of smart minds, they were at the forefront of developing electronic funds transfer payment systems. Gray was prone to thoughtfully considering a matter under discussion before responding. Graeme, although more loquacious, was no less deliberate. The two men were meditation practitioners and it showed. They exuded and could retreat to calmness at will. Their ability to do so kicked up a mild envy in most observers.

Following a briefing to gather more detail, I fronted my bank-fraud team contacts to get further details on what happened to the funds. I learned that just over two-and-a-third million NZ dollars had been transferred from First Equity's ASB account in Auckland to an account in the name of Exista Foundation held with BNP Paribas in Basel, Switzerland. A decent amount of that money had been invested by the three men who were to issue me recovery instructions. I had no idea how big the case was to become.

I sat with Murray, Gray and Graeme and we had a serious discussion about how to proceed. I had taken written statements from each of them outlining the nature of their investments, representations made about how their funds would be invested, and affixing bank-transfer and financial documentation showing what had happened. It became apparent that my clients appeared to have been the victims of an international fraud. More specifically, a Ponzi scheme.

Such frauds operate by using the funds of new investors to pay dividends to existing investors. No funds are actually invested anywhere; it is just a money-go-round where the promoters of the fraud receive the funds and those working within the fraud operation receive a clip or commission for what they can extract from unsuspecting investors. Characteristics of such frauds are high returns, cold calling, impressive websites and documentation, flash offices displaying the accoutrements of wealth, glib account managers, statements showing fat returns, confidentiality attaching to techniques, complexity to confuse investors, requests for progressively larger amounts, and repayments of small amounts to engender trust.

I wasn't entirely sure if I could get my clients' money back or how I would do it. I did know with absolute certainty the money had to be followed and if it wasn't, it was gone for sure. The only positive was that the money had been transferred only two days previously. The trail was fresh.

"I know it's a tough call," I said, "and it's going to cost you more on top of what you've lost, but to get any result I need to travel to Switzerland — like now."

"Hmmm," came from Murray. Then: "Hey, if you think that's the best way to go we have confidence in your advice and ability."

That was it: I felt humbled by their belief in me and felt a responsibility to get them a result.

I received the nod early Friday afternoon and booked to fly that night. The statements were in draft, but there was a scramble to locate certain outstanding bank-transfer documents to complete the evidential suite. Having these was a must as they were the crux of the evidence and would be picked up within the fraudsters' Swiss account.

Travelling the thirty hours to Europe is always a bane. New Zealand is at the bottom of the world. To get anywhere is at least twelve hours, except Aussie, which doesn't count. I landed in Geneva and hired a car for the trip to Basel. En route I was contacted by my office and advised that the money had been transferred to the BNP Paribas branch in Geneva, not Basel. The initial information from the ASB fraud team had been wrong. Not a major in most circumstances, but after travelling so long the jet-lagged mind is a conjurer weaving shadowy uncertainty around facts.

Through contacts I had settled on the Geneva law firm De Pfyffer

& Associés as local counsel; I had full use of the Geneva law firm's office at 6 Rue François-Bellot. Their partner and acting counsel was Jean-Cédric Michel. He embodied refinement. Late thirties, slim and impeccably groomed, he was the consummate professional. Jean-Cédric had an uncanny ability: when I briefed him in English that was highly legalistic he would take notes in French.

The Swiss judicial process is inquisitorial in nature and fundamentally different from the English system upon which New Zealand law is based. The English system relies on an adversarial approach, meaning competing litigants put up their version of what has occurred and the matter is determined by the court, which assesses the competing merits of the adversaries. The inquisitorial system by comparison relies on an inquiry as to the matter at hand. The Swiss judges are trained to be judges from the start, as opposed to an avocat (lawyer). In determining a case, the Swiss judge explores the facts and then makes decisions as to what legal order or measure they will adopt to gather further facts to determine the case. This gathering of further facts, as opposed to applying the law on the facts that are available, is a fundamental difference from our system. Law schools within English common-law jurisdictions always teach this application of the law to the facts. This is at odds with investigative steps which necessarily are designed to gather further information, which may change how the case looks.

The Swiss judge has an athenaeum of resources to apply to cases, such as seizure orders, search warrants, interception or bugging warrants, discovery orders and examinations under oath. The system works well with international financial-crime investigations, as the judges are really investigators, searching out the actual facts of the matter brought before their court. In New Zealand and the other non-inquisitorial legal systems, investigation is often seen to be inconsistent with the practice of law. This perception is changing, however, with an acknowledgement that a full body of gathered facts makes any determination, in whatever form, easier. The changes in investigation and how it affects legal systems is likely to accelerate with scientific developments of processes such as brain-scanning, which will be able to determine what is in someone's mind to ninety-nine per cent accuracy, virtually eliminating the bringing of inaccurate or vexatious claims.

Money, money, money — that's pretty much all that's spoken about in Geneva. No wonder, as Switzerland houses one third of the world's private wealth, amounting to around eleven thousand billion US dollars, most of it in Geneva's one hundred and fifty private banks. Financial terms and hushed, fervent deal discussions hung everywhere in the air, including at my accommodation, the Art Deco Hotel de Rhône (now the Mandarin Oriental). The hotel is nestled on the banks of the Rhône River, just around the corner from Lake Geneva. It became a regular base for me in Geneva. Being greeted by name by the smiling cocktail-bar bartender after a long day strategising is an abiding memory of the place.

I arrived in Switzerland on the Friday, and following an order issued by the Court of Justice on the morning of the following Wednesday, 11 October 2011, the BNP Paribas Exista account was frozen. Because of related transfers there was also another account caught and frozen, in the name of Raft Foundation.

Frustratingly, the Swiss asset-forfeiture process is such that the amount blocked in the account is not revealed. Through a groundswell of intelligence received from various prosecution agencies I understood the amount lost in this fraud could top one hundred million US dollars. Given I was receiving a percentage contingency on funds recovered, the amount seized was more than relevant. (I later learned that in addition to my funds of interest, fourteen million US dollars of terrorist funding sent by Al Qaeda were identified during the process of forfeiture.)

By now I knew this international fraud was most probably the work of the Russian mafia. Fraud was but one enterprise they engaged in, along with human trafficking, prostitution and drugs. Aside from Fauci, the nominated prime suspects in the fraud were two Russians, Andrei Koudachev and Gary Farberov. Koudachev, cunning and manipulative, was the mastermind behind the fraud. A former adviser to Boris Gromov, the governor of regional Moscow, he was chief executive of Mosoblgaz, a state-owned gas company with eight thousand employees.

The case was gaining momentum; affected victims were making

contact with my office. I flew back to New Zealand to co-ordinate victims and assemble evidence. Both the Serious Fraud Office and the Police Fraud Squad were aware I was acting and had referred complainants on the basis that the matter was international and outside New Zealand jurisdiction. This was new ground: I formulated a plan to manage the case, daunting as it was. There were times I felt growing apprehension concerning my ability to handle what was becoming a leviathan case.

The month before, Al Qaeda terrorists attacked the World Trade Center in New York. Ainsley and I numbly watched the horrific events live on CNN. I clearly remember saying, "This will change investigation and security forever." How prophetic those words were. Not only was the whole investigation and security industry redefined globally, but my own professional life would never be the same again.

Evergreen and First Equity had been based in the World Trade Center. Visiting investors (soon to become fraud victims) from all over the world were transported from the airport in limousines and greeted in opulent offices at New York's premium address. Nattily dressed staff hovered over the latest computer systems. Bright eyes watched sleek monitors upon which circled fictitious numbers. Although not there permanently, a priest often sat quietly on a plush meeting-room sofa — his collar, no doubt, providing divine comfort to hapless wealth-seekers.

Boiler-room frauds or Ponzi schemes have a gestation of around eighteen months. That's the optimum time to extract maximum funds from victims, collapse the operation and disappear. Unfortunately for Evergreen and the Russian mafia, the operation was not quite there despite having bagged around one hundred million US dollars from unwitting investors around the world.

When the Twin Towers went down, investors made contact. At first they were concerned about the brokers they had been dealing with and the welfare of other Evergreen staff. A secondary concern, however, began to assume prominence and that was the welfare of their funds. Naturally, many investors thought it might be appropriate to make a call on their funds. There were no funds to fulfil these requests and no new victims were being lured to the honeypot. The pot was cracking.

I organised victim meetings in Auckland and Melbourne. I considered it important that the victims had a voice and needed representatives I could report to, who could adopt my recommendations and control group funds. A victim group was formed named Evergreen First Equity Recovery Group (EFERG). Mike Bush, who went on to become police commissioner, was then a detective senior sergeant and attended on behalf of the police. This helped my credibility. Murray, Gray and Graeme were committee members; the first group chairman elected by victims was Dick Karreman, who owned a quarry in Queensland. He had emigrated from the Netherlands and made himself a fortune. He owned the largest private fleet of dump trucks in Australia and was as hard as those machines. Approaching seventy he presented as a big, strong, fit man. Fools were not even mildly tolerated by Dick.

He expertly weaved accented English around his swear words. The fraudsters were always described as "those fucking pricks". Dick appeared to rate bankers only marginally above fraudsters: "I make those fuckers come up from Brisbane to see me. I then make sure I'm working under a machine so they can fucking wait. I then shake their puny fucking hands with a grease-covered mitt and crush their fucking soft white office paws."

Dick had become interested in horse racing late in life and brought a Midas touch to the game. He had studs in New Zealand and Australia, with stallions standing in both countries and in Ireland. His demand for high standards meant success came on the track too.

I clashed with Dick a little in the first stage of our relationship but that was soon sorted and I came to like and respect the man enormously. He brought a pragmatic approach to the loss of his funds, saying, "It's my fucking fault for trusting those fucking little pricks."

This approach was not shared by all victims and I was surprised to learn that some of my clients could not acknowledge their shortcomings in being duped, but would instead level anger at me, their lawyer. This jaundiced view was not shared by Terry Ward, the next chairman. Terry shared Dick's pragmatism, saying, "It's just one of those things. We now have to do what we can and see what we can get back."

Terry was a very successful businessman, the former worldwide chief executive of Heinz. Tall, with an unmistakable air of authority and confidence, he hailed from Melbourne but had spent a number of years in London. He spoke fluent French and had holiday houses in Cap Ferrat and Monaco. We had a shared affinity with cars and speed. Terry had a Porsche 911 and a Bentley in France, with matching vehicles at his Melbourne home. That was downright cool, but particularly so when I learned he shipped a Bentley around the world to do runs and had completed an off-road race through Malaysia.

The EFERG group grew to three hundred and thirty-two victims from thirty-one countries. With the group coming together, I flew back to Europe to chase further leads on funds arising from the Swiss action. I nested in my hotel base and met with Jacques Bour, a former banker who acted as an investment adviser, covering Geneva and Lichtenstein. Slim, tall and perennially healthy looking, Jacques shared the same birth year as me. Brought up in a privileged, strict German household, he found comfort in formality. Even when travelling, his shirts were ironed and folded in a particular manner. When he visited and stayed with us in Auckland he wore a perfectly pressed shirt buttoned at the wrist, with a lemon-coloured jumper tied loosely around his neck, to a barbecue on the back deck. Slightly incongruous, as cooking a barbie over a few beers in New Zealand is the least formal event on the planet.

I teased him with, "Geez, mate, you didn't need to get dressed up!"

"I'm not really," he said. "I'm not wearing cufflinks."

I liked Jacques and got on with him well. With his knowledge of the Swiss financial system, his sage advice was invaluable.

Intelligence to hand indicated funds had also been diverted to Australia, Austria, Hungary and Latvia. Not knowing if the motherlode was already subject to seizure in Geneva, my objective was to trace and lockdown these other accounts.

"A small gratuity should suffice," said Mag, whom I had retained to provide advice and open doors. He held the title President as the former head of the Vienna police. Everyone in Austria seemed to have a title, the ubiquitous Doctor or for lawyers the prefix Mag.

"We will go down to the police station and you can make a formal statement about the fraud. The modus operandi of the fraudsters will be pertinent." He looked towards a waiter and, switching to German, ordered a cigarette. The President was a chain smoker. Judging by the hazy smoke levels in the bar of the Hilton Plaza in Vienna, so was everyone else in the room. Tall, rangy and wearing a rumpled Burberry coat, he had an authoritative presence honed by years of command roles. "What do you think about Budapest, Carl?"

The President's question was directed to a stocky, black-suited man who was also smoking. Carl, an East German, was a former Stasi agent. Nothing about him could be considered friendly. He personified "mean", from the slightly faded scar on his left cheek to his slightly scuffed shoes.

Carl's current role was repossessing stolen buses from Albania. They had been taken from other parts of Europe by organised-crime gangs, and recovering them held about the same level of risk as facing a gladiator in the coliseum. Carl was on board in case things got rough. His recruitment arose from an earlier comment from the President: "My Europol contacts advise that the Russian mafia are not too keen on their bank accounts being shut down." Europol was the European Union's law enforcement agency set up to fight serious international crime and terrorism, so this information was credible.

"Let's deal with here first, then see how it goes over there," replied Carl matter-of-factly.

Carl nosed the black Audi 8 out of the Hilton Plaza's forecourt and headed towards the Polizei at Wattgasse 15. Vienna is a majestic city. Stunning architecture adorned with finely sculpted statues stare over the wide avenues. The previous night we had dined at a restaurant formerly used by the House of Habsburg, the historical rulers of Austria. Elegantly styled exotic plants reached up to luminous pink- and blue-neon lighting. Our dinner guests included administrators of the Austrian and French rugby unions. A sublime feast of fish was matched by a feast of rugby chatter. The delightful Russian wives present closed the circle on an evening of beauty and style.

A very formal and efficient Austrian detective took my statement.

She was curt as opposed to cute, with square-rimmed glasses and her hair tightly in a bun. Plain silver rings on each hand danced over the computer keyboard as she recorded my answers. Very professionally she added just enough extra information to what was in the bundle of documents I had provided her.

"Thank you, Herr Mark, we will be in touch," she said, proffering the statement for signing and indicating the briefing was over. True to her word, within twenty-four hours I heard back that two accounts had been identified, but the fraudsters had emptied them within the last two weeks.

Further troubling information had come from Europol the previous day. I knew from PNB Paribas Geneva that Gary Farberov had tried to withdraw all funds from the Exista and Raft Foundation accounts the very afternoon of the day the account was frozen. The timing was within a few hours of the account being locked down. But for the seizure order the victims' funds would have been lost, disappearing into Russia. This, according to Europol, had caused a reasonable degree of unhappiness within mafia circles. As a result the word was out that my damaging conduct needed to be stopped by any means.

I figured the Austrian banks would have advised their account holder of my measures and that my foe knew I would be moving on the Hungarian and Latvian accounts. The personal risk levels for the next foray into Budapest were therefore elevated. I spoke to Carl and we both agreed an extra level of protection was required. I contacted New Zealand and told Ainsley to get on a plane. I needed her: the one person I trusted implicitly, skilled in threat assessment, counter-surveillance, trained to kill and unhesitatingly would meet violence with deadly force.

The Hilton Plaza bar was the venue again for a briefing once Ainsley arrived. Between cigarette puffs the President said, "This is at such a serious level we need to deal with the Hungarian Organised Crime Unit rather than the local police or banks. These are not the sort of guys you want to take lightly, and they're hurting." Crushing out his cigarette, he pulled at his coat before shifting in his chair and looking around for a waiter.

"I can sort weapons for us at the border," said Carl impassively. "We need to leave early."

I kept Dick and the committee posted as to what was happening. When camped at the Hotel de Rhône I had a fax machine in my room to receive documents. As events unfolded and different documentation was required, the time zones between Europe and New Zealand worked well. With twelve hours' difference, I could finish the day in Europe with instructions to my office as to what was required and it would be done during the New Zealand business day ready for me in the morning. Effectively, administration and office support was operating twenty-four hours a day. One slight problem ensued, though: I would receive telephone calls and faxes at three and four in the morning my time. The quick ring and buzzing of a fax being received in my room was like feeding barbed wire in one ear and out the other.

We stopped at a coffee house en route to the Austria-Hungary border. "This is one of my favourite places. Austria has the best coffee houses in the world. You must try the Sachertorte, our most famous culinary delight. It's the best," said the President, his hand fishing inside his coat for cigarettes. As on every other occasion the President was right. I love chocolate cake, but the Sachertorte version took, well, the cake.

The more time I spent with the President the more likeable he became. He was prone to making sweeping philosophical statements. His pearls of wisdom came easily. "The aye rabs are the biggest threat to the world," he said, with emphasis on the "aye".

Halfway through his Sachertorte the President said, "These crooks we're dealing with, there's an old German saying: fear makes the wolf bigger than he is." After a pause everyone commenced eating again.

Looking at his cake fork as if it were providing inspiration, he said, "We only have today. That's all we've actually got — yesterday has gone and tomorrow hasn't yet come."

Then: "Everyone wants to eat but no one wants to hunt."

The hunting analogy and notion of human game had come up again. It wasn't lost on me that these comments were being made with the risk levels about to increase. I looked at Ainsley and knew she was thinking the same thing.

"Shall we go?" said Carl, rising from the table.

As we walked past the coffee-shop counter I heard strains of the Travelling Wilburys song *Tweeter and the Monkey Man*. That song always reminds me of working undercover. There's one line that sears and makes me feel uncomfortable, the one about the undercover cop being found face down in a field.

Working undercover there were plenty of trying, anxious and downright terrifying times, but there was also humour. Rick would quickly rise to a laugh, and often there was bonhomie with a few beers on board among genuinely good company.

Johnny Nicholson was the archduke of the strip-club scene in Auckland. Affectionately called Johnny Nick, the wiry don of flesh was one of life's true characters. To avoid any confusion, Johnny Nick's club, the Las Vegas in K Road, sported a huge poster of a naked girl. Despite numerous complaints over forty years, the Vegas Girl endured to become Auckland City's most famous billboard.

Rick and I had been out south doing a successful heroin deal, so to celebrate we turned up at Johnny's for some entertainment. After an enthusiastic welcome Johnny thrust porcelain cups into our hands. As he didn't have a liquor licence, Johnny would fill delicate tea cups with gin as refreshments for selected customers. Dressed immaculately in a black pinstripe suit and red silk tie, he resumed his seat on his usual stool in the small office at the top of the stairs. "Got two pheasants last week, Marcus," he said proudly. Game-bird shooting was one of Johnny's passions.

Johnny didn't tolerate any shit in his club and was more than capable of dealing with trouble. Although now in his mid-forties, he'd been a boxer in an earlier life and wasn't afraid to mix it up. Many a pissed smartarse had underestimated Johnny. His club was a fiefdom and he exercised ultimate control. I liked seeing Johnny; he was a good joker and always amusing. His views on life, and in particular the female role in society, always called for reflection.

Moving again on his stool he opined, "I can't believe how women are being treated these days. You know, they've even got bitches in the police. It's not right they should be doing that. They should be looked after and protected. Just like I do with my girls."

After I terminated, I still maintained a relationship with Johnny when I was in the CIB. Johnny had the ability to deal with criminals and the police in the same way. Neither sector saw it as a problem. Johnny thought it was hard case that I had come to the club when undercover and later as a detective. He loved the subterfuge. It helped me with the girls, too.

Ainsley had dealings with him when she was in uniform, making inquiries about a car of his that had been stolen and recovered. She had information that would benefit him. As if that would make any difference to Johnny's attitude to a woman in blue.

Johnny lived in an apartment atop a block of shops in Balmoral. Access was up a set of rickety wooden stairs. It was basic shopkeeper-style digs. Ainsley parked her marked police Holden in the street, left her male partner in the car and made her way up the ramshackle stairs. She was about to knock when a muffled "Fuck off!" came from behind the door. Johnny must have watched her approach.

Talking to the door, Ainsley assured him that she was there on a basic inquiry that would help him and there was nothing to be concerned about.

"I don't want to know about it," was Johnny's response.

"If you just open the door I can explain the situation to you," Ainsley said.

"I'm not going to talk to a woman cop. Send the man up and I'll think about it."

Returning to the car, Ainsley briefed her partner. "Fuck him. If that's his attitude, I'm not going up," was his blunt assessment.

Ainsley could be forgiven for having some animosity towards Johnny but the reverse was true: she liked him.

The irony with Johnny was that whatever derogatory term he used about women, it somehow sounded normal and without negativity when coming from him. In many ways he mythologised women, creating his own small utopia within the walls of the club.

Pearl was his top lady. Early thirties, Maori with a toned athletic body, she wore her hair in long pigtails which swung across her back when she danced. *Brown Sugar* by the Stones was her signature song. With high cheekbones and large brown eyes she was traditionally beautiful. "Johnny is a sweetie," she told me. "I love him. I wouldn't have been here so long otherwise. He looks after us and genuinely cares about how we are. I always feel safe here. Now and again you get the odd fucken drunk idiot trying to grab you but John always sorts it out. I like it here. I like performing. Some girls might say it's temporary or the means to an end but not me — I like being on stage."

This night with Rick I asked Johnny, "Had any issues lately, mate?"

"Nah, not really. Just the usual eggs who have to be taught the error of their ways. I had to baseball-bat a cunt last week who got out of control. He crossed the line, was disrespecting the girls. I tell you boys, there's just no respect or honour among these young pricks today."

"Yeah, amen to that," murmured Rick.

"I don't know where it's going to end. The fucken fleas can do it out there but it ain't happening in my club."

"It's impressive how fit you keep, mate," I commented.

"I need to, Marcus. Things can get out of control here pretty quick. Gotta stamp on it straight away. I run ten kays every day, rain, hail or snow. It's an investment in protecting the kingdom. Can't show any weakness and you gotta be able to back up the talk."

Johnny was exactly right. Because it was a strip club some jokers thought they could behave like dogs. Just like a canine they needed to be shown a firm hand. Once the rules were set and backed up, everything went smoothly.

"And you need to be fit for your hunting," I added.

"I love getting out in the bush. It's respite from my world here. I'm out with nature and the birds. There's no conflict or stress. Even though I'm shooting them, I love those birds. They are beautiful creatures."

"Good on ya, mate. You're a classic," I said, clapping him on the shoulder.

Nodding to Johnny, Rick and I headed out to the club floor and to seats up against the wall. Pearl had just left the stage and after the obligatory flashing lights the next girl, Brandy, was announced by Johnny's man Adrian. Mimicking a boxing announcer Adrian's introductions were a hoot: every girl hailed from some exotic location and was given a drawn-out rapturous welcome. As we sat down, Topaz, one of the other girls, came over and gave each of us a fresh china tea cup followed by a kiss.

The club was briefly plunged into darkness before a single spotlight illuminated Brandy. You couldn't call her mammoth but she was definitely hefty. Quite a departure from Johnny's usual stable, who were all well above average. I'd courted a couple who fitted very nicely into the scene. What was disconcerting, considering Brandy's size, was that she sat atop a swing. Her outfit, purportedly that of a nurse, was not flattering.

The swing was moving at a good pace, arcing from the back of the stage out over patrons in the front rows. Brandy had a knack of not only keeping, but gathering, momentum. At the apex of her arc, Brandy opened her legs provocatively. Dependent upon your taste, the move was either tawdry or a nice touch. *Magic Carpet Ride* by Steppenwolf blared from the sound system.

Rick leaned over and said, "Glad we're sitting at the back, mate, coz if that fat bitch flies off that it's gonna be a fucken bloodbath."

Things began to go awry a few minutes later. Almost in slow motion, the rope affixed at one end of the swing gave way. Swinging down towards the audience, seating displaced, Brandy did admirably, athletically avoiding a crash landing in the crowd. Clinging to the ropes she twisted to her left, rose higher for a fraction then dropped directly to the stage, her white nurse's sneaker flying into the audience. The front row scattered, broken china spraying liquor indiscriminately.

The border crossing went without incident. About twenty kilometres inside Hungary Carl pulled the Audi into the car park of what looked like a three-star hotel and disappeared into the darkened reception. Shortly after, he returned to the car, opened the rear passenger's door and handed me a black canvas bag. Unzipping it revealed two 9mm semi-automatic Glock pistols and holsters. At the bottom was a Mossberg pump-action 12-gauge shotgun with a pistol grip. "I'm set," said Carl, rearranging his jacket over his shoulder holster.

Ainsley and I checked the pistols, took our jackets off and slipped on the holsters. Ainsley didn't seem to mind that her holster didn't have a flower.

"We'll leave the shotgun in the boot as backup," said Carl. I liked that we had a shotgun. It was my weapon of choice, just like when I was in the scene. Good at close range in confined areas. Pretty difficult to miss a target and does plenty of damage. Ever since I had terminated from undercover, in every place I lived there was a shotgun under the bed.

As we sped towards Budapest I couldn't help but think how a black Audi S8 4.2 V8 like the one in which we were travelling had featured in the movie *Ronin*. It was life imitating art. I'd had that feeling before and regarded the thought as friendly.

"We need to rendezvous with an Organised Crime Unit agent who will take us in to their base," said Carl. "Things are so hot at the moment they regularly move and have a high level of security around their base."

Carl had been executing counter-surveillance moves since we arrived on Hungarian soil. He'd crashed a few red lights and suddenly exited off freeways. On the outskirts of Budapest he turned into a service station. In a parking area away from the pumps sat a grey Opel Astra sedan. Carl glided the Audi into a park three along from the Opel. After waiting a couple of minutes he got out, approached the Opel and spoke with the driver.

"Sehr gut," said Carl, indicating satisfaction as he got back in and buckled his seatbelt. "We need to follow this agent. He will take us where we need to go. Let's cause some more problems for these guys, hey Mark?"

From the other front seat came, "Yes, these men need to be wary of old men in a profession where men usually die young." Followed by a chuckle from the President, punctuated by a cough. Levity was welcome.

Our lead car travelled at a decent clip, just fast enough to make us difficult to trail, but not so fast as to let us lose him. As we travelled deeper into the city, typical Art Nouveau Budapest architecture slipping by, the web of streets became tighter. Carl stuck to the Opel, its brake lights coming on and off with each swerve.

Alongside a line of commercial buildings, the Opel braked, turned off the road and dropped over the footpath down an enclosed driveway that ended with a grilled roller door. On our approach, the door creaked up and both cars eased into the darkened basement garage. We were escorted out of the garage and back on to the street, where we approached a drab concrete four-storey building without any signage. Greenish moss clung to concrete ridges which were the building's only features. The agent knocked and an eight-foot-high wooden door, one of two, opened slightly. A guard's uniform cap appeared in the gap.

After greetings, we were permitted entry into the building's foyer. A marble floor led up to two tall steel doors. To the right was a guardhouse booth. The guard, whose uniform was military, collected all our passports and went to the booth where he made a telephone call. We stood in the foyer waiting. There were no seats or any other furniture. I took a moment to examine the steel doors. Maybe they were bomb-proof? They were the sort of doors that could keep out marauding ancient armies. Inappropriately, or maybe not, the doors in the spoof spy movie *Get Smart* came to mind.

One of the steel doors opened and another guard appeared, gesturing for us to follow. The marble floor continued inside the doors towards a wooden staircase. We followed the guard up two flights of stairs and into a waiting room. This time there were chairs, but that was the furniture limit.

Five minutes later a woman in her early thirties entered quietly. With the grace of a dancer she moved across the room towards me. "Sorry to keep you waiting," she said. "Come through." She could have daintily stepped from the pages of a fashion magazine. Her perfectly coiffed long blonde hair rested on a tailored tweed jacket covering tight, fitted black slacks above black kitten-heel shoes. Carl became the most animated I had observed thus far.

The woman led us into a smallish office with a document-covered desk bookended by filing cabinets. There were three chairs in front of the desk. Carl frantically assisted the woman in carrying through a further chair.

"Just a few more minutes," she said before leaving. If the game was to impress with secretaries, I thought, eleven points out of ten to Hungary.

Moments later she re-entered the office, threaded through our chairs and took a seat behind the desk. Leaning against it was a Hungarian-manufactured KGP-9 submachine gun.

"I am Captain Petra Varga, head of the Organised Crime Unit," she said.

Carl shifted in his chair.

"How can I assist you, Herr van Leewarden?"

I was somewhat shocked that the woman I thought was the secretary was actually the boss of the unit.

"First, thank you for seeing us, Captain. Your assistance is greatly appreciated," I replied, thinking of the oft-quoted quip that assumption is the mother of all fuckups. "I understand you have some knowledge of this international fraud."

"Yes."

"Perhaps I could give you a summary of the fraud and what we are trying to achieve," I said, opening files and preparing to launch into my usual spiel of trying to encourage assistance from bodies that didn't necessarily have to assist.

"No need," she said. "What are the bank account numbers you want frozen?"

"Ahhh." I couldn't believe what she had just said. "Just a minute." I rapidly flipped through the file and pulled up the banking details. On cue, a male colleague of Captain Varga entered. He looked just like my old mate Morrie Raskin — maybe he'd come back from the grave to help on the case. The pair had a quick discussion in Hungarian before he left the room

"Lieutenant Kovacs is calling the banks now," Captain Varga said reassuringly.

Carl took the opportunity to strike up a conversation with her. No matter what the language, it's easy to tell when a bloke is trying to crack on to a bird. Captain Varga didn't seem receptive but Carl persevered, before finally petering out.

Kovacs returned and reported: "There were five accounts in total. They are now all frozen. We will have the balances of the accounts in a couple of days."

Sweet, I thought, it doesn't get much easier than that.

The money trail was exhausted, apart from Latvia which we were still working on. There was only two hundred thousand dollars in Australia and that was locked down. As it turned out, there were only minimal balances in the five Hungarian accounts. The theme prevailed: funds transferred into Russia and the trail lost.

I consulted with Dick and the committee. I felt it was worth a crack at the offenders themselves to see if some sort of deal might fly. Given I represented the majority of victims, perhaps there was some leverage regarding charges, providing a decent recovery was in the offing. It was worth a shot, so I jumped on a plane to New York.

◄ NINETEEN ►

"Very bad times have befallen us."

FOLLOWING 9/11, PLANES HEADING TO New York from Europe were virtually empty. Arriving at JFK airport, the enormity of what happened to the city was sheeted home to me both physically and emotionally. As I emerged from the terminal I was greeted by an acrid, metallic smell. I had detected wafts of it in the terminal and wondered what it was.

"It's the smell from when the towers went down," said the cab driver. "It hangs in the air all the time, man. It's a constant reminder of the bad shit that went down here."

There was a collective psychological pain shared by the Big Apple locals I met. They were shocked and haunted by what had happened. Whispered conversations traversed feelings of confusion, paranoia, uncertainty and fear for the future.

"Hello," came down the line in an American accent.

"Is that Mr Justin Fauci?" I asked. I was speaking to the primary First Equity offender.

"Yes. Who is calling?"

"It's Mark van Leewarden speaking, I'm a lawyer from New Zealand, I'm looking—"

"I know who you are. What do you want?"

"I'm in New York and thought it might be worthwhile catching up for a chat."

"Oh. Okay," he said slowly.

"Maybe there's an upside for you. There's certainly no downside," I suggested.

"I'll think about it and get back to you," he replied, finishing the call.

Within an hour Justin called me back setting an appointment for two days later at a lawyer's office in Manhattan.

I had also sorted an appointment with the Eastern District of New York US Attorney's office, which had started to investigate the fraud. The US Attorney's Office deals with federal as opposed to state criminal offending, so is responsible for the most serious crimes, particularly those with an international footprint and organised-crime involvement such as Evergreen.

With a couple of days to go before the meetings I visited Ground Zero. The cab driver dropped me about five blocks out from the disaster site, explaining that the emergency services did not let anyone drive any closer. The site still remained a massive crime scene. I didn't envy the investigators picking over evidence in such difficult circumstances. On foot I could approach to within about two hundred metres of the pit.

Wispy smoke drifted up from the twisted metal and concrete. Feelings of shock, awe and incomprehension all danced together. With an absence of reference points and never having seen something so tragic and overwhelming, it wasn't easy to process the sight of the catastrophe. Three rows of people stood before me at the wire boundary fence. No one spoke.

I didn't stay long. Hands deep in my pockets, I walked slowly away from the destruction, immersed in thought. After a block or so I found myself before the window of a leather shop. A brown aviator-style calfskin jacket with a space-shuttle breast patch hung in the shop front. I liked the look of it; it roused me from my melancholy.

I entered the shop and was faced with a small, elderly, stooped man with glasses balanced on the tip of his nose. He was busy at the back placing items in cardboard boxes.

"Hello," I said, attracting his attention.

"Yes, yes, son, how can I help?" He craned his head back so he could see through the precariously balanced glasses. "Very bad times have befallen us," he said before I could reply. "Had this shop for thirty-two years. It's been my life," he added wistfully.

"I like the look of the jacket in the window," I said.

Either he didn't hear me or chose not to. "Today is my last day of trading. It's all over for me, thanks to those demons that attacked my city. Anyway, let's get that jacket down so you can try it," he said, brightening slightly.

I tried the jacket and asked the price.

"That's a nine hundred dollar jacket, son, but you can have it for a hundred."

"Are you sure? That sounds pretty cheap."

"Yes, I'm sure. I close forever in an hour. You will be my last customer. Wear that jacket and remember what happened here."

I wear the distinctive jacket whenever I can. Should people comment on it, I recount the story of the old man and 9/11.

The lawyer's office was austere but had a clear view of the Statue of Liberty. Unlike most New York lawyers, Sam Cane looked dishevelled: top button undone, tie loose, creased shirt and crumpled tie matching a wrinkled face. "How can we help?" he asked. His Bostonian accent and the edge in his voice belied his appearance.

Sitting in chairs to his right were Justin Fauci and Mamed Mekhtiev. Fauci was the Evergreen broker responsible for dealing with the Australian and New Zealand investors. Fresh-faced and dressed in a preppy style with a similar bearing, he had remained quiet since my arrival. Mekhtiev — thin, swarthy, with angular features — was the operation's chief trader and purported currency dealer. He wore a dark suit and was also silent, his gaze fixed somewhere on the floor beside me.

In response to Cane's question, I gave a case rundown and covered the funds seizure in Europe. I concluded by saying I acted for a number of victims who might choose a particular path regarding certain individuals, dependent upon what might be delivered, either by way of evidence or further funds-recovery. My objective, I said, was to open the door to assistance.

I was on high alert before and at the start of the meeting. I didn't know if it was a set-up and had no information on exactly how Fauci and Mekhtiev featured in the fraud.

After about five minutes of discussion, the mood in the office imperceptibly mutated into something more sinister. The temperature seemed to drop by a few degrees, sound was more acute and colours clearer. I could see the statue over Mekhtiev's shoulder; the liberty symbolism telling. I knew at that point that the two men in the room with their lawyer were central players in the fraud I was investigating. They weren't peripheral players or potential witnesses, but major cogs in an international scam.

No deal was going to be done. These men were in too deep. As soon as civility allowed, I took my leave. Descending in the lift I shook my head, mulling over a meeting where most of the critical communication had been non-verbal.

There is a survival sense developed and honed from working undercover. I learned to rely on that sense and it served me well both in the programme and subsequently. It's like a broad alert and it activated in that New York law office. The same sense came to bear in assessing people. A mistake in summing up a person in the scene could be perilous to your health.

I liken it to a sixth sense developed through necessity, as acuity develops in a blind man's hearing. How it actually works is unfathomable, but within a pot of negatives it was one of the benefits I derived from working undercover. I nurtured that sense and treated it as a trade-off against personality alteration and the physical manifestation of leading a double life in dangerous and stressful situations, such as the "startle response" I will have until the day I die. I move suddenly or jump every time I am surprised or startled.

Whether spurred by my meeting, or an angle about to be adopted, Fauci and Mekhtiev ran to the FBI. Armed with thousands of pages of Evergreen documentation, they pleaded ignorance of any deception. It's not uncommon for criminals facing charges to flip. There is a last-chance saloon before prosecution and jail. The warmth of reception at the saloon is dependent upon a number of factors, including how strong the case is, the nature of evidence being brought, who the main players are, and whether the offending is ongoing. In this instance, my targets' move proved to be folly. They were going down no matter what co-operation was forthcoming.

My next stop was Brooklyn. At One Pierrepont Plaza sat the US Attorney's office for the Eastern District. The head honcho was the Harvard-educated Loretta Lynch, who would later become Attorney General of the United States. I met with two of her staff, male and female assistant US attorneys, who delivered a perfunctory update about the status of the case. I wasn't expecting anything startling, as I was ahead of them and had already frozen funds in Switzerland. The prosecutors, however, were courteous and helpful; the lines of communication were open.

During the visit I met Randy Cox, the federal agent assigned to working the case. Attached to the US Attorney's offices nationally are agents who conduct investigations. They sit at the top of the law-enforcement tree, as they assess cases brought by the various federal enforcement agencies' investigators. They can prioritise and influence cases that will be tried criminally.

I immediately warmed to Randy, a former NYPD detective. His face was that of the scurrilous, mischievous kid in the school playground. His short and stocky build somehow aligned with his easy manner. A distinctive New York accent betrayed his local roots.

"Dang, as an ex-detective you're one of the brothers, I'll help you any way I can on this case," he drawled. His words were music to my ears. "Tonight I'll take you to a local haunt, chow down on ribs, drink some Bud and chew the fat about the case."

I didn't need to be asked twice.

The haunt was a neighbourhood Brooklyn eatery nestled among distinctive two-level brownstone apartments. From that night on, Randy helped me however he could, even with some surprising information.

Air New Zealand flight NZ1 spirits Kiwis back home from Los Angeles. I jumped on that bird back to Auckland to regroup, consult with the committee and plan the next inquiry steps. By now the media had their teeth into the case. The storm of interest was something I had never experienced before. Local television and print journalists made repeated contact; the international contingent included the *Australian Financial Times*, *New York Post*, *New York Times*, *UK Guardian* and German television.

"Would you consider coming over and joining our team?" I said tentatively down the phone.

"Yes, I would," came Denise Graham's reply.

Denise was regarded as Auckland's top legal secretary. I had met her when in legal chambers with Phil Grace and John Long. They shared her as their secretary and PA. I knew she had left the chambers and for three years had called her to see if she would come and join me. I wondered if a fourth call was worth it, and with encouragement from Ainsley gave it one last shot, finally getting the right result.

As an avowed petrol-head and racing fan, Denise bore the nickname Diesel. She hailed from West Auckland, a born and bred Westie. All Westies love V8s, black T-shirts and bare feet. Most bad crimes happen in West Auckland and it is rumoured there are bodies of murder victims buried everywhere around the Riverhead Forest out there.

Diesel drove a red 1987 convertible Corvette. As a true Westie, she chose one year to take a new sports exhaust system for the Corvette as a bonus. Wearing a ponytail and fit from her boxing classes regimen, she was to efficiency what sand is to a beach. She was an expert in shorthand and typing from her time as a court stenographer, but that was only the beginning of her skills. When working in chambers, she prepared first drafts of most legal documents, topping the skills of pretty much every junior lawyer in the city. She was savvy, too: holding down three jobs when she first started working allowed her to accumulate a portfolio of residential and commercial properties.

Diesel shared her life with at least six cats, the number swelling occasionally depending on the number of transients. An assemblage of cat-themed objects, pictures and cartoons surrounded her workstation, the most prominent being the image of a cat looking inside the book *To Kill a Mockingbird* and saying to himself, "WTF? There's nothing in here about killing birds."

Very soon after she started, Diesel was finishing my sentences and could read my handwriting, a crippled style ever since I can remember; even I found it hard to read. She was invaluable in assisting with all facets of cases: strategically, preparing documentation, conducting research, handling clients, liaising with agents and managing fees. I knew I couldn't handle the high-level cases of the future without her.

Scrambling to assemble further evidence before returning to Europe and accordingly misplacing documents, I resorted to my default position: "*Diesel!* Where's the authority document for that Irish claimant?"

"It's right there," came the ever-calm response. It surprised me then, and still does, how Diesel can immediately find particular documents within leviathan files, plus source historical filings pinpointing the exactly required reference.

I drew up the leather-backed stool to the bar. The enthusiastic welcome from the Hotel du Rhône barman was largely lost on me this evening. I was still thinking about word I had received from Randy just after I arrived in Switzerland. There were murmurings that the US Attorney's Office might try and seize the funds I had already frozen at BNP Paribas Geneva.

Ordinarily not a problem: you want prosecution authorities to act, as your victims should benefit from subsequent distributions. In this instance, however, without my freezing of the account the funds would have disappeared into the fraudsters' coffers. Furthermore, I needed control of the funds as I was on a contingency fee, seven-and-a-half per cent of the amount recovered plus my usual daily rate and disbursements.

If the American authorities had the funds, there were two issues. One, they had no legal obligation to return funds to investors; they could be absorbed by the US government consolidated fund and my victim group would receive nothing. Two, if they did decide to distribute they could do it directly to the victims and take fees for the privilege. Either way, there would be no contingency fee for me.

The following morning I met Jean-Cédric in his offices and explained what I'd heard. "There's no way the funds will leave Switzerland," he said categorically. "Let's check with the judge, though, to make sure," he added.

Jean-Cédric's first calls in French appeared to have been fielded by the judge's underlings. After a longish pause, there was dialogue between my assisting counsel and the judge who had blocked the bank accounts. Concluding the call, Jean-Cédric swivelled his plush high-backed leather chair towards me in. "The judge says, as there is a Swiss seizure order in place the bank cannot release the funds to the Americans."

Well, that couldn't be any clearer, I thought, as my Swiss colleague and I left the law offices and took the brief walk to a cafe nestled in a cobbled city square.

Two days later I received the bad news. The money, which I now knew totalled seven-and-a-half million US dollars, had gone. The US government had grabbed the funds pursuant to a Mutual Legal Assistance Request to the Swiss government. Such requests are legal devices whereby governments can get assistance from each other in criminal matters.

An urgent meeting with my Swiss associates produced shrugs, head-scratching and murmurings of discontent, but nothing concrete in terms of potential remedial steps. The funds were in the US and any recourse had to be sought there.

The issue was one of competing legal orders: whether a Mutual Legal Assistance Request could supersede a country's domestic order. It was a vexed question of international law. None of the academic nuance interested me in the slightest: what did was that the millions I had seized for my clients were now in another jurisdiction.

The answer to what was a serious problem lay in New York and that's where I headed. As it's only a twenty-hour diversion I went back to Auckland first. I got Diesel to get banking-law research underway, as I wanted to look at the liability of Chase Manhattan Bank in New York who held the First Equity account. Wherever we might find gold, that's where we'd dig.

The potential legal liability of Chase Manhattan turned on the bank-transfer documentation. When victims sent bank-transfer instructions to pay funds, the telegraphic transfer instruction specified the beneficiary as First Equity, but also included the instruction "For further credit to" and specified the victim's name. Our argument was that the instruction on the transfers was such that it created an obligation on the bank to protect the funds for the client's benefit, or otherwise reject the deposit.

I jetted back to New York. This time I stayed in midtown Manhattan near the banking lawyers I had sussed out. Bryan Skarlatos, a specialist in banking law, was acting for one of the American victims of the fraud and had commenced proceedings against the bank. We hooked up at his Manhattan office and debated the respective merits of taking action.

We discussed the mechanics of my client group possibly joining his action. Armed with a view as to the likelihood of success and the potential ramifications of an adverse finding, I consulted with my group's committee.

Taking on banks is like hunting in bear country; you wonder if your gun is big enough and whether you have enough ammo. After due consideration it was decided the risk of a group mauling remained a tad high.

I commuted over to Brooklyn to see a line-up of assistant US attorneys. I complained loudly about what had happened and reiterated strongly that but for my steps in Switzerland, there would not have been any funds recovered; the fraudsters would have got their greedy paws on them. I tabled that in the interests of fairness, the funds should be disbursed to me for ultimate distribution to my clients. There was a nodding acquiescence that this sounded right, but no commitments.

Tactically it was a difficult situation. Did I litigate in the US courts against the US government and challenge the veracity of the order, or should I try to get a negotiated arrangement with the Justice Department? As the US is not averse to invading countries on a whim, I considered that taking them head-on might not be the smartest move.

The criminal prosecution mounted by the US authorities ground on, progressively crushing each player in the fraud game. A pretty face provided no immunity. Polina Sirotina was the operation's chief financial officer. Her perfectly manicured fingers pulled the financial levers. She diverted the savings of unwitting victims to the various criminal participants who used the money for personal gain — cars, boats, apartments, art, antiques, travel, investments — or simply spent it. Sirotina considered herself to be a fine creature, and few would argue with that. Fine creatures need finery: hers was furs and jewellery. Half a million dollars' worth in a year was her threshold.

Eight individuals — including Koudachev, Fauci, Mekhtiev and Sirotina — were charged with mail and wire-fraud conspiracy, mail fraud, making false statements and money-laundering conspiracy in connection with the loss of a hundred million dollars. Gary Farberov pleaded guilty to money-laundering conspiracy on 7 December 2001.

During the hearings FBI Assistant Director-in-Charge Kevin P. Donovan was moved to state: "Deceit, deception and duplicity were the ethical standards by which these defendants operated. This investigation has revealed a mountain of false representations and sham transactions used by the defendants to defraud the investing public."

Convictions were secured against all defendants, who were sentenced to prison terms ranging from five to fourteen-and-a-half years. Negotiations with the US Attorney's Office regarding the funds I had frozen took about three years. During that time I appeared in the US courts and argued my victims group's case for a direct distribution in support of what were very civil and productive negotiations. To facilitate the decision, I drafted and submitted to the courts a distribution agreement outlining how the paying out of funds would work. This was ultimately accepted and the total funds were forwarded to me. I appointed forensic accountant Dennis Parsons to accept the funds on my behalf and carry out the logistics of paying each victim their pro-rata share.

The result was professionally pleasing. Satisfaction stemmed from being able to snatch stolen funds from the mouth of an international organised-crime syndicate with a small team based at the bottom of the world.

◀ TWENTY ▶

"My client wants his money back."

WARDEN CONSULTING LIMITED WAS INCORPORATED in Auckland in July 1995. With the amount of investigation work coming to me as a barrister, the idea was to channel this work through the company and grow an entity which would have value. The company obtained private-investigation and security-consultant licences. Through its life, the company's primary focus was investigation, but over time this also expanded into elite uniform-security services.

From the beginning I developed a particular focus on covert operations, specifically undercover work. My own history had shown how effective such operations are at producing evidence which is virtually irrefutable, subject to evidential and procedural compliance.

I structured a corporate undercover programme based on the police programme but adapted for the private sector. When senior corporate managers get wind of serious criminal offending within their organisations, the deployment of an undercover agent into the heart of the suspected problem will produce valuable intelligence.

There are two primary ways operations can go: evidential or intelligence. Evidential is like my police operation where stolen property or drugs are bought directly from the offenders. The transactions are recorded in statements and exhibits managed with a view to future arrests and prosecution. Where appropriate, corroborative evidence might be obtained through wires or surveillance of the transactions. Police co-operation and assistance is required when the operation terminates, but this is always forthcoming as it means quality arrests without initially having to gather evidence. The police are there for the execution of search warrants and the interviews.

Wardens conducted the country's biggest private-sector undercover operation in 2002-03 on behalf of NZ Post. It was evidential in nature, with three agents deployed over an eighteen-month period. The agents — Jackal, Raptor and Wolf — worked as couriers there and were able to get alongside targets, ultimately purchasing one-and-a-half million dollars' worth of property stolen from the postal network.

When the operation terminated, ninety police worked on the case with twenty-one search warrants executed simultaneously at addresses throughout New Zealand. Twenty-five people faced the courts, charged with property and drug offences. All pleaded guilty due to the overwhelming evidence.

The second type of operation is intelligence. In an evidential operation the agent is disclosed as having been deployed and is often fronted before the offenders. With intelligence there is never any disclosure an operation existed. The agent will be dropped into the organisation, gather information and then simply leave when the operation is completed. Other investigative techniques can then be adopted to sanction targets such as surveillance, covert cameras or other technical means.

Over time, this has become the preferred course of the business community. Emphasis has also shifted from theft and drugs to business intelligence. The driver is questions such as: What is happening in my business? Do our systems work? Are our employees safe? Are our managers effective? Who is thieving time? Who are the disaffected? Who is undermining the business? Who is supportive? What improvements can be made?

Clever executives love the tactic. There is no dilution about what is happening. What's delivered up from the agent is one hundred per cent accurate; from the horse's mouth. Crime is still important, but operational emphasis is around forty per cent as opposed to historical levels of eighty to ninety per cent. A properly tailored operation will net evidence of crime in any event.

For years Wardens has sourced and trained undercover agents. Generally, new agents are referred from colleagues and associates. They are initially screened by a series of "rough" interviews by senior Wardens staff.

These are designed to put pressure on the candidate. You want to flush out uncertainty or potential weakness in a male agent? Use a woman, preferably more than one. She'll see things in his character even he didn't know about.

If they make it through the interviews, they will be psychologically screened by Mantis, our consultant clinical psychologist. Mantis is a good mate. With us from the beginning, he understands the business. He was a former police detective himself before he started mending broken minds, and we spent a considerable amount of time identifying desirable covert operative traits. I trust his judgement and ongoing monitoring of agents.

If they get past the Mantis, the next step is live training. Only then will we let them loose operationally.

With eight operations under his belt, Jackal was the company's most successful agent. An auto-electrician by trade, tough, uncompromising, with an abundance of street credibility, he adapted seamlessly to each scene.

After three rings Jackal answered his cell phone. "Jackal, it's Emu, I'm in need of your particular talents."

"Yeah, mate, what's up?"

"A spin to Oz to nail a fraudster."

"Cool, when?"

"Tomorrow."

I'd had a call from a finance company client who had funded a car dealer to the tune of four hundred grand secured over motor vehicles. The problem was, he had decided he'd had enough of New Zealand and car dealing, so thought he might use the money for himself. He also had a nineteen-year-old girlfriend he needed to impress.

The word was that the target, Mr Harrison, had fled to Australia with his big bag of cash. The trail was hot, as inquiries at his address revealed he had left the day before. Contacts confirmed he had left Auckland on an Air New Zealand flight bound for Sydney. Bank inquiries revealed he had transferred the four hundred thousand to an account in Sydney. Through their fraud unit, I dealt with bank management. After some discussion, the bank agreed to freeze the account on the basis of money laundering and an indemnity from my client.

Jackal and I jumped on a plane to Sydney. As we emerged from Customs, I received a call from the Sydney bank manager. "Our man's been in trying to withdraw his funds. He turned up at our Glenelg branch in Adelaide this morning. I instructed the manager to tell him to come back later in the afternoon and the cash would be arranged."

"That's great, thanks. I'll get to Adelaide as soon as possible. If he turns up can your manager continue to stall him?"

"Yeah, we'll try."

I purchased tickets for the next flight to Adelaide. Luckily, we had to wait only about half an hour for the short flight — I was concerned that the delays might have spooked our prey and he wouldn't turn up back at the bank.

As soon as I turned my phone back on after arrival in Adelaide, it rang. "He's at the branch now," said the manager breathlessly.

"Okay. Try and stall him. I'm on my way."

Jackal and I ran to the Avis rental car counter, snatched the keys to a Commodore and ran out to the car park. Tyres screeching, we came sideways out of the airport exit. We did the fifteen-minute trip in seven.

As we braked into the seaside village of Glenelg, the phone went again. "He's left the bank," said the manager.

"Shit, the game might be up. I'll call you back," I replied quickly.

Engine heat and the smell of brake pads crept into the Commodore cabin as we drove slowly along the street. On the right three blocks up I could see the illuminated bank sign. There was an ATM machine in a shop front immediately opposite the bank.

We had only a description of Mr Harrison, a portly German male in his forties. His companion: nineteen, slim with long blonde hair.

A couple fitting the description were standing by the ATM. The male, looking quizzically at the machine, was inserting and removing a bank card.

"Fuck, Jackal," I said, "that's gotta be him."

Fortuitously, there was a vacant car park on the street right where the ATM was. Jackal slid the car into the park. The passenger's window glided down.

"Mr Harrison!" I called to the suspect, who was a mere couple of metres from the car.

His head jerked back in shock, confirming his identity. The girlfriend took a couple of steps around behind her suitor.

I followed up with, "My client wants his money back."

"Um, ah, how did you find me?" Harrison stuttered.

"Might pay if you jump in the car and we can discuss the situation," I said, alighting from the car and opening the rear passenger's door.

Visibly disturbed with his hands slightly shaking, Harrison got into the car. His girlfriend, trying to invoke a cloak of invisibility and pulling down on her short skirt, joined him.

"This is not a good situation, Mr Harrison," I said solemnly. The statement was met with a slow nod by both back-seat occupants.

"But it is simple. You have two options. Either we go across the road to the bank and you send the money back to my client, or we can go the three blocks down to the police station."

After a longish pause came, "I think I'd like to go to the bank," in a quiet voice.

"Very sensible," I said. "Let's go then."

I led the pair across the road. Jackal remained behind us, gently reminding them of his presence. Ushered into the manager's office, Harrison sat in front of the manager's desk. I'd been dealing with the Sydney manager so hadn't spoken with this banker. Wishing to protect himself, he adopted a formal approach. Looking at Harrison he said, "Now are you sure you wish to make this transfer back to New Zealand?"

"Yes," replied the German fraudster.

"You're absolutely sure?" pressed the manager.

Any more of this and our man might become fortified and think he doesn't have to comply, I thought. Stationed standing behind the manager, I looked Harrison in the eye and nodded, reminding him of his obligations.

"Yes, I'm sure," he said, then added to me, "I'll have no money if it all goes back. Do you think I could keep a few thousand just to survive?"

Yes, he is fortified, I thought, but not enough to be damaging.

"I'm sure my client would authorise the retention of ten thousand dollars."

Hell, my client was getting virtually all his money back. Throw the dog a bone and have an unimpeded transfer. And that was it, done deal.

◀ TWENTY-ONE ▶

"Something bad has happened with the case."

"You remember what happened to the tiger?" said the Irishman.

"Yes," said his lawyer, extending the word to give it emphasis. "Do you really think we should be talking about this here?"

"Yeah, it's no problem. Even if it is recorded and translated they won't follow up on it."

The recording device in the Taiwanese jail interview room silently captured the discussion.

"PC has crossed a line that doesn't get crossed. There are consequences for that, which he well knows. A call needs to go out to our man in Amsterdam," said the Irishman.

"You sure?" asked the lawyer.

"Of course I'm fucking sure. A message needs to be sent," said the Irishman venomously.

Stephen Cook was the puppet master of an extensive fraud scheme spanning the globe, but based across Thailand, Malaysia and the Philippines. His deception had earned him close to half a billion dollars. He used two women to look after the fruits of his efforts. Each controlled a hundred million dollars, ran their own money-laundering operation and were protected by hand-picked security teams of former Special Forces operators.

He was one of the world's top boiler-room operators, a boiler-room being the telephone sales room of a fraud operation where calls are made promoting investments. (The tactics are high-pressure, hence the term boiler-room.) The purported high-return investments being promoted are fraudulent.

I was acting for two victim groups who had been deprived of funds by

Cook, one based in New Zealand comprising mainly Kiwis and Aussies, plus a European group sprinkled with South Africans. I made a global tour cementing the groups. Diesel made arrangements for me to meet victims in Bangkok, Penang, London, Frankfurt and Johannesburg.

The total losses from both groups was a touch over fifty-five million dollars. Cook had overstayed his welcome in South-east Asia and was looking for a new base. He chose Taiwan.

He made one fundamental mistake in travelling there, following an advance guard of his minions: he used detectably false documents to enter the country. I had been tipped off by a former CIA agent familiar with the case. We knew when he was travelling and alerted the Taiwanese police. Cook was snapped at Taoyuan airport and held in custody.

He wouldn't be in jail long on the passport charge. Long enough, however, to prepare and submit evidence supporting an international fraud case. The idea was to submit the case, pressure him with the prospect of a long prison term in Taiwan and drive him to settle with my client groups.

I flew into the bustle of Taipei and met with the local police. After deliberations on the merits of the case, I was referred to Taipei prosecutor Josie Hsu. A tiny woman in her early thirties, she had an excellent command of English and quickly grasped the fundamentals of the case. She arranged for an urgent translation of my clients' affidavits. After an appropriate assessment by the authorities, charges of international fraud were laid against Cook.

He remained in jail for a couple of months, but as it transpired the fraud charges levelled against him carried a maximum sentence of only ten years in prison. Under Taiwanese law he could in these circumstances apply for bail. We knew that if Cook was bailed he would flee Taiwan. His resources meant he already had plans afoot to be spirited out of the country by private jet: my CIA contact had confirmed that Cook's associates were on standby and false documents had been prepared.

The situation was tricky. Any leverage we may have had concerning continuing incarceration had evaporated. Creativity needed to be applied to this situation. We knew that there had been a falling-out between Cook and one of his lieutenants, Philip Cole. Cole was head broker and a pivotal player in Cook's worldwide fraud schemes, but had decided to make off with the client list. This list is central to any boiler-room or Ponzi scheme, and contains individuals who, through profiling and initial contact, are identified as susceptible to being scammed. Among the cardinal sins of fraudsters, stealing the list is at the top.

Even though he was a fraudster, Cook was not shy about using extreme violence to further his ends. Although it was never proved, there were suspicions he had arranged the killing of an associate, Tiger Travis. A Thai assassin riding pillion on the back of a motorcycle fired two bullets into Travis's head when he was stopped at lights in central Bangkok. He was dead before his head dropped to the steering wheel.

It was worth talking to Cole as he could have information of value. Expanding our range of inquiries, I asked the police whether there was any bugging of Cook's communications. An affirmative response meant a good line of inquiry and possible paydirt. The discussions between Cook and his lawyer had been recorded. It didn't take long to pick up the chat about "what happened to the tiger" and a potential hit on Cole. The talk of attempted murder meant the chance of laying more serious charges against Cook. Charges which carried life imprisonment, meaning Cook's bail would be refused.

I discussed the prospect of further charges with prosecutor Josie. "Yes, we can lay further charges," she said, "but we need evidence from Philip Cole. We need as a minimum a full statement from him and he must agree to come to Taiwan and give evidence at trial."

"So when you get the statement you will go ahead and charge Cook with attempted murder?"

"Yes, if the evidence in the statement is good enough."

It was a race against time. I had to find Cole, get him to co-operate, get him committed to writing and get him to agree to testify against his former boss. All before Cook was bailed on the passport charges. Hell, it couldn't be that hard, I thought, trying to minimise the magnitude of the task.

The "our man in Amsterdam" Cook mentioned was a Dutch hitman named van Os, nicknamed Axe either because he looked like a six-foot five shaven-headed axeman or because an axe was his purported weapon of choice. Either way, he had devised a plan to kill Cole. He would rig the brakes on Cole's pickup truck so they failed on one of his regular trips over the hill between Phuket Town and Patong beach — the very hill I'd spent so much time running on.

The plan, however, went astray. At the last minute Axe changed his mind. The reasons were not clear. Perhaps he'd found God, maybe the stars weren't aligned, more likely he'd reviewed the merits of being in the employ of Cook. Anyway, Axe sat down with Cole and gave him the good news about his life being potentially shortened.

My CIA contact had turned up a number for Cole. It's always dicey making initial contact with a witness, especially with heightened pressure to get a comprehensive and quick result.

"Paris, I'll only meet in Paris," Cole spat.

As if that was an issue. It didn't worry me — I'd go anywhere in the world to meet him.

"Bon soir," muttered the muscled security guard as I exited the Westin hotel in central Paris. A red Security armband adorned his perfectly tailored back suit. I flipped up my collar against the cold night, folded my arms and set off towards the Place Vendôme.

Looming larger as I approached was the column atop which stood a statue of Napoleon. The monument dominates this section of Paris. The Ritz hotel sits on the edge of the square. Its opulence is manifested throughout the cobbled square, which is dotted with high-end fashion boutiques and jewellery stores. Walking past the Ferrari and Lamborghini parked out front, I looked through the main entrance at the foyer's revolving doors. Doors through which Princess Diana walked for the last time, before her life was cruelly extinguished in the Pont de l'Alma tunnel car crash. I nodded respectfully before moving on.

At Rue Daunou I took a right and walked the hundred metres to Harry's New York Bar, which I had suggested as a meeting point. The iconic, century-old joint had contributed in no small way to the planet's drinking culture by inventing the Bloody Mary.

The back corner booth provided a perfect view of the door and adjacent bar. My order of a Brooklyn lager was met with enthusiasm by the white-tunic-clad waiter. "Très bon, an excellent choice, monsieur." Overflowing with vim and theatrical gestures, he wheeled and half-skipped back to the bar. Pennants of US universities were pinned around the walls; at eye level were old crests of English academia.

From surveillance photos, I recognised Cole as he entered the bar. Momentarily stopping at the door, his blinking eyes flickered around the bar. Skinny, almost junkie-skinny, with pale jeans twisted at his waist, he looked like a hunted animal — which of course he was. I observed him for about five minutes before approaching him. Back in the booth, we discussed his predicament. He was more open than I expected, born of resentment at being targeted.

"I never thought that prick would try and have me taken out," he said. "He thinks he's omnipotent. He's lost the plot — the high life and money have fried him. He's like the master manipulator, deceiving everyone so he doesn't know what the truth is any more. He started bullshitting us doing the job, just like the hapless pricks we were taking for a ride. I tell you, man, I'm pretty pissed off about what's happened."

Cole's attitude and tenor was exactly what I wanted. I had to get a statement while he was still of a mind to assist. Following gentle encouragement he agreed to come back to the hotel to do a statement. We sat for around five hours and I teased out the details of his relationship with Cook and the attempt on his life. He left promising to return the next morning. I rang Diesel back in New Zealand to dictate the statement. She formatted and emailed it back. After two drafts it was ready for signing.

In the early hours the phone rang. It was Ainsley. Even though I'd just been jolted from a deep sleep I could tell by her voice something was wrong. "What is it?" I asked.

"I got this weird call from Phil Grace. He said he needed to meet me urgently but not at the chambers. I got into the city as soon as I could and we met at that cafe in Vulcan Lane."

Phil wasn't one to grandstand or exaggerate. He wouldn't summon Ainsley in this manner without serious justification. "What did he say?" I asked, trying to sound calm.

"He said he had been contacted by someone in the intelligence world who said you need to be very careful over there."

"Fuck, I already know that," I croaked sleepily. "What's the nature of the threat?"

"I pressed him really hard but he didn't come up with anything specific."

I snapped, "It's a bit hard to meet a risk when you don't even know its form."

"I know," said Ainsley in a small voice. "All it's done is make me really worried. It might have been better if he hadn't said anything."

I felt a spike of fear. I hated hearing my wife's fear and vulnerability. "Please don't worry," I said, mustering a crumb of confidence. "Just be careful. Keep a closer eye on the kids and do counter when you're moving about. Remember, the shotgun is under the bed. Don't give second chances with people around the house, especially at night."

"Yes, okay," came Ainsley's quiet reply.

"I just wish I was back there," I said.

"Love you," came the delayed response.

"Love you too."

I had no idea where the threat had come from. With the number of cases I had done, even tracking back to my police days, there were a number of potential problem sources. As it happened I learned nothing more about this threat and never found what it was about.

Risk was a factor attaching to the life I had chosen but that was my call. My real concern was what might happen to my wife and children. Ainsley knew and accepted the risks — but our children were innocents in the game.

I am always jumpy that a witness may not return and commit to signing their statement. Cole, however, was there right on the agreed time. He signed at a cafe around the corner from the Westin overlooking the Tuileries Garden on Rue de Rivoli.

Josie accepted the statement gratefully and Cook was charged as planned. Doing a deal was back on the table. To try to facilitate this, I sought the help of the New Zealand government through diplomatic channels. This resulted in my meeting the Taiwanese minister of justice. Although the minister and his office could offer no promises of help, it perfectly positioned the case.

About three weeks later I received a call from Josie. I was pleased to hear from her, as it meant there must have been a development.

"Something bad has happened with the case," she said down the crackling phone line.

"What do you mean? What's happened?"

"Mr Cook is dead."

"Dead? How?"

"He was found dead in his cell yesterday morning. We are still waiting for information on the cause of death."

It didn't matter to me how he died. Heart attack, snake bite, boredom, or perhaps Cole got him. Dead was dead. With Cook's death, the chances of recovery died along with him.

◀ TWENTY-TWO ▶

"Trust comes on foot but leaves on horseback."

"From the inquiries we've done so far," said the chairman, "it looks like he's flogged about a hundred thousand."

"If that's what you've picked up, it could well be ten times that, around a million," I replied.

This deflated the chairman somewhat, but it was counter-productive to try to soften the blow. Experience showed that initially detected losses would inevitably translate to around ten times the amount in actual offending. This was hard to swallow and the formula was sometimes met with scepticism, but it meant that he and his audit team would keep looking.

Winston McKay, the chair of Westlake Finance, was sixty-five and had the bearing of an American bald eagle, complete with a shiny pate and a ring of tufty hair which extended from ear to ear. He wore a black pinstripe suit. The stripes were slightly wider than the norm, giving it a contemporary feel. His blood-red tie was slightly askew at the neck, giving him a formal but jaunty look.

"If you can't look after yourself, how can clients expect us to look after their money?" was one of Winston's favourite sayings, which he would preach to his forty-five employees. A self-made man, he had built up a sizeable empire comprising merchant banking, stockbroking and financial advice. A money man to the core, his expertise was built on a strong academic footing: a BCom from Auckland University, a master's in economics from Oxford and an MBA from Yale. He'd cut his fiscal teeth as a young trader in Switzerland.

"Really!" he said in a clipped manner betraying his English roots. "That's no good at all and leaves me more than slightly aggrieved." He tugged at his cuff-linked shirtsleeves. "The man should be hanged."

The man he was referring to was Max Delaney, general manager of Westlake Finance for the past decade. Winston looked upon Max fondly, like a son, a member of his family. Betrayal affects people in different ways, but it is always wholly unsavoury to witness.

There is a Dutch saying: *Vertrouwen komt te voet, maar gaat te paard* ("Trust comes on foot but leaves on horseback") meaning it takes time to gain trust, but it can be lost quickly. Being ripped off by his trusted lieutenant touched Winston with bewilderment, deflation, confusion and sadness.

"What are the next steps?" he asked.

"I need a rundown on exactly what Max has been doing. In the meantime we will undertake a complete background on him and I suggest a period of surveillance. See what he's up to, where he's going, who he's meeting. You and your audit team need to keep looking, further explore his MO and try to get to a quantum of the loss," I replied.

Two hours later I left Westlake Finance's Queen Street office and headed for the Auckland Harbour Bridge. No matter how many times you cross it on a sunny day, the glistening beauty of the harbour and CBD backdrop never disappoints. Straight up the northern motorway is Albany. Exiting at Greville Road I skirted through to Triton Drive. As you roll up Triton the Warden Consulting logo comes into focus on the left. The gold-and-blue six-point star is emblazoned on three sides of the modern office building.

In the car park were marked vehicles. A black customised Jeep Wrangler, stars on the doors with Investigation & Security signage and a matching liveried Ford Ranger Ute. Diesel's red Corvette was in its usual space, as was Ainsley's violet Porsche 911. Poised, rather than parked, was my latest acquisition, a black Dodge Viper. How such a beast legally made it into production is a mystery. Fire-breathing excess power made it almost impossible to drive. I liked it.

Punching the code into the black security door beneath a watchful CCTV camera, I entered the large open-plan office area. A regular sweep ensured that the premises remained eavesdropping-device free. The smiling Bee greeted me. Hailing from Cape Town, at twenty-six she had a master's degree in resource management. Petite and pretty, she possessed an unerring ability to receive and assimilate information. A licensed private investigator, Bee had developed rapidly, moving into briefing and preparing evidence for fraud cases.

Ainsley sat at her desk in the corner intently tapping her computer keys. Behind her on the wall was a black-framed contemporary art piece acquired on a recent art tour in Venice.

Diesel's work station in the middle of the office allowed her a complete survey of the bustle.

Against the far wall, Raven sat on her perch. A specialist in supply-chain losses, she brought a feisty, tenacious and persistent attitude to her PI role. Attractive, diminutive, with a brutal sense of humour, Raven would entertain the office, recounting her latest suspect interview success complete with nuggets of profanity. In fact, swearing often floated on the office air conditioning and was not frowned upon. Political correctness was a foreign concept within the office walls.

"Stingray's here for the briefing," said Diesel.

"Okay, let's get this thing done," I replied.

My daughter Charlotte was seated facing Triton Drive fielding a call from Australia on an industrial-espionage matter. From the look on her face, the issue was either frustrating or difficult. Perhaps it was both. She was code-named Horse after a 1960s TV puppet character called Charlie Horse. The moniker was first attached by my Dad, her doting Poppa. Over time it was shortened.

Charlotte had followed my footsteps into the law and had risen to become Warden's investigations manager and a specialist investigating lawyer. She held a practising certificate as a barrister having been admitted to the bar on 28 October 2011. As an extremely proud dad, I moved her admission in the Auckland High Court before Justice Christian Whaata.

The business was in Horse's veins. She had grown up surrounded by operational planning discussions, erudite pontifications on the law, visits from undercover agents, urgent travel and late-night sojourns.

At fifteen she ventured with me to the US, the UK and Switzerland on a fraud case. She met international lawyers and bankers. This included sitting at a dinner in Gland, south of Geneva, where three of the four guests were billionaires. By seventeen she was working on audits and learning her craft. While still in her twenties she controlled major national and multinational clients, managed some thirty staff including surveillance and undercover agents, had both investigated and acted as legal counsel on major frauds and was tapped into an international network of former spies and Special Forces operators. Few of her contemporaries held such power. One string-pull of her delicate young fingers could destroy lives.

Horse's brother Ben, aka Silver Snake, started even younger. At six months old the fledgling agent was used as cover for his mother who led a multi-agent national undercover operation gathering intelligence. With his pram as transport, there were no worries about his compromising the job by saying the wrong thing.

Sitting beside Raven discussing the collation of investigation files was Kitten. One of the new breed at twenty years old, fresh-faced, tall and slim, the classic "girl next door", she had started on trial but showed considerable promise and was appointed as a trainee investigator. A cackle of laughter indicated amusement somewhere in the body of files.

The reader might now be thinking, That sounds like a lot of women in a male-dominated industry. Such a reflection would be correct. Women excel in a confidential inquisitorial environment. Loyalty, a fundamental to any trust-based environment, is pledged more easily and completely by a woman. Couple that with intuition, vision, commitment, cunning, attention to detail, a collaborative approach and viciousness — voilà, the perfect private investigator. Estrogen is not always the answer, however. Muscle can be good... very good. A pinch of intimidation goes a long way. And there is always a place at the table for a hard-bitten former detective.

"Right," I said, wheeling a whiteboard in front of the board table.

Seated were Horse, Diesel, Bee and surveillance expert Stingray. As a former detective, he had a wealth of experience, including within the police undercover programme. He had operated two agents with considerable success. Aside from surveillance, his discretion and skill meant he was used on sensitive "black operations". Slim, his greying hair bleached from surfing under the Queensland sun, he had just jetted in from Brisbane. He had an endearing and distinctive habit of speaking with pauses between his sentences. The quirk somehow highlighted the importance of whatever he was saying. Everyone liked Stingray.

"We're dealing with a fraud case at a local finance operation, Westlake Finance," I said. The meeting participants leaned forward over their notepads. "Our suspect is the GM, Max Delaney. It appears he is using a number of MOs, including diverting client investments to himself, setting up ghost employees and establishing fictitious vendors. We're not at a quantum yet, but it's gonna be decent. The suspect is unaware he is under investigation so we have the opportunity to dive into an initial covert phase. Stingray, we will need two-up coverage from first thing until lights out. Diesel will complete your op orders with addresses, photos and the usual by the end of the day."

"Okay, I'll kick off the recce tomorrow," Stingray said. "Any issues with his home address — dogs or anything?"

"No dogs, but it's a good address in a quiet no-exit street. Exposure could be an issue, so you'll have to become invisible, like you usually do. He has no surveillance awareness that we know of, but this joker's a decent thief who is still offending, so we need to be aware. The property has CCTV but it's limited. His wheels are a black late-model Range Rover, plate Kilo, Alpha, Yankee, Three, Six, One. He is married with three teenage kids. The missus drives a green Land Rover Discovery, personalised plate Papa, Echo, Tango. Don't know what that's about, maybe she's the *Penthouse* kind."

"Okay, no problem. Duration?"

"Let's kick off with a week and see what intel we pull up. If it's looking good, we'll run another week. The key will be who he's meeting, to identify anyone else who's complicit, and where he's going to get a bead on where the ill-gotten gains are. Financial institutions and unknown addresses. If we even look like being burned, pull off him so we don't compromise any later steps. Horse will be your point of contact."

"Yep, sweet. We'll get it done."

"Diesel, we need a full background on this joker. Personal, credit, directorships, corporate links, real estate, cars, boats, investments and associates. Let's do the wife too. She might be holding investments and real estate on his behalf."

"Are we going to go as far as an I2 chart?" What Diesel was referring to was an Intelligence Analysis chart.

"Not at this stage. We may need to later, dependent upon what unfolds."

Diesel scratched a shorthand note in response. The edge of a crinkled wrapper peeped out from under her pad, evidence of her favourite delicacy, chocolate.

"Bee, could you attend to the social-media inquiries?"

The question was met with a silent nod.

"Facebook and the usual platforms. We need to monitor them all. Let's also grab all postings coming from the subject address. Tie him up like a gnat's arse."

With Winston's audit completed, we reviewed the findings and suggested a few further steps including the pulling of our target's email traffic. The quantum of loss came in at one-and-a-quarter million dollars, in line with predictions.

Learning of the final figure did nothing to alter Winston's mood. "Can we get the money back?" he implored. "Plus I want his head, I want him in jail," he added, accompanied by heightened sleeve-tugging.

"We'll do our best to get it back. In a negotiated arrangement we don't usually get a recovery and jail. If the target is facing jail, there's no incentive to pay it back. Avoiding jail is the leverage. Let's face it; any white-collar criminal is a scaredy-cat when it comes to prison."

Facebook monitoring turned up Delaney planning a holiday to Hawaii with his wife and children. Subsequent posts confirmed a return date of 10 June. Winston confirmed the leave period but was not aware of the overseas travel.

Diesel unearthed real estate we were unaware of: a modern beach house at Omaha Beach north of Auckland. Weirdly, it was held in Delaney's own name, meaning we could put a charge over it without any issues. The icing on the cake was that the property was unencumbered — no mortgage. An estimated value of one million was the third hit.

The surveillance had been on foot for a bit over a week. My cell phone buzzed with Stingray's moniker appearing as the caller.

"Hey, mate, how's it going?"

"Yeah, good. Hey, this target has led us a merry dance. He's just taken us from Albany across the top to out west. Had plenty of pace on, cracked the speed limit the whole way. As you know, if he's going quick we have to fly. Had to crash cherries in the suburbs, but got over here in one piece. Anyway, we're now propped at a boat-builder. I have eyes on our boy in the yard walking around what's a pretty decent powerboat. Looks like the build is nearly finished. If that's his, which it looks like from the interaction with the boat-builder, it's gotta be three or four hundred grand."

"Good work, mate. Brilliant. That thing's now in the recovery pot. Might have to get in a bit of fishing in the gulf before we liquidate it!"

I had a roundtable with Winston, brought him up to speed with the inquiry and recommended grabbing Max at the airport on his return from Hawaii. Winston agreed with the approach and finally emitted a wry smile at the disclosed assets position.

As 10 June loomed we were ready to move on our target. By virtue of a Caveat Against Dealings we had locked down the Omaha property. Discreet inquiries with the boat-builder revealed Delaney as the owner of the identified boat valued at three hundred and seventy-five thousand dollars. It had been fully paid for apart from around thirty-five thousand dollars. I had briefed the police Company Fraud Unit about what we were doing in case their support was required.

An obese file had been prepared covering each fraudulent transaction and the relevant supporting documentation. I had distilled the evidence down and compiled an interview plan including prepared questions. Corridors of questioning would hopefully lead to admissions. In most instances, in the face of incontrovertible evidence, a denial is as good as an admission. As far as possible, the target had been profiled and the temperature of the interview would be set to best match his personality and likely leverage points.

Stingray and one other surveillance operative were stationed at the airport to pick up the suspect upon arrival. We also had an airport cop monitoring Customs to give us a heads-up when the family were being processed. To ensure privacy and allow the interview to take place at the airport, we had booked a conference room by the airport's main restaurant. Discreet access to the room was provided by a door immediately inside the entrance.

Max Delaney's world was about to implode. And he had no idea. Maybe thieving to fund the holiday, boat and extra property was worth it to him. All would be revealed with his conduct stripped bare and highlighted under the cold light of dispassionate scrutiny.

"They're coming out now," came Stingray's laconic call.

Max pushed a trolley laden with bags. His tan didn't hide an uncomfortable demeanour. A jacket to protect against the Auckland winter covered a bright Hawaiian shirt. His petite wife walked to his right wearing a fluffy hooded sweatshirt. The three offspring trailed their parents with teenage insouciance.

As the family reached the arrivals seating area, I approached the suspect. "Mr Delaney, my name is Mark van Leewarden. I wonder if we could speak."

His face dropped, followed by his head. "I wondered when you'd catch me," he said in a soft, tremulous voice.

"It may be best if your family go on home and we have a chat here," I said. "We can organise transport."

"Yes, yes, I'll advise my wife."

Stricken with a look of shock and confusion, Max's wife had heard the discussion. She offered no resistance to leaving her husband, no histrionics or cries for legal advice, which would have complicated matters. I was suddenly struck by the thought that she may be complicit in or at least aware of the offending.

Safely in the conference room, Max came clean on everything, even tacking on the theft of laptops, of which we were unaware. Almost immediately after sitting down came a tearful apology. After a full admission the mechanics of repayment were nutted out. Assets would be liquidated and we would take an unregistered mortgage over real estate to ensure compliance.

"So with this deal I won't be referred to the police or Serious Fraud Office?" said Max hopefully.

"Well, you know if you are, you'll spend a decent stint in prison."

"I don't know if I could handle that," he said, his bottom lip quivering.

While the fraudster was at a nice low ebb, I launched into my spiel. "My client is most appreciative of your assistance. Winston doesn't want blood, but wants you to bear some personal pain, just like he has experienced. In addition, of course, to making complete reparation, including the costs of the investigation.

"I think I could arrange for you to just be charged by the police with a small amount, say theft of ten grand. You would need to plead guilty. There would be no prison, just a sentence of something like community service. I think I could get Winston to accept this, as from his point of view you have been convicted and have a criminal conviction for dishonesty."

"Thanks," he replied miserably.

Winston would be pleased. He had received a complete recovery of his loss, plus a conviction for Max.

◀ TWENTY-THREE ▶

"This place is getting a hold on us."

THE CALL CAME IN FROM Seoul. "I'm prepared to meet," said the female voice. "Only at a neutral place, though. Nowhere in Asia and not New Zealand."

"Okay, that's no problem. I'm grateful you're prepared to have a chat," I replied, trying not to sound too enthusiastic. "I can be in London next week if that works for you."

"Of course. Just let me know when and where."

"Fine. I will come back to you with the details."

I disconnected the call with a smile, followed by an anticipatory hand-rubbing.

The caller was Lynda Park, wife of fraud offender Brian Collins. For a couple of months we had been trying to get Lynda to meet and provide information about her husband and his dealings. She was a key witness. The planned meeting was a breakthrough.

My client was Star Industries, a New York-based marketing company that made promotional products. Driven by low manufacturing costs, Star had their products made in Hong Kong, Taiwan and mainland China. Collins, an expat Kiwi, was their man in Hong Kong co-ordinating product manufacture: he was fluent in both Mandarin and Cantonese, having spent ten years operating in China. The Star office in Hong Kong had six employees all reporting to him. His right-hand woman and fraud co-offender was Zoe Yang, a Hong Kong national. They were partners in crime and love. He had left his wife Lynda for her. Lynda's percolating scorn had finally driven her into our camp.

Collins' deception was based on concealing from his employers the true costs of product manufacture. He would recommend to Star that a certain quote be accepted, yet would have another manufacturer make the product at a lesser cost. He would then render a false invoice in the name of the company with the high quote and direct payment to bank accounts controlled by Zoe and himself.

Payment would then be made to the lower-cost manufacturer and the difference pocketed. Star therefore were paying falsely inflated amounts for their product with the benefit going to Collins and Yang. The bank accounts to which the Star funds were paid were opened by Yang at HSBC in Hong Kong using false names styled to resemble true manufacturers. Through this technique they fraudulently obtained fifteen million US dollars over two-and-a-half years.

The principal of Star Industries was Virgil Miller. Also working in the business was Virgil's son Dylan. Joining his father after a career in commercial law, he brought youthful acuity to the business. Virgil had established Star right out of Columbia Business School. He didn't see much point in working for someone else. He'd do it himself. And that's what he did, creating a successful global company.

Virgil was brought up on a ranch outside Point Pleasant, West Virginia. He could drive a pickup truck at seven and was roping calves at nine. There aren't too many sissies in West Virginia. According to folklore, Point Pleasant was the home of the legendary Mothman, a man-sized bird-like creature sighted numerous times in the late Sixties. His arrival was supposedly linked to a bridge collapse that killed forty-six people. The Mothman legend was the subject of a 2002 film starring Richard Gere.

I visited Point Pleasant on a motorcycle trip in June 2012 and experienced the weirdness of the place first-hand. Accompanying me on that ride were Hornet, an old mate and a former Kiwi detective who had been very successful in the aviation business; John and Wayne, custom motorcycle builders from Galax, Virginia; Road Captain John from Indiana, a nonchalant ageing biker who loved the road; and Donnie, of West Virginia, one of life's genuine good guys.

Donnie, an engineer, knew how everything worked. Wiry with grey hair and a beard, he would wear some quirky cool hat whenever he was without a helmet. He had three favourite sayings which were delivered in his distinctive southern drawl: "Itta be awright", "Good God" and "Whaddya put in a burger in West Virginia? Ssslaawww."

About an hour out of Point Pleasant we stopped at a diner. Road Captain John had a map spread out on the footpath so people had to walk in a big arc to get around him. On hands and knees he was carefully examining the veins of roads. Wayne stood behind him. "Hey, Road Captain," he said. "That map's upside down."

"Fuck, no wonder we're lost."

We rode into Point Pleasant and lined the bikes up on the deserted main road. Our rag-tag collection of choppers and bobbers usually attracted attention, but not here. Walking up to what looked like the centre of the small town Hornet said, "There's something weird about this place, man. It's spooky." In unison everyone nodded assent.

Cautiously unhurried, like a line of sheep, we traipsed into the only diner on Main Street. Just enough stools meant we could all sit along the counter. Before us was a middle-aged waitress. She wore an old-school checked smock. Pinned on her front was a name tag… only it was without a name. Her red hair was curled Sixties-style. With small talk and efficiency born of considerable experience, she prepared our coffees and teas. The rest of the diner was empty.

"You know this story about the Mothman. Do you think he was real?" John asked her.

"Yes, of course!" she said emphatically, folding her arms.

"Did you see him?" asked Hornet.

"No, I was young then. Others saw him, though. He had a birdman body but a human face. One distinctive feature was burning red eyes. I *did* see the men in black. I remember them."

"What men in black?" probed Wayne.

"Well," she said, leaning forward conspiratorially. "They were all over the town. They came in black cars with tinted windows and were talking to people. This was when the Mothman was here and he caused the bridge collapse. They were also over at the old North Power Plant which was used as an ammunition factory during World War Two. That's where the

Mothman lived. I don't know exactly what they were doing, but they were here for about a week."

She leaned down under the counter and produced a dog-eared scrapbook. Opening it in front of us, she flicked through the pages. "These are newspaper articles from the Sixties when the Mothman was here," she explained.

Faded excerpts with headlines about strange happenings filled the book. Our Mothman sage treated the book like a bible.

"Where were the men in black from?" asked Hornet.

"Well, they wasn't from right here."

"Do you mean aliens?"

"I can't say, but I know their language didn't come out right. They never blinked their eyes and didn't know how to shake hands. I saw one playing with a pen like he didn't know what it was."

By this point I wasn't the only one feeling uncomfortable. "Let's take off," said Road Captain John.

When we emerged into the wide street, the place was still bereft of people, except for an old, hunched woman with a small dog and a bald, spectacled man walking intently towards us. "Excuse me," he said. "I am the town's local photographer. I wonder if I could take photos of you gentlemen. There will be no cost and I will send you the shots once they are done. My studio is just along the road, if you'd like to accompany me."

Road Captain John looked at each of us and was met with shrugs. "Okay," he said. "We've got time. Be good to have a memento, I suppose."

We followed the photographer into his small studio. "I'll start with you individually and then do a group shot," he advised, gesturing to a black curtain across the back of the studio.

Shit, I'm not going in there first, I thought. Might be a one-way trip to another dimension.

Hornet stepped forward and disappeared behind the curtain.

Adorning the walls were photos of couples, families, a man holding a fish. Wayne bumped my arm and pointed to a college graduation photo of a smiling young woman. "Look at the date," he whispered. "That's today!"

The date alongside the woman was 21 June 2015. The same day we were there but three years later.

We left the studio as soon as politeness would allow and walked at a decent clip back to the bikes. Road Captain's bike wouldn't start, which was odd for a relatively late-model Harley which hadn't been plagued with any such issue previously. Donnie's Yamaha rat bobber wouldn't start either.

"Good God, this place is getting a hold on us!" Donnie had said what we were all thinking.

Then after a couple of minutes, suddenly and simultaneously both bikes started. Road Captain John led us out of town. The traffic light on the town fringe was red. Red it stayed, and stayed, and stayed.

"Fuck this, we're outta here," yelled Road Captain John as he throttled through the light and across the intersection. With considerable relief we followed in formation. As we sped away from Point Pleasant, I took a sneaky look in my rear-view mirror. The light was still red.

I had been briefed on the case in New York by Virgil and Dylan. I was there on another matter and fortuitously the instructions had come in at the same time. Virgil wasn't keen on meeting at the Star offices, so we convened over lunch at the Iroquois Hotel. Situated on West 44th Street close to Times Square, the boutique Iroquois was once home to James Dean. I was camped at the Penn Club just along the road, so the location couldn't have been better.

Extending a huge paw, Virgil greeted me with, "How ya'll doing, son?" I suspected he called everyone son, even those older than him.

He'd swaggered into the restaurant, a gait perfected over sixty-four years. Slim and fit-looking, he wore expensive tailored jeans, shiny cowboy boots and a checked sports jacket. Dylan was dressed more formally and looked older than his thirty years.

"You come highly recommended by our New York lawyers," Virgil said.

"Thanks. I hope we live up to your expectations. We'll certainly do our best to resolve your issue."

Virgil ran through the specifics of the case. "We know Brian and Zoe have left Hong Kong and are in New Zealand. We think they are in Auckland. Will you be able to find them and prepare a case on our behalf?"

"Yes on both counts. If they're in New Zealand we'll find them," I replied.

Putting on his legal hat, Dylan interjected, "We don't want the police or FBI involved. We would rather reach a solution outside the criminal arena."

"Okay, that's fine, as long as we know the strategy from the outset. We won't tell our targets that, though. At this stage it looks like we have at least five jurisdictions involved — the US, New Zealand, Hong Kong, Taiwan and mainland China. Not counting other countries to where funds may have been transferred. It will be more costly and a bit more of a challenge to not utilise Interpol or international enforcement authorities. The number of borders crossed by funds transfers means it would be easy to attract interest from Interpol on the money-laundering front, but we will act as instructed."

My head swimming with different case angles, I retired to the comfortable lounge at the Penn Club to devise an investigation plan. Email instructions were sent back to Diesel at the Wardens office.

It took two days to find Collins and Yang. Their bolt-hole was a designer beach-front town house north of Auckland. Having done a deal on it at two-and-a-half million dollars, Collins was the new owner. We locked the property down: thanks to his astute real-estate purchase we had a good chunk of the stolen funds we were looking for. Furthermore, the Auckland property market was running hot: it didn't matter how long it took to liquidate the property as it was bound to appreciate. We had the pair's movements monitored with round-the-clock surveillance. They weren't going anywhere without our knowing.

Each financial transfer needed to be scrutinised and matched with surrounding documentation, so considerable forensic analysis was required to prove what had occurred. I dealt with the Star CFO and prepared a substantial affidavit from him including flow charts displaying the money flow. It became apparent that the fictitious Hong Kong banking arrangements were handled by Yang. She was the manipulator of the funds movement and concealment. In this she was assisted by handy allies, namely her brother, a cop in Hong Kong, and a cousin employed by HSBC.

The five-star Park Tower Hotel in Knightsbridge is across the road from Hyde Park. Harrods department store is just along the road. I like the old London black cabs and had settled into the capacious back seat of one for the thirty-minute trip from Heathrow. In my mind I tumbled the final strategy for dealing with Lynda — if she fronted.

The architect who designed the hotel in the early Seventies must have been drunk. If he wasn't, the person who approved the design surely must have been. The circular concrete high-rise monstrosity could easily be mistaken for a prison or a car park. Despite appearances the hotel was endearing, well located, with friendly staff. The comfortable, quiet cocktail bar was a perfect spot to meet with Lynda.

Just a couple of minutes before our appointed meeting time she turned up wearing a simple blue dress. Tall for a Korean woman, in her mid-thirties with long black hair to her waist, she exuded fragile confidence. She introduced herself in a clipped English tone, perhaps an indicator she had been educated in London.

"I've been wrestling with whether or not I should meet with you," she said. "In the end it came down to betrayal. Brian betrayed me and it's time to set the record straight. We have two children together. He doesn't give me or the boys anything and now I learn he's with that vixen and they've had a child together. I held out a false hope he might do the decent thing and look after me and our children, but he only cares about himself. I know he's taken all that money from Virgil. I feel bad about that too. He doesn't care if he hurts other people."

"Did he speak to you specifically about stealing money from Virgil and Star?" I asked.

"Yes. He said it was easy, that he could do what he wanted. He thought Virgil was making too much money and that he deserved a piece of the action; that he wasn't being looked after properly. He's always been selfish and focused on his own needs, but I never thought he could go this far. You know, it's probably his disregard for other people's feelings, including those closest to him, that allows him to commit a fraud like this. I have always been loyal to him but that only goes so far."

Lynda's sentiments encapsulated every fraudster's attitudinal traits of greed, selfishness and egocentricity. Nothing about what she said was surprising. Touching on what would undoubtedly down the track come as some type of justification argument, I asked, "What would you say to his potential argument that he was entitled to do what he's done?"

"Without a doubt he knows what he has done is fraud and clearly wrong. Because he was so far away from the US and with limited supervision, he thought he could get away with it. He told me that once he had the Hong Kong office set up, he worked out there were big holes in the Star ordering process that he could take advantage of. You should also know Brian is close to his brother Dave. I wouldn't be surprised if he was involved in this somehow."

"Tell me about Dave. Where does he live and why do you think he might be involved?"

"He lives in New Zealand. He's running some big IT company there. Like Brian, he's a bit too smart for his own good. The two of them are as thick as thieves — literally. Dave worked in the Philippines, based in Manila. He left an IT company there under questionable circumstances. Something about financial irregularities, the loose translation being he's a thief like his brother."

For a further two hours I mined Lynda for further enlightenment on our targets. Her profiling of Brian, Zoe and Dave painted a personality picture and gave valuable information on how they might react to potential courses of action.

I rode the lift to my hotel room and nutted out an email of instruction for the office. Diesel dived immediately into financial-transfer documentation, working backwards from the settlement of the Auckland property held by Brian. This revealed that the funds to settle the purchase had come from a local Westpac bank account in the name of David L.

Collins. This firmly placed brother Dave in a money-laundering mire. The disclosure, a strong pinch bar of leverage, would be invaluable when it came to interview the recalcitrant Brian.

The Auckland surveillance of Collins and Yang produced nothing startling. Their daily routine circulated around taking their child to daycare and periodic visits to Dave's sumptuous residence in Mount Eden. Late-model European cars were sighted at Brian's place, raising the question as to how they were funded.

Diesel set up a Skype conference with Virgil and Dylan to discuss the way forward. I recommended fronting our targets in an attempt to resolve the matter.

"If they are going to be approached I want to come out there and be present when it happens," said Virgil.

"You sure, Dad?" pressed Dylan. "Do you think you can be impartial? I'll go if you want."

"No, I want to be there. I want to see the whites of their eyes," said Virgil stubbornly.

As far as I was concerned the jury was out on whether Virgil coming was a good idea. It was unusual to have clients actively involved in the operational aspects of a case. It could introduce one more quotient of conjecture in a game where the variables need to be limited as much as possible. But Virgil was the client, and what the client says goes... within reason. I wasn't about to raise an objection; his presence might work well. If I did, it would be met with a query as to why. I couldn't very well say, Coz you might fuck it up.

"If you're coming, Virgil, you need to come soon. Our surveillance places them at the Auckland address and we don't want them to fly the coop and skip out to Asia."

"Okay. I'll get there as soon as I can," replied Virgil.

Stingray's call came crackling through my earpiece. "Targets have touched down back at home address. Two up, minus the child."

"Roger, copy, we'll be there in twenty. Let us know if there's any further movement."

The beach-front properties along Auckland's East Coast Bays possess commanding views out over the Waitemata Harbour. Our quarries' bolthole in Campbell's Bay was no exception. A modern two-storey structure, it stood alongside another of similar design on a shared driveway. Chest-high electronic gates secured the driveway entrance.

Accompanied by Ainsley and Virgil I approached the property on foot. I whispered to Ainsley, "Geez, it might be like the Lucas warrant." She said nothing but lifted her arm and gestured to a scar on her wrist.

The Lucas search warrant was executed back when we were on CCU. Part of our role was acting on tip-offs and intelligence received mainly about drug activity. Some of the information was scant, but we got search warrants and kicked down doors anyway to see what was turned up. Information had been received that one Christopher Lucas was dealing drugs from a particular address, with gear and firearms at the property. Any information linking Lucas and crime would always be accurate. Lucas was a bad bugger. He was a user as well as a dealer: his innate unpredictability was dependent on his level of substance intake. He was an associate of Rick's, so we were casually acquainted. (When Rick killed Paula, Lucas was hovering in the area in the immediate aftermath. How he ended up in a vehicle outside the Station Hotel after the murder is a mystery. His attempt at assisting Rick to flee the scene was foiled when Ainsley ordered him from the area.) I never saw much point in getting alongside him in the scene due to his volatility and the fact that he looked as if he would die at any time. Not thin but skeletal, his eyes buried rather than sunken.

I had a sledgehammer when we ran up Lucas's drive to the front door. A typical drug-dealer's door; although it had sections of glass, it was reinforced.

"Police, open up!" I yelled, simultaneously swinging the sledgehammer backwards. I wasn't about to give him too much time to destroy his gear. Ainsley and fellow squad member Wayne Wright were behind me. The forward swing smashed into the door below the handle, splintering glass and aluminium. It didn't budge. I swung at it again. At the second impact, high-pitched screaming came from behind the door. "It's open, it's open!"

"Emu, Emu!" implored Ainsley beside me, reaching for the door. While I was cocked in a backswing ready for the third attack on the door, she leaned forward, depressed the handle and swung the door open. Blood on the inside of her wrist betrayed a six-stitch wound inflicted by a glass shard from my futile second strike.

Virgil scaled the electronic gate, easily belying his years. Ainsley bounced over it, thereby earning the code name Ladybird. I followed but remained wary of the spikes protruding from the top of the gate.

The look of surprise on Brian's face when he opened the door to us on my third knock was something. "V-V-Virgil," he stuttered. "Wh-what a surprise."

I introduced myself and said, "Brian, you are probably well aware what this is about. We would like to have a discussion about what has been happening with Star in Hong Kong."

"Yes, yes of course. I was wondering when you would turn up. I'm glad you're here, Virgil, so this can be cleared up," said Brian, attempting to compose himself.

His eyes were furtive behind his glasses; his thinning hair touched his protruding ears. He wore a denim shirt and jeans on a slim frame. I didn't like him. Not just because of what I knew about his actions — it was a gut feeling. One I never discounted. It had served me superbly in the past.

"Who is it?" came a female voice from the stairwell.

"It, it, it's Virgil," replied Brian.

"What!" was the shocked response. Zoe emerged from the stairway into the foyer. Short in stature, dressed in track pants, T-shirt and expensive sneakers, she burst into tears and ran towards Virgil throwing her arms around his neck. "I'm so sorry, Virgil! I didn't want to do it, I didn't want to hurt you," she sobbed. "It's been awful. I'm so pleased to see you."

Virgil said nothing.

I wrested back the initiative. "Look, the idea here is to sort this out in

Virgil's favour without things getting messy — if you know what I mean."

"Well, of course, I understand. I'm sure this can be resolved," said Brian, completely composed now, with a slight edge in his voice.

"We can sell property and get cash from bank accounts," blurted Zoe.

"How much can you get together immediately?" I asked.

Brian interjected, "That will depend. We will need to look at it."

"Okay, that's fine," I said positively. "It's pleasing you concede there's a problem and that you owe Virgil."

Zoe's sobs diminished to a whimper as she moved back alongside Brian. "Come upstairs," he said.

The stairs ended at a designer kitchen and dining room. Full-length windows along the side of the house framed a commanding view over the harbour and foreshore. Set in stark white decor sat a lacquered table surrounded by white leather chairs. The kitchen bristled with Gaggenau appliances. Tasteful art decorated the walls. It's strange how a pall attaches to opulence funded wrongly, I thought.

Brian asked me, "Could Zoe and I speak with Virgil by ourselves?"

"Let me consult with my client."

I took Virgil to one side in a room off the dining area. Ainsley remained with the fraudsters who were now communicating in Mandarin.

"I don't like this, Virgil," I said. "I'd rather be present during any discussions with these two."

Virgil scratched his stubbled, jet-lagged chin. "I think it'll be okay. They're talking about repaying their ill-gotten gains. I reckon I can handle them and get my money back. Anyway, they look pretty scared about what's going on and what might happen."

"Yeah, but that's at the moment. These things can change quickly. I don't trust Brian one bit. Or her, actually. They've already shafted you."

"It'll be fine. I'll deal with them," Virgil said, turning away towards the kitchen.

While Ainsley and I waited anxiously in the ante room, Virgil spent half an hour with the villains. The longer the meeting went on, the more worried I became that Virgil would be manipulated into an agreement that wasn't in his best interests.

"They've agreed to come to the Wardens offices tomorrow morning first thing," said Virgil upon emerging from the meeting. "We can then arrange the formal transfer of this property to me and they'll bring bank statements showing balances and where the money is."

"You're happy they'll come and not try and flee?" I asked.

"Yes. They both seem genuine to me."

"I recommend we put a guard in here overnight to keep an eye on them and protect what is essentially yours."

"I don't think that will be necessary," said Virgil assuredly.

The following morning Collins and Yang were no-shows. I implored Virgil to get the authorities involved, explaining that on the basis of a police complaint we could have them stopped at the airport and questioned. We had sufficient evidence to have them arrested. But Virgil was resolute and with Dylan's support was intent on moving against them civilly through the New Zealand courts.

The next day Collins and Yang flew out of Auckland. Still, thanks to a caveat on the house and injunctions on the bank accounts, they were minus a house and twelve bank accounts in Hong Kong, Taiwan and the Philippines.

"Hey Sean, it's Emu!"

"Gidday, mate, how's it going? Haven't heard from you for ages."

Sean was the chief executive of Alpha Systems, an IT company with eight offices throughout New Zealand. In a previous senior role, he had been a client. We sorted a widespread internal theft issue through the deployment of a female undercover agent.

"You got a joker called David Collins working as your CFO?" I said.

"Yeah, we have, as a matter of fact."

"You might want to take a close look at him."

"That right?"

"Yeah."

With that, Dave's career in IT was harpooned.

◀ TWENTY-FOUR ▶

Drive a black Mercedes. Tell lies.

SITTING ON STOOLS IN THE Wardens office kitchen, Raven changed the subject from the perennial issue of problematic Auckland traffic. "Who is the Bat anyway? What's his name?"

"I don't know and I'm sure not going to ask," replied Bee.

"Maybe he's more than one person," opined Raven.

The term "murky figure" does not do justice to the Bat. He operates on another plane altogether. For over a decade I had used Bat on "sensitive," "off the books", "black" or "the secretary will disavow" operations. A former decorated Special Forces commissioned officer in the South African Defence Forces, Bat's particular expertise was in combat demolition. Those skills took him worldwide on covert hit-squad missions. A helicopter and jet pilot, he had, while in the United Kingdom, held accreditation as a supplier of aviation services to Her Majesty the Queen.

Of average height and build, he exuded an inescapable fitness born of repeated engagement in physically trying situations. Often dressed dapperly, his appearance belied a deep-rooted sinister side. A large laundry basket of blood-soaked keffiyehs, collected from past missions, confirmed periodic openings of the door marked Sinister. Chameleonic, with a wicked wit, the Bat appealed to the female of the species, something he embraced with vigour. There was an unspoken understanding of respect and loyalty between us.

After a stint working in New Zealand the Bat, fluent in Arabic, returned to the Middle East, location of numerous missions as a hired gun for intelligence agencies, covered head-to-toe in traditional Arab dress, brown contact lenses concealing his only potential giveaway: blue eyes.

The case was a fifty-million dollar advance-fee fraud with a simple premise: you pay upfront to get a loan, the loan is never forthcoming and the fraudsters pocket your fee. To make it work the fraudsters need a viable and credible cloak of legitimacy. In this instance, the fraud operation was based in the Middle East, specifically Bahrain. Internationally, certainly in Australasia, the Middle East is viewed as awash with cash. A good starting point to begin structuring fake capability.

Overlay this with apparent links to local royalty, a sheikh or two.

A fabricated background in international high finance.

A premium financial-centre address.

Opulent, vast, art-adorned offices stacked with minions.

Produce compelling promotional material.

Deal only in large loans. Offer low interest rates. Require extensive due diligence.

Refuse to hold fees in escrow or trust. Make borrowers come to the office. Use delay.

Make them wait for meetings. Charge two per cent of proposed loan. Add "insurance" fees. Add "due diligence" fees.

Have fees paid to different countries. Use different banks.

Promise to repay if no loan. Avoid the US. Pay brokers a good percentage of fees.

Have a slick online presence.

Choose smart, impressionable, malleable staff. Split responsibilities. Tell staff nothing.

Spend on PR. Make threats. Shift money. Falsify references.

Retain quality auditors. Instruct prominent lawyers. Formalise document signing.

Negotiate to buy a football club. Lease a jet. Buy racehorses. Get a boat.

Tease borrowers with limited access. Associate with politicians. Splash out on entertainment.

Fly first-class. Act rich. Dress formally. Pay bribes. Have good security. Dine at the best restaurants. Date a good-looking bird.

Drive a black Mercedes.

Tell lies.

It is challenging getting into the Criminal Intelligence Directorate in Bahrain. The compound faces two streets on the edge of Manama, the capital. Typically, the streets are unnamed.

Your only guide is a number. The low clay-coloured buildings, matched by the hue of the dusty street, are shielded behind a high wall with red steel-barred gates. A shield in the middle of the gate is the only clue to officialdom. An appointment is needed to initiate the entry process. Bat had tapped a police contact and arrangements were made.

Directed first by a uniformed cop sitting on a collapsible chair in front of the gate, automatic rifle comfortably across his knees, Bat and I entered a sparse room with chairs around the outside and uniform police sitting behind a counter. Chattered Arabic from Bat formalised our presence.

After passing through a metal detector and being relieved of our phones, we were escorted to another building. En route across the expansive dusty yard we passed armoured pickups with 50-calibre machineguns mounted on roll bars. As we entered the building welcoming aircon washed over us, a relief from the forty-two degree afternoon heat. Our escort punched the sixth-floor button on the lift and we rode upwards silently.

We came out onto a pale linoleum hallway with light-coloured walls. Functionality reigned as it does in police stations all around the world. Wariness, however, often with a garnish of unease, is a constant companion in Middle East dealings. We passed a number of offices to the right of us. Opposite them were rooms set out like courts.

Outside the fourth office we were stopped by our escort and directed into one of the court-styled rooms to wait. A long table with a red leather top ran the length of the room, separating chairs on each side. A small elevated judicial bench rose from where the table ended. A portrait of the king hung prominently on the wall behind the bench. The king's image was ubiquitous, featuring in all governmental buildings.

"Come through, please," called our escort, showing us across the hall into a brightly lit office with two desks. Just inside and partly hidden by the office door sat Lieutenant Abdullah, a handsome man in his late thirties. His strong, angular features were accentuated by his perfectly laundered keffiyeh.

His robe was fastened at the neck by a black button that looked like a precious stone. The stark white of his garb was almost luminescent against the drab office. His limpid brown eyes stared intently at us. His look was direct and bore a particular menace. A cultured Arabic menace.

I had submitted a written complaint of fraud and spoken to other Anti Economic Crimes Unit investigators, but their superior was not particularly interested in formalities. He had heard enough about my suspect.

"Two weeks," said Lieutenant Abdullah in slow, measured English. "Two weeks and we will have him in here. It will be quick, we will deal with him. If he doesn't talk, we will torture him," he said unblinkingly.

Unsure quite how to respond, I said, "Thanks, thanks for that. I am most appreciative."

"I am happy to help," said Lieutenant Abdullah, his right hand over his heart in the Arabic gesture of sincerity. "Inshallah."

Two months later, sharing a drink with Bat at the fittingly named Sherlock Holmes Pub in the Gulf Hotel, we discussed developments in the case. There was little to discuss as no action had been taken by the Anti Economic Crimes Unit.

"That's the way it works here," said Bat. Dressed crisply in his usual ensemble of black suit, white shirt and dark-coloured tie, he nursed a cocktail. "This country is completely controlled by the royal family. Like any family it has its gripes, foibles and prejudices. Trouble is, here they're imposed on the entire populace. Is there corruption here? Well, not in our sense of the word as it's considered normal. There's no doubt, Emu, it's a challenging environment."

Just along the bar were two young Arabs in traditional dress. From the volume of their discussion, the glasses around them and the pained expression on the barmaid's face, they looked as if they'd been there for some time. Alcohol was legal in Bahrain but not in Saudi Arabia, so it was common for Saudis to drive across the border and seek entertainment. The resultant trouble was often cause for local consternation.

"I don't like those fucking Saudis coming over here and causing shit," said Bat suddenly.

An altercation had arisen between Bat and two Saudis outside a local liquor store. Bat was there to buy a bottle of wine for his girlfriend — or one of them. Desperate to get hold of liquor, the Saudis had parked their late-model Audi right behind Bat's car, blocking its exit. Stewing for twenty minutes before the Saudis came out of the store, Bat was in an agitated and unhappy state, not the best scenario for those concerned.

Being told the error of their ways seemed to embolden the larger of the two men, who mistakenly threw a punch at Bat. The strike response from Bat shattered the man's jaw and drove the bones into the top of his head. He collapsed in a coma. His colleague also had a swing but was instantly dispatched to the ground.

Before the police attended, Bat put on his reading glasses and claimed he was a mild-mannered businessman defending himself in dire circumstances. Too late the Saudi had learnt the universal lesson: there is always someone meaner and tougher than you.

The lack of action by the Anti Economic Crimes Unit didn't perturb me greatly. We had managed to freeze proceeds of the fraud in Switzerland: five million US dollars in six Zurich Credit Suisse bank accounts and an apartment valued at three million in Hergiswil on Lake Lucerne. Another three hundred thousand was found in accounts in the Bahamas and Amsterdam. Taking our offender down in Bahrain was largely personal. This dude deserved to do time and if we could attach a few assets along the way, so much the better.

I stopped in Doha, Qatar, before making the final leg to Bahrain on Gulf Air. Despite the late hour, Bat met me at the airport immaculately turned out in black suit and silver fern tie; a New Zealand flag tie-pin sat proudly on his lapel. He dropped me at my usual haunt, the Sheraton Bahrain, with the promise we would meet the following day for lunch.

The Capital Club is Bahrain's premier business and social club. Sitting on the fifty-second floor of the East Tower, Bahrain Financial Harbour, it affords a sensational view of the Arabian Sea and downtown Bahrain.

It is an expat enclave, sprinkled with local senior business leaders and politicians. I had been invited by the Bahrain government to give an address there on international financial crime, so I was familiar with the surroundings and really liked the place. I'd also been invited to Dubai and covered the same topic.

Bat was in fine form when we sat down to lunch. He began a treatise on life, investigation work and the Arab world.

"I always say, Emu, you can't train intelligence. If you've got someone smart you can train them to fight, kill or be an investigator, but without intelligence you can't do anything. It's a Special Forces mantra and basic requirement. The Arabs have a saying on this: 'Lack of intelligence is the greatest poverty'."

Pondering this I had to agree. It certainly applied to undercover agents we had recruited for private-sector operations. The best possessed an underlying acuity allowing curiosity, aptitude and an ability to quickly assimilate information.

Bat liked to illustrate his conversation points by referencing a saying or proverb. He collected them like his bloodied keffiyehs. When a point perfectly meshed with an appropriate saying he physically swelled with pride.

"Salaam alaikum," interrupted the waitress with the traditional Arabic greeting.

"Alaikum salaam," replied Bat, before settling on a drinks order. He continued, "Western culture can never be applied to the Middle East, mate. It is so fundamentally different here, culturally and sociologically. There are differing ideological arguments in play, but most of what happens here is about money. Money's the main driver. The country is desperate to be a force as a major financial centre, hence the interest in fraud. They have to, really, as Bahrain missed out on the oil the rest of the region has."

"Shukran," said Bat, thanking the waitress as the drinks arrived. Then he changed the subject. "I know you were betrayed cruelly by one of your best mates. That's hard to take."

"Yes, it was pretty tough," I replied, not wanting to revisit a dark episode that involved a trusted friend selling out our lines of inquiry in a high-profile case.

"For money too?"

"Yeah, that's right."

"The Arabs say, 'It's better to have a thousand enemies outside the tent than one inside the tent'. And 'Be wary around your enemy once and your friend a thousand times. A double-crossing friend knows more about what hurts you'."

"Yeah, that's for sure," I said trailing off, hoping the subject might follow the sentence.

"Jealousy drives narks and traitors too, Emu."

"That's right, but I've always thought if you have no enemies you've done nothing of consequence."

"It's like managing people. You can't always be friends," said Bat. "You have to have the gumption to use the whip. The horses ain't gonna pull the cart for the fun of it. It's like I said to the CEO of a big corporate in Saudi I was consulting to: 'Your triple FFF management system is killing your company. Family, Friends and Fools'."

We ordered lamb sourced from Saudi Arabia. The breeding stock was probably originally from New Zealand. "Now that you're being philosophical, Bat," I said, "what do you think about death? Are you afraid of dying?"

"Let me answer that with a story, Emu. I was in Tal Afar, in Iraq, lying almost dead on a basement floor in a building knocked down in an air strike. Hurt and delusional, I imagined I saw an angel in the room looking down on me. The angel looked at me, assessed me and then said softly, 'I came to take you with me, but I'm going to give you another chance at life. Worry about nothing, just be happy. For every day you are happy, I will give you one extra day of life. For every day you are unhappy, I will take two away; and be warned, the next time I come, I *will* take you with me.'

"There was a strange, ancient, canvas-like smell circulating about him. When I sense that smell in the air now, I know instinctively that death is near and that someone is dying or will die. Every time I sense that same odour, someone nearby does actually die.

"I reckon I have some life credit, just don't know how much. Don't know when the accounting started and I have never bothered to tally it up. I just focus on the now of life. I have no pensions, plans, investments, or anything else. But I don't go hungry."

"That's a good story, mate," I said. "Yeah, the Grim Reaper will come for us all. The question is only when, where and for what reason? The game of life is so rough it ends up killing you."

"It's funny, different people's attitudes to death," Bat said. "I remember working with a Pom on a mission. He said to me, 'I'm dead tired, I can't go on'. I said to him, 'If you don't go on you won't be tired, just dead'. I picked up his Bergen rucksack and kept walking. If he came he would share his food and water with me; if he didn't come, it wouldn't go to waste."

"Hah! Nice!" Then I started to get deep. "What about God, do you believe in a higher being?"

"I reckon there's a God, there must be. Have you ever heard of a man who was drowning, dying in the desert, trapped on the side of a mountain, on a sinking ship, in a raging bush fire, or anywhere else on the precipice of death who doesn't believe in God?"

The waitress appeared with our meals. She came back with a metre-long pepper grinder.

"Excuse me," said Bat.

"Yes, sir?"

"Do you think you could bring us the big pepper grinder?"

Once the laughing stopped Bat got serious. "There is a new case Henry, a friend of mine, would like help with. He has been relieved of one hundred thousand pounds and would like you to deal with it for him. I'll assist, of course, and do whatever you instruct. Henry is originally from the UK but has been here for over twenty-five years.

"The offender is a local Bahraini named Omran Al Musawi. He's a relatively prominent businessman, owns a large commercial building and a restaurant. He promoted this investment to Henry promising a three hundred per cent return in three months. Omran, acting as a finance broker, has bitten a lot of other people here too. The word is he took over thirty million pounds from one hundred and thirty-five different residents. The funds he took in were sent at his direction to bank accounts in London.

"The cash went to the benefit of a UK company called Porton Group controlled by a Pom called Harvey Boulter. It's believed to be an entirely fraudulent investment operation. Boulter is said to have bagged over two hundred million quid from victims around the world."

"Okay, sweet. Where's this cat Boulter based?"

"London and Dubai, I understand. He apparently has a pretty decent pad in Dubai, worth over ten million."

"We'll kick off with backgrounds on Omran and Boulter," I said. "I'll get hold of Diesel, then we need to put the bite on Omran. He's got to be our main target. Remind him of the error of his ways."

"Roger that," said Bat, eyes burning with anticipation.

The backgrounds confirmed Porton as a fraud operation into which Henry's funds had been sucked. Following a briefing with Henry, we devised a plan to put heat on Omran. I made contact with him twice by telephone, subsequently arranging a personal meeting. He made repayment noises, but ladled a fair amount of obfuscation into our chats. I decided to front him in person.

Bat and I walked into the Le Chocolat Cafe in the Seef District at 9.16am. As we made our way up the steps leading to the entrance, we passed Bull standing about twenty metres off to the right. Shaven-headed, dark-glassed and black-suited, Bull was a Maori involved in personal protection and surveillance. Wardens had him operating both in New Zealand and the Middle East. Muscular, but not ripped, Bull was reasonably distinctive. Maori are not exactly thick on the ground in Bahrain — but at a pinch he could pass for an Arab. Omran was expected at 10am. Bull's role was to monitor the environs for his arrival, note his vehicle, who accompanied him and see who might be hanging around.

Running along the length of the cafe was a glass atrium. I chose a table in the back corner with glass on each side. It was a good spot to monitor approaches from left or right and I could see the entrance. Bat sat with me and did a final check on his covert audio recording equipment.

At 9.55am my phone beeped with the text "touched down".

Thirty seconds later Omran walked into the cafe and took a seat at the opposite end from where we were sitting. Portly, wearing a stylish sports jacket and jeans, he was alone. Good. No lawyer or other adviser to spoil the party. In the circumstances, he appeared reasonably comfortable. After a couple of minutes I asked Bat to go and get him. By now Bull was seated three tables away.

After introductions and small talk I embarked on the interview. "As you know, Omran, Henry is looking to get the money back he gave to you for investment. You promised to return it to him, but he hasn't seen even one dinar."

In an apparent gesture of nervousness, Omran moved the sunglasses that were sitting on his head. "Yes, I've promised Henry I will return his money. I have given him my personal guarantee, which is not something I have given to anyone else."

"So there's a number of other people that you have taken money from?"

"Yes. I admit there is. There's probably over a hundred and thirty. The money went to Harvey Boulter and the Porton Group. I'm not so sure of Harvey's operation, though. Harvey bought technology companies really cheaply, then he inflated the price and sold shares in them. I think he planned this from day one."

"But despite your guarantee Henry has not seen his money."

"I will get it to him, I promise. Henry is a friend of mine. At least, I regard him as a friend."

Things were progressing well: he was talking. But I needed admissions from him on one particular point.

"So, Omran, you've said you took money for investment from Henry and other residents of Bahrain. Did you act as a finance broker then?"

"Ah, yes I did," moving his sunglasses again but also scratching his head.

"Did you have a licence to act as a broker or approval from the Central Bank of Bahrain?"

"No. I admit I didn't. I was just doing it in my own name."

Bingo! An unqualified admission gobbled up by the audio.

I pushed further. "What about commission payments for what you did? How did that work?"

Omran looked down at the table, his shoulders slumping. "I was paid ten per cent of the amounts invested. I received around two million pounds as brokerage fees. The fees were paid by Harvey to my personal Bahrain bank account."

I had researched the law in Bahrain and established that recent changes had criminalised unlicensed finance broking, allowing for serious penalties and the recovery of funds lost to such activity. Given his admissions, this was probably something of which Omran was unaware.

"So when exactly can Henry expect his hundred thousand?"

"I'll get it together as soon as possible."

"Well, listen carefully, Omran. If you don't, there will be serious consequences for you personally. For good measure, I will take your wife down too. Just to be clear, I'm not bluffing."

"I understand."

Understand... obviously Omran did not. He chose not to repay Henry.

I prepared a criminal complaint of unlicensed finance broking. Framed to focus on the narrow fact situation and simply cover the offence ingredients, the complaint, translated into Arabic, made no reference to the wider international Porton fraud. Attributing liability to Omran in the wider offending would be difficult to prove and complicated by jurisdictional issues.

The prosecutors ran with the complaint. Omran was arrested, charged and convicted. Bahrain's Lower Criminal Court imposed a sentence of three years' imprisonment, a fine of fifty thousand dinars (a hundred and thirty thousand US dollars) and confiscation of the proceeds of crime. The court allowed referral of civil proceedings to the Competent Court, opening the way for civil recovery of losses. Pretty much a slam dunk. His wife joined him as a convicted criminal. Omran was finished. Like others before him, he had bet that I was bluffing — and lost.

◄ TWENTY-FIVE ►

"Would it be fatal if I was to tell you I had been in the police?"

THE MCDONALD'S AT GREENLANE sits just off the motorway exit by a Countdown supermarket, which allows easy parking. On a cold June day in 2006 Ainsley sat at a table on the edge of the restaurant. Sitting across from her was Ricki Goodin. He had served twelve years in prison for murdering Paula. Twenty-seven years had elapsed since that fatal day in 1979 at the Station Hotel. Now sixty, Rick still wore his hair long, but the onset of grey gave his mane a salt-and-pepper look.

Under her code name Ladybird, Ainsley was running a team acting on behalf of finance companies, and purely by chance had come across an inquiry involving Rick. Initially reluctant, she nevertheless saw an opportunity to speak to the man who had cast a shadow across her husband's life. It was serendipitous that she was privy to the inquiry and so was able to trace Rick, as he was notoriously difficult to find, and that he even agreed to meet.

From her days in the police she was well aware of the notoriety surrounding Rick as a major crime figure and the general view that if you came across him, it could be the last time you drew breath. On the cusp of the meeting she was expecting to feel hostility, anger and revenge at the price her husband had paid for being a police undercover agent. Upon meeting him, though, a diametrically opposed reality kicked in.

She felt warmth and sensitivity. Rick was nervous and almost shy. When they sat down at the table, Rick accidentally spilled his coffee. He immediately stood up and worried he may have spilled some on her clothes, becoming solicitous and concerned. As he stood and moved, she noticed his pronounced limp. His obvious concern displayed an inherent vulnerability.

After disposing of the pretext financial inquiry, their discussion ranged for twenty minutes over a variety of subjects. She was unprepared for the realisation that she liked him. They developed a rapport, a connection.

Rick spoke of his life as an old-school criminal and the code that governed his conduct. You didn't rob old ladies, like the thugs of today. You didn't squeal to the coppers.

Without braggadocio, he described how, as an old-school capo and elder statesman, he had been called in by prison officials to calm warring gang factions at Paremoremo's D block.

He talked about his childhood, how he had been brought up like an animal, literally being chained to a table like a dog. He wasn't trying to evoke sympathy but Ainsley felt it all the same.

"Would it be fatal if I was to tell you that I had been in the police?" she asked.

Rick was genuinely shocked. Sitting back in his chair, he replied, "Well, okay."

His response was understandable. Before him sat an attractive, courteous, refined, well-dressed woman who drove a Mercedes, which he of course had observed arriving. She was the antithesis of the kind of police he was familiar with.

Having disposed of that potential damper on the conversation, Ainsley said, "I am aware of what happened with Paula's murder. I was one of the first police on the scene."

Her fears that Rick might shut down at the mention of that night were unfounded. "I really loved Paula," he said. "Every single day I think about her and regret what happened. I couldn't believe it when I got to the mortuary and saw her there dead. And it was because of what I did."

Then he asked quietly, "So you saw her outside the hotel?"

"Yes, I did. She looked peaceful."

Ainsley felt compelled to add, "There was a guy I used to work with who was an undercover agent and might have known you. His name is Marcus."

"Marcus. Yeah, I knew him. We were pretty close. I just couldn't believe he was an undercover. Even when he told me himself, I still wouldn't believe it. I trusted him completely and he stitched me up good and proper. Paula didn't trust him, though. I should have listened to her.

"The thing I couldn't believe was how many people he caught. I don't know how he did it. I didn't think I told him anything, but he made all these connections and did heaps of buys.

"Thinking back on it now, I have a grudging respect for what he did. It was a really good job and I was taken down fair and square. At the time, though, I wanted him clipped and arranged for it to happen."

Ainsley said, "If there was an opportunity to meet with Marcus, would you be prepared to do that?"

Struggling with the question, pain etched on his weathered face, Rick took a full two minutes to answer.

"It's all pretty raw even now… but maybe."